Planned Press
and Public Relations

PLANNED PRESS AND PUBLIC RELATIONS

Frank Jefkins

International Textbook Company

Published by International Textbook Company Limited,
450 Edgware Road, London W2 1EG
A member of the Blackie Group

First published 1977

ISBN 0 7002 0264 1 cased
      0 7002 0272 2 paper

Printed in Great Britain by
Robert MacLehose and Company Limited
Printers to the University of Glasgow

Contents

Preface

This book attempts to bring together practical, research and teaching experience to offer ways of improving professionalism in the planning of PR programmes aimed at achieving tangible results. It is intended for both practitioners and CAM, Institute of Marketing and other students of communication.

The book is in four parts – planning, media, creativity and case studies.

The practical approach is shown in the emphasis on planning by objectives, which makes the assessment of results possible, and in the need for strict budgeting. One chapter is devoted to skeleton costing schemes.

In the planning and creative sections will be found easily remembered formulae and check-lists. There is the Six-point Planning Model, the Seven-point Formula for planning a house journal, and another Seven-point Formula for researching and writing feature articles. With the Seven-point Formula for writing publishable news releases there is a step-by-step application of the method, and a separate chapter explains the importance of the 'opening paragraph'. Invented and real examples of news releases are given as practical demonstrations.

But PR is not limited to press relations, as the middle section shows with its analysis of the variety of media which can be employed to reach different publics for different purposes.

The four case studies demonstrate the versatility of PR and show the application of the principles set out in the book. They show PR at work for British Airways and Concorde; Flymo; ITT Europe; and the Open University. Within the text are smaller case studies about CPC Europe. Elf Oil, Goodyear Tyre and Rubber, John Haig, Knorr Soup,

Zambian Information Services and the Zambian Ministry of Rural Development. These are modern and international examples which I hope will make the book useful to readers in many parts of the world.

This book would not have been possible without the generous help of all those who sent me examples or quotable material or granted me interviews.

Frank Jefkins

Croydon, August 1975

Part One
Planning PR Programmes

CHAPTER ONE

The Purpose and Philosophy of PR

Public relations is a constantly misused and misunderstood expression. A simple explanation is offered by reversing the words to say 'relations with the public'. The PR practitioner is concerned with organizing and conducting communication to achieve better understanding between an organization and the numerous groups of people with whom it has or desires to have contact. Many skills are required by the practitioner if he is to be successful. Some of the misunderstandings occur because it is not always realized that these skills extend a long way beyond journalism and the ability to read a wine list.

This is because PR touches every aspect of any organization; it should be a management philosophy, the first PRO should be the chief executive, and the primary place for PR instruction should be in business and management schools.

Every organization has PR whether it likes it or not, for PR is like the weather, sex and the poor and it won't go away. Everyone in every organization communicates: the practice of PR seeks to integrate and undertake communication purposefully. Consequently, PR should be neither haphazard nor intangible. The need to plan objectives against which results can be evaluated is described with a six-point planning model in Chapter Four.

It follows that PR concerns all types of organization, commercial and non-commercial, as was made very clear with the reorganization of local government in 1974 and the appointment of so many hundreds of press officers, information officers and PRO's that there is now a *Hollis New Authorities Guide*, which lists the PRO's of local, new town, area development, health service and water authorities. Every kind of organization from the Government to the local tennis club is involved in public relations. PR embraces the total communications of the total organization, as we shall see in Chapter Three which defines publics. Moreover, more than just the PRO or PR consultant are actively engaged in PR operations and need therefore to be appreciative of PR techniques.

The three most difficult areas in which to establish a clear understanding of PR are (1) management; (2) advertising and (3) the news media. Management, because it is usually ill-trained in communication processes, tends to regard PR as some form of protection, means of influencing the media or device for obtaining cheap or free publicity; advertising pretends that PR is some sort of below-the-line publicity seeking; and the media regard PR with suspicion as something with biased, ulterior motives. This is not to say that some organizations are not blessed with management from which PR originates – such as the success story of Marks and Spencer – and there are advertising managers and advertising agents who are thoroughly appreciative of the value of PR and how it differs from advertising, and also journalists who rely on respected PR sources for their information. But in general PR suffers from being wrongly defined.

And so management expects PR to do the impossible, advertising regards PR as a poor relation, and the media label anything they do not like as 'a PR exercise'. With the latter adopting such an ostrich-like attitude it is not surprising that journalists turned PRO's (with no training in PR but typical press misconceptions which they perpetuate with great harm to the PR profession) tend to do what management expects of them. The weaknesses of the journalist turned PRO are that he is purely creative, seldom knows how a newspaper is printed, and has never heard of budgeting and campaign planning. Nor does he want to.

The Institute of Public Relations and the CAM Education Foundation have a very long haul if between them they are going to succeed in converting the ten thousand people engaged in PR in the UK into skilled professionals. The best that can be said is that a lot of intelligent people are working hard for minimal salaries, deserving no more because their humble status reflects their PR knowledge, abilities and usefulness to their employers. The professional PRO is of management status and answerable to the board of management, and in large organizations he will be on the board. He should at least hold the qualification of MIPR, and ideally he should also possess the CAM Diploma. Anyone less qualified may be an associate member of the Institute (meaning he has three years comprehensive experience). Others may be supposed to have either very little practical experience or be unacceptable by the IPR. 'Good Fleet Street contacts' is no qualification for a press officer. It could mean that he is merely an expert at running up expense accounts.

However, this is not to imply that PR is a closed shop in Britain, although in an increasing number of countries an official licence to operate is required. If licences were required in Britain, the new local authorities would have had grave difficulty in recruiting their new PR staff for journalists could scarcely be licensed as PR practitioners!

Membership of the IPR confers not only recognition of professional status but requires adherence to the Code of Professional Conduct which is both self-disciplinary and self-protective. This important Code gives the PR practitioner the strength of professional reasons for refusing non-ethical assignments from employers or clients, and he is also entitled to expect the media to understand that he will maintain standards of integrity when dealing with them. When PR was maligned in the press because a self-styled PR consultant was gaoled for corruption, the IPR very quickly pointed out that this person was not an Institute member and was not therefore bound by a professional code. It is therefore a matter of both professional pride and protection to seek membership of the IPR if one is elegible. To be an experienced practitioner but not an MIPR is to invite clients, employers and colleagues to ask a very pertinent 'Why not?'

Similarly, the CAM Education Foundation is making it possible for new entrants and those engaged in PR to become proficient in the practice of PR.

The above remarks are introduced early in the book because when PR is criticized it is only fair to the professionals to emphasize that undesirable practices which give PR a bad name are usually the result of management employing either untrained PR personnel or outside PR services lacking experience and professional skills. Let us take one everyday instance. Every morning newspaper and magazine editors, news agencies, and radio and TV news departments fill large plastic dustbins with useless news releases. At least 70 per cent of all releases are rejected, chiefly because they are unprofessional. Often, they have been written and distributed by people with no training in press relations; in many others they have been wrongly written because management has insisted they be produced that way. An incredibly common fault is that so many releases fail to state the subject in the first three words, which is the most elementary and the most ignored rule in news release writing. A professional would not submit the sort of release that makes editors think all PRO's are idiots. The authority of a professional should be accepted by an employer on the principle that one does not keep a dog and bark oneself. Unfortunately, the daily output of useless PR material submitted in all seriousness to astonished editors invites the suspicion that professional PRO's are rare. But there is another side to this: proficient PRO's may seem rare because they are likely to send fewer and more relevant stories to the right media at the right time and their work will appear less often on the editor's desk! Bad PRO's sometimes try to justify their existence by sending out as many releases as they possibly can. Let us hope that the high cost of paper will deter such tactics and encourage the conservation that has long been overdue in the PR business.

This is therefore a book about *professional* PR, It is intended for those who want to earn fees and salaries equal to their abilities to conduct PR that achieves precise objectives. This is cost-effective PR whether it be aimed at averting vandalism, recruiting the right calibre of staff, improving dealer and customer relations, establishing confidence in a share issue, educating the market so that advertising works, or simply establishing a correct impression of what an organization is and does. The range of PR objectives is limitless.

As will be explained in Chapter Four, it is the responsibility of the professional PRO to define areas of activities, recognize the constraints on finances, labour and physical resources, and produce programmes which can achieve feasible objectives. We are talking about planning press and public relations, not dabbling in it. Too many consultancy fees are round-figure estimates for highly generalized and unspecified purposes, while employers often expect their own PROs to do everything on practically nothing. The biggest single lesson that management has to learn about PR is that it is labour-intensive, mostly painstaking work, and the biggest cost is manhours. A fee of £10,000 may seem a lot of money but if (including salaries, overheads and profit) it represents only 500 working hours it means less than two days a week per year of service. Not much can be done on that sort of money, especially when a reasonable amount of time has to be spent on talking to the client. The only way to get PR budgets onto a practical footing is to estimate what it will cost to achieve a given objective: that also means that objectives must be defined. They seldom are.

Public Relations and Marketing Strategy

A businessman is concerned with either gaining a greater share of the market or, at worst, maintaining his existing share. How can PR help him to do this? If PR can contribute in any substantial way to the greater prosperity and stability of the company he will be prepared to invest money in it. But he will not waste money on a fad or a fashion. That PR is a viable proposition as a serious marketing aid is not always properly understood. Too often it is considered as a bit of a gimmick on which a negligible sum may be spent to gain some 'free' editorial publicity – forgetting that editorial space is priceless and that even the negligible sum is a cost. The value of the press coverage is seldom known, and is generally difficult ot appraise in the same way as advertising. Sometimes it is a matter of spending a few thousands to compete with other firms in the editorial columns. Keeping up with the competitors is a very unsatisfactory use of PR. Unsurprisingly, then, PR is not regarded as seriously and as fundamental to good business as it deserves to be.

As already indicated many different kinds of organization employ PR techniques, but here let us consider the use of PR (not just press relations which is a comparatively minor though poorly practised aspect) as a method of communication essential to the total marketing strategy. To do this we must first analyse marketing strategy in order to give PR its rightful place.

Marketing embraces every activity from the conception of a product acceptable to the public at a profit-making price to the results of selling which may include after-sales service, consolidating replacement sales, together with testimonials and complaints. In between come production, packaging, naming, pricing, distribution, and advertising. But at any point in the marketing exercise there can be PR activity, and every part of the marketing mix has PR implications for the marketing director, product manager and advertising agent. There is a PR element in every facet of marketing, see *Marketing and PR Media Planning* (1.1).

A salesman who bullies, exaggerates, cheats or lets down customers is a PR liability as is advertising which is tasteless, irritating, unethical or out of character. Dirty delivery vehicles, indifferent servicing, poor packaging, careless workmanship, and industrial strife due to poor communication are all forms of anti-PR leading to ill-will and a sullied reputation. They create a bad image or impression and they must be rectified so that the well-deserved image can be presented and readily accepted.

PR is therefore concerned with the human factor in marketing. Advertising may seek to persuade people to buy, but you cannot persuade people against their will. PR can create the situation whereby prospects are well disposed towards the products or services.

Much of PR is thus to do with gaining credit for achievement and of establishing an image which is a clear and correct impression of an organization, its policy, products or service. This is a very big task and it has to be planned and executed in a logical way. It also has to make sense to the businessman.

If we assume a situation of economic rationality in which the businessman seeks to make maximum profits and the consumer seeks to gain maximum satisfaction, PR can be accepted as the means of relating one to the other in the most effective manner. This mutual response depends on understanding, communication and goodwill. Thus PR as a marketing aid can be defined as the process of assessing consumer wants, establishing communication, and fostering goodwill so that the consumer wants or needs can be profitably satisfied.

This is very nearly a definition of marketing, and there are those who will declare that marketing and PR are synonymous. In many respects they are – in the human relations aspects – but marketing also deals with other things. It takes the results of PR communication and converts them into marketable products; it uses special techniques such as advantageous packaging, pricing, advertising and merchandising to speed up acceptance and ensure an economic level of production. PR is ubiquitous in the marketing scene even when special marketing techniques, those different from PR, are being exercised. A simple definition of PR is offered by Roy J. Leffingwell (1.2), when he says 'public relations is that part of management's responsibility which involves all people-to-people relations'. All forms of management, including marketing, are to do with PR. We might say especially marketing management since so many different people in the sales and servicing departments, the distribution network and the consuming public come into the marketing orbit.

That is why wide-awake marketing people are becoming aware of the limitations of advertising (making known in order to sell) and are seeking methods which convince rather than persuade. New types of advertising agencies have emerged which do not necessarily use media advertising, and in moving away from the commission system to professional fees they are able to offer promotional campaigns based on below-the-line media such as sales promotion and merchandising. (Above-the-line refers to the media on which advertising agencies receive commission, below-the-line to everything else.) Some industrial advertisers have found that advertising pays less well than a good many PR techniques such as technical seminars, documentary films, video-tapes and external house journals, showing that PR can contribute handsomely to marketing strategies. The consumer protection agencies, official, voluntary and EEC, are criticizing traditional advertising in favour of more plainly informative announcements and this may be in line with the growing scarcity of commodities and less competitive marketing. In this atmosphere, PR should provide services more diverse than mere press relations. This became rapidly apparent with the introduction of independent local radio and the need for radio interview and radio news services as provided by Universal News Services.

Nowadays, the manufacturer has to get closer to people. Hence the popularity of sales promotion and merchandising at the point-of-sale where the manufacturer can deal directly with customers through money-off, free gift, premium offer and mail-in schemes or sampling and in-store promotions.

In getting closer to the consumer the manufacturer may also subdivide the market into segments, the publics of PR. To reach these different groups he employs the PR techniques of press relations, documentary films, house journals, seminars, works visits, private demonstrations, touring exhibitions, educational literature and other aids. Moreover, he has to consider those who influence opinion, the trade channels, and all communication media that express ideas and news, meaning quite an important swing away from the bombast of advertising to the subleties of PR. The reason for this change is that people want to be convinced, not pushed and persuaded. Advertising depends on advocacy and its bias is accepted, whereas PR techniques should be impartial. The example can be taken of the greater influence achieved by road test reports than display advertising for cars. The big ads will arouse curiosity, and interest people to look at the car in the showroom. Inside the showroom the distributors now have video cassette screens and give visual demonstrations, an excellent PR technique. Since most motorists have no technical knowledge, they depend on the advice of motoring correspondents and car-buyer's magazines which give comparative summaries. The motoring press becomes the buyer's second opinion, supplementing the prospective buyer's wishes with expert knowledge.

The editorial must be impartial and credible, not just a nice write-up because the manufacturer is advertising in the same issue as this does the advertiser no good. The product must deserve good opinions, but since few things are ever perfect the manufacturer must not mind constructive criticisms.

It is significant that long-running London shows are often the ones that were panned by the critics. Unstinted praise reads like an advertisement, the antithesis of PR.

Public Relations and Advertising

Because sharp distinctions have been made between PR and advertising the author hastens to make it clear that he is not attacking advertising. But, advertising is not the only way to communicate commercially. There are times when PR can be more effective than advertising and vice versa. The distinctions are necessary because PR is neither a part nor a form of advertising, but a technique which can be used irrespective of, instead of, or in addition to, advertising. It is significant that students preparing for the CAM Certificate now have to study both advertising and PR, so that advertising and PR students understand both. It is also essential to appreciate that although advertising budgets may be larger than PR ones, advertising is but one aspect of a company's activities and only one ingredient in the marketing mix, whereas PR concerns all the many forms of communication of the whole organization, including advertising which can be good or bad PR.

The difference is chiefly that PR informs and educates people so that they understand and know what advertising is persuading and reminding them to buy. In fact, PR helps to strengthen the buyer's power of choice. For instance, it is the PR task to provide knowledge and create understanding of, say, eye care, and for the manufacturer to advertise his brand of eye lotion. This does the PR job of overcoming ignorance, apathy, hostility or misunderstanding. After this, advertising can work more effectively, perhaps on a smaller budget or with less dramatic appeals. People tend to prefer the things with which they are familiar, and PR is a familiarizing process. This does not mean that PR is a 'soft sell', a common misconception of advertising and marketing people. When a child is taught mathematics it is not being put through a soft selling operation in favour of making a career in banking or accountancy. We must see PR as operating on its own plane and establishing knowledge, understanding and confidence on its own merits. People must make up their own minds about the information presented to them.

This is a good place to mention a problem which bothers those concerned with both advertising and PR. There are times when 'blackmail' attempts are made to sell advertisement space in return for editorial coverage. There is no harm in the smart advertisement manager trying it on, and he has to be forgiven for ignorantly regarding editorial mentions as 'free' advertising, but strictly speaking there is no relation between the two. If two hats are being worn, the publicity manager should refer to himself as the PRO or press officer when dealing with editors and producers. Editors are apt to be suspicious of news releases from the advertising fraternity.

Here is a typical 'blackmail' letter, followed by a suggested reply which can be adapted to suit the circumstances:

Dear Sir,
Over the last 12 months or so our editorial department has been inundated with press and information releases concerning XYZ products and enterprises.

We are always willing to use such information in our columns but we consider it rather unfair that other journals in our field get advertising from XYZ when our journal – one of the longest established of its kind – is passed over.

You will appreciate, no doubt, that we cannot continue to give free editorial publicity to XYZ unless some periodical advertising is received also.

Perhaps you would be good enough to comment on the points I have raised.

With best wishes,
Yours sincerely,
John Smith (Editor).

(The appeal for commiseration should be ignored, but the recipient might ask himself whether he may not have spoilt his welcome by sending out too many news releases.)

Dear Mr. Smith,
Thank you for your letter addressed to our Advertising and Publicity Manager who, incidentally, is in no way responsible for the company's press and public relations.

News is sent to you from time to time by this department and if this is of interest and value to your readers you will no doubt print it on its merits.

On the advice of our advertising agents in London, our advertising department books advertisement space according to a planned and approved schedule. Our advertising agents are . . . . if you wish to contact them about next year's schedule.

There is no connection between the advertising and PR departments, since they serve different purposes, and we do not seek 'free publicity' since editorial space cannot be purchased. If we can co-operate with you in any way with news or pictures about the industry we shall endeavour to give you information that is reliable and in good time for your deadlines.

Yours sincerely,

James Jones (Public Relations Manager)

In other words, we leave the advertisement manager to deal with the advertising agency, and the PR manager to deal with the editor. The lesson has to be learnt that advertisement space must be bought for its own special purpose, and it could happen that while a feature article referred to the PRO's company or product, an advertisement would be useful to persuade readers to apply for sales literature, invite a call from a sales representative or purchase the product. Both advertisements and PR editorials serve different purposes – one does not justify the other. When an article about a product is accompanied by an advertisement for the same thing, credibility and reader-value of that editorial column can be nullified.

Some journals invite articles, or offer to publish interviews, and then follow this up by saying that the length of the feature will depend on the amount of advertisement space which will be bought. That is a naked racket.

It is also blackmail when space is booked in various publications and the marketing manager expects editorial coverage in all the journals on the schedule. The schedule may indicate publications which may be interested in PR material, But the PRO cannot lean on the editor because his firm is taking advertisement space.

Very suspect are those newspaper features or supplements in very well-known newspapers, produced solely to sell advertisement space, which mention in the editorial only those firms that buy space. Many of these supplements are of minimal value, being read by only a small proportion of an already small circulation, the advertisement rate consequently being disproportionately high!

Perhaps it is very fortunate that the press is becoming less dependent upon subsidized advertising, and more dependent upon the cover price. When income is derived mostly from readers the editorial can be truly independent of advertising.

The only way a journal can stay in business is to publish what people are prepared to pay money to read, unless it be a freesheet or controlled circulation journal and even they must be read if advertisers are going to get response.

Public Relations as a Management Function

PR practitioners, and the Institute in particular, frequently refer to 'PR as a management function', and there is a tendency for those who are principally engaged in marketing operations to regard this as a somewhat tongue-in-the-cheek attempt to put PR on a more lofty plane than 'mere selling'. These people say that the purpose of a business is to sell and make a profit, that PR efforts should be directed solely to profit-making, and therefore the PR budget and all PR activity should come within the marketing function. This results in a company's entire PR operation being planned and bought or staffed by the head of marketing. Even worse, PR is sometimes bought through an advertising agency as 'below-the-line' expenditure within the advertising appropriation. This is nonsense, and management is at fault in permitting this blinkered approach to PR. Management should have a separate PR budget, allocating sums to marketing and other sections of the organization which require expenditure on PR. Advertising agencies – excellent though they may be in their specialized field of advertising – are often so remarkably ignorant about PR that their 'advice' is a disservice to their clients. We have only to see the elaborate news release headings and the lavish press kits created by advertising agencies to realize how out of their depth they usually are concerning PR.

Those advertising agencies which have realized that PR is a very different world have wisely set up separate subsidiary companies as PR consultancies which handle agency and other PR accounts. Co-operation with the advertising campaign is sensible, for advertising is part of the total communication effort. It may be necessary to see that the advertising does not incur dislike or criticism that could harm the reputation of the company. In today's atmosphere of consumerist attack on advertising, and official consumer protection through increasing legislation and the activities of the Office of Fair Trading, the PR implications of advertising have become more important. An over-zealous young copywriter, not very familiar with the British Code of Advertising Practice or the sixty or so statutes affecting advertising, could inadvertently bring a firm before the Advertising Standards Authority or even the courts, provoking adverse publicity and nullifying the efforts of the PRO. For many well-known companies, advertising has become a very vulnerable area and it is worth recalling Hubert Oughton's comment 'public relations, of which advertising is a part'. He said this when serving as president of the Institute of Practitioners in Advertising.

As will be seen in Chapter Three, a company may deal with many categories of people who have no connection with the marketing function. As well as marketing, a company has to finance itself. It has social responsibilities. Some companies are not out to maximize profits and are engaged in satisficing as Simon puts it (1.3). Community relations, staff recruitment, staff relations, supplier relations, stockholder relations should all come within the span of the PRO's and the PR consultant's activities. A great mistake made by uncertain users of PR is to employ only a press officer attached to the marketing department, or to allow marketing to buy five or ten thousand pounds' worth of press relations service from a consultancy, and rashly call it PR. It is rather like a man putting a flower in the button hole of his shabby old suit and thinking how smart he looks.

Public relations is not just a supplement to advertising but an aid to the entire marketing strategy.

The Image in PR

'Image' is an expression as much maligned and misunderstood as public relations itself. This is partly because of several slightly different meanings) of the word 'image'. In PR we mean a correct impression.

There can be different kinds of image. The *mirror* image is how a company sees itself; the *current* image is how others see the company; the *wish* image is how the company would like to see itself; and the *optimum* image is the possible one that can be achieved bearing in mind the competition from other claims on public attention and interest. An *image study* is a survey to discover the nature of the current image. A *multiple* image occurs when different representatives of an organization, e.g. salesmen, each give a different and perhaps personal image of the organization. Advertising will set out to establish a particular image – a distinctive image that may not be the complete picture – which identifies the product or service as being, say, the cheapest, strongest, most reliable, most exclusive or whatever may be the most advantageous and sales promoting characteristic. There is a so-called intellectual disinclination to admit the validity of image-making, as if it were immoral, but this attitude is irrational and not particularly intelligent.

If a company wishes to market a product it is essential that prospective purchasers should know what kind of product it is and for whom it is intended. Critics who pretend that it is an abuse of freedom of choice to persuade are really sceptical of the ability of human beings to compare the choices and make up their own minds. A bad product can seldom be sold twice to the same victim. Image advertising is therefore very often in the interests of the consumer for it positions the product in the market.

A lot of nonsense is talked about the 'persuasion business', and book titles such as *The Hidden Persuaders* have been misapplied to PR. It is nevertheless a very interesting book, and in it Edward Bernays is asked to consider the possible application of motivational research to PR. But that doyen of American PR, Edward Bernays, has both written some excellent books and confused the non-American PR world with expressions like 'engineering consent' which may have an innocent meaning in the USA but sounds very devious in the UK. Similarly, John Marston, author of a much-admired book, *The Nature of Public Relations*, defined thus: 'Public relations is planned, persuasive communication designed to influence significant publics'. Again, this may suit Americans but it is anathema to others. Some people outside the States try to apply this sort of definition to PR without understanding the differences in definition either side of the Atlantic. People trying to adopt PR techniques in the Third World are often baffled by the disparity within what is loosely called the 'Western World', one that includes Australia, Europe and North America.

The reason for disparity lies in the constitutional status of the press. In the USA it is the fourth estate. It does not hold that role outside the USA and certainly not in Britain where there is a myth about 'freedom of the press' coupled with the prejudiced and mercenary double role of the press. Years ago, the British press consisted of political propaganda sheets, mostly sold in coffee houses or illicitly transported across the country. Today's press is the most class divided in the world, notwithstanding the revealing A, B, C1, C2, D and E social grades of JICNARS. The British press has been the path to fortunes and titles. PR material will be judged by its ability to please readers and sell papers, and it is a waste of time convincing ourselves that the press performs much of an altruistic public service. One may question whether Lord Thomson subsidized *The Times* because he believed Britain needs and deserves such a paper or because it pleased his vanity and ego to own one of the world's most famous newspapers, even if its circulation figures suggest a constantly decreasing reader interest in it. But dual standards are also apparent: journalists as distinct from proprietors and editors tend to be radical and ready to denigrate anything from PR to multinationals as examples in this book will show.

It is by understanding the business nature of the press that it becomes obvious how tactless it is for British PR to be *persuasive*. The press prints persuasive messages or puffs in the advertisement columns and charges advertisers accordingly. As we shall discover in Chapter Fifteen all persuasiveness, all superlatives, all generalities, all self-praise must be replaced by cold-blooded factual information, offered without the slightest comment. Having said this it is immediately clear that when our stories do appear in the media they are not 'free advertisements'.

This does not mean that we are purely informative, full stop. We are informative in the service of proper understanding, which is a highly necessary part of an organization's activity. A hospital may not be thought to be 'selling' its services under the British national health scheme, but it will not function fully unless its specialist services are known in the right quarters – you don't take an adult accident case to a children's hospital – and this depends upon communication.

PR practitioners are sometimes accused of being *selective* about the information they issue, as if they are deliberately withholding information. While they should not attempt to whitewash unpleasant incidents, it is necessary to select the information which is relevant to particular media. Criticism can indeed be made of *unselective* information, as when the same story is sent foolishly to the technical press, popular newspapers and the Press Association. Material has to be selected to suit all three.

There is no point in marketing a product which no-one understands or about which people are sceptical, apathetic, prejudiced or hostile. This could lead to grossly wasteful expenditure on unsuccessful advertising, and this has happened time and again with new product launches that have failed because the market had not been educated, and an image established, in advance of promotion. PR *educates*: it does not *persuade*. It presents facts so that people will be made aware. But people tend to like the things they know and understand best, and therefore people are more likely to buy the known than the unknown. PR can aid the arts of selling, advertising and merchandising by breaking the barriers of ignorance, without urging any action beyond asking for further information or beyond encouraging prospects to go and study the goods for themselves. This is the subtle difference between PR and advertising. PR is neither a substitute for advertising nor a kind of advertising. For this reason it is false to say that mention of a product in a press story or TV or radio news bulletin would be 'advertising' since the more complete PR message would have no sales content. On this point there is confusion over publicity and advertising which are not synonymous. Publicity is a result. Advertising is an intention.

But just as there are advertising people who find it difficult to recognize the subtle difference between PR and advertising, and cannot see PR as anything else but another weapon in the promotional and persuasion armoury, so there are PR people who fear the closer association nowadays being forged between PR and marketing because they think information is likely to be presented less honestly, more persuasively and therefore with greater bias. Perhaps because so many marketing ideas have been imported from the USA, they fear that PR may become Americanized on persuasion lines. There need be no foundation for these fears if we recognize that PR is a far greater field of activity than those activities, like selling and advertising, in which persuasion is a necessary part.

But even within advertising some interesting new thoughts are being expressed about persuasion! People are often more independent than their protectors imagine. Brainwashing does not work, given access to choice. Motivation research, as pioneered by Ernest Dichter, has revealed some home truths about buying motives, often using elaborate clinical techniques to prove the unacceptably obvious!

Conversely, Christians are Christians, Moslems are Moslems, mostly because the dogma was inculcated when there was no other choice. Many of us are subject to a form of mental conscription simply as an accident of birth. Get a child young enough and it can probably be taught to believe anything, but later in life the awkward questions can arise. Not many people do enjoy much choice in their political or religious views unless they have a very liberal education and enlightening personal experiences outside their birthplace environment which invite comparative thought. Lack of comparative thought has led to tragedies like that of Northern Ireland. Genuine free thought is an exquisite luxury liable to lead to great personal unpopularity. Advertising and public relations have to be seen against this difficult background, not picked on as isolated bad influences in an otherwise pure world. For these reasons the image of a product may vary from country to country. Beer is a good example. In Britain it is a traditional drink associated with food and pleasure, but in West Africa or the West Indies it is associated with health and strength and sexual prowess.

While it is not the function of PR to persuade, PR is concerned with image-making if we frankly take this to be the establishment of a correct impression of an organization, its policy, products or service. This is rather broader than the advertising concept of an image – e.g.

Guinness is Good For You – which is usually limited to a brand image rather than that of a total organization. Thus, it is the PR task to clear lines of communication so that our subject is known and understood for what it is.

A misguided criticism sometimes levelled at image-making is that it is a means of obscuring the truth. In other words, we are accused of saying things are better than they really are. Malcolm Muggeridge once described PR as 'organized lying'. How do we reply?

The fact is that everything in life is liable to misuse: murder can be committed with a useful tool such as a hammer. Without laws, codes and rules there would be anarchy, and we are one another's keepers. Is it therefore unexpected that businessmen with a keen eye to profit and a blind eye to ethics will misuse the ability to communicate ideas and information to the public and have no scruples about presenting a false image which is to their financial advantage?

But the PR practitioner and the press officer must have scruples, and they must be prepared to refuse their services to those who would abuse them. Good PR relies on this ethical adherence being understood by editors, journalists and radio and TV producers, reporters, interviewers and others. The importance and value of the IPR Code of Professional Conduct has already been stressed, and it applies again when we are asked to falsify images. One way to create a good image in place of a bad one is to use PR techniques such as opinion research and problem analysis to discover how the causes of the poor impression can be removed. Then, when a good image is deserved it can be made known and established by PR methods such as press relations.

The principle has to be clearly understood and upheld. Expressions such as 'image-making', 'polishing tarnished images' and 'creating favourable images' are bandied about as if PR was a form of wizardry. How can one polish a tarnished image? It is impossible. The truth will depend on the available information and how it is disseminated. This is the biggest problem in image-making: there are limitations on both the output and the input of information, on the ability to dispense it and the willingness to accept it. Consequently, a dilemma of PR is that everyone inevitably is restricted to imperfect images about everything, and it is the PR responsibility to try to correct the misapprehensions that most people have about many things. The immensity of the PR task is therefore quite stunning.

Yet another situation occurs when it is necessary to change an image or create a new one. Times and products change.

An organization which began making, say, simple wireless sets may today produce sophisticated electronic and Hi-Fi equipment.

It is, of course, very much a management responsibility to determine what image or character the organization should have, and this is closely linked with marketing policy, and with the determination of the means of distribution and the type or class of buyer to whom the products or services are aimed. Stores are particularly good examples of businesses that have individual images or characters. The images that people hold of, say, Harrods, Selfridges, Woolworths and Marks and Spencer are distinctively different and more or less universal.

Press Relations and Public Relations

The creative aspects of press relations form Part Three, but this is a good place to distinguish between *press* relations and *public* relations. The initials *PR* are so commonly used that it has become easy to confuse press relations practice with its parent public relations, especially when so many people from company directors to editors either see no difference between the two, or believe that press relations practice is the beginning and the end of PR. It may sometimes be the end, in the sense of the end product, but it is certainly not the beginning.

In PR we do not address ourselves to the public, or the general public, but to particular defined publics. Unlike consumer advertising, consumer PR is addressed to different sub-sections of the mass buying public such as past, present and future customers of various age groups, social grades and either sex. Publics also extend from the extremes of the local community and the scattered consumer public, taking in staff, suppliers, investors, distributors and opinion leaders. Many other techniques besides press relations are needed to communicate with all these different publics.

This means that while press relations is a valuable technique, and one that can be used extremely well in industrial countries that are well-endowed with press, radio and TV communication media, there are other techniques such as documentary films, internal and external house journals, educational literature, exhibitions, sponsorships, seminars, conferences and so forth that come within the gamut of comprehensive public relations practice.

References

1.1 JEFKINS, F., *Marketing and PR Media Planning*, Pergamon Press, 1974
1.2 LEFFINGWELL, R. J., *International Public Relations Review*, October 1974
1.3 SIMON, A. H., *American Economics Review* **49**, 3, pp 25-83, June 1959

CHAPTER TWO

Special Uses
of PR

To demonstrate something of the breadth of PR usage this chapter will consider a variety of commercial and non-commercial uses beginning with the most common one in industrial society, product publicity. It has developed out of the need to publish news about the host of new products which came on the market in the 50's and 60's, once wartime shortages and controls came to an end. It is perhaps hard to believe that before this era of prosperity most houses had been built without a garage and only a minority of people owned a motor car, that holidays abroad were almost unheard of, and detergents, washing machines, plastic paints, television, transistor radios, central heating, Hi-Fi, and many other things now taken for granted were either unknown or little known. In less affluent countries, the more common uses of PR may be in the Government services which use the techniques to improve production, raise standards of health or promote education. Basically, the reason for using PR is the same: information has to be spread about things new.

Product Publicity

A study of what is called 'product publicity' will help to show the difference between news and puffery.

In the 1820's and 1830's, when early newspaper advertising for commodities and services was better known as 'puffing', it was hard to tell editorials from advertisements because the art of displaying advertisements was a sophistication yet to come. It belonged to the day when the space broker found it was easier and more profitable to sell space if he also had creative talent, and especially a gift for writing slogans.

In the early 19th century, advertisement copywriters were famous authors and poets, like Charles Lamb. Puffery was a valuable aid to marketing, although much despised by men like Carlyle who could not understand that a trader or manufacturer must make known in order to sell, and that newspaper advertising was an economic means of broadcasting a sales message to buyers distant from the mill or factory.

To the newspaperman, puffery has continued to mean literary advertisement, and the attempt to present advertising as news has incurred the wrath of editors convinced that their editorial columns were being invaded and misused, although a great many things advertised are also of news value.

A puff, or a 'free puff' as it is more often described, means an unmistakable advertisement appearing in the editorial columns. It is the term used by an alert editor when he thinks that somebody is trying to gain from a reference in his columns. It is also used less specifically by advertisement managers responsible for selling space who regard editorial mentions as announcements improperly occupying space which they could or should have sold. For these reasons we frequently see the absurdity of a legitimate news story from which all commercial names have been obviously deleted, usually to appease the advertisement manager. The press is, regrettably, inclined to be dominated by the advertisement side rather than the editorial for the simple reason that many publications exist very largely on their advertisement revenue. However, with competition from TV and radio, high production costs and reductions in advertisement revenue due to economic crises, income from cover prices is becoming more important, thus encouraging greater editorial independence. And, unless the editorial secures adequate sales the advertisement manager will be unable to sell his space. A good editor, as we shall see, may well rely on good press officers providing him with material which helps him to achieve a successful journal.

We therefore have to balance the fears of the editor that he is being 'got at' by those seeking free publicity with those of the advertisement manager that organizations may be getting away with unpaid advertising. In reconciling these fears the general antipathy of the publishing world towards the growing practice of press relations has to be overcome which is sometimes seen to be a menace to both their independent editorial functions and their profitable space-selling enterprise. These are not entirely unfounded fears because users of PR often erroneously believe that press relations is simply the means of achieving free and favourable publicity. Publicity is like swings and roundabouts. *Favourable* reports have to be deserved: they cannot be contrived. And the media have a wicked way of repaying those who perpetrate non-stories for the sake of publicity.

A four-sided situation confronts us. It comprises the organization, the press officer, the editor and the advertisement manager, and the situation can be resolved only if we accept the fundamental principle that it is the press officer's duty to establish good relations with the communication media on behalf of his organization. In the supply of genuine news to editors, producers and script writers he is doing nothing to offend advertisement managers, and he has every right to expect his organization to be named as a proper and necessary part of the published story. This means, then, that the press officer's sole concern is in satisfying the editor. The employer or client not only has to understand this principle, and the relationship that follows from it, but also appreciate that publicity derives from a story which is published on its merits.

This is imperative now that PR is becoming less of an information service and more of a system of communication necessary to marketing strategy. But it also applies in the newly PR-conscious world of the local authorities and among the numerous public services and nationalized industries that have to explain themselves. In times of great political and economic change it is necessary for governments to use the frankness of PR rather than the political pornography of propaganda. We are so inundated with media which penetrate our letterboxes, drawing rooms and motor cars that the news will be rejected if it lacks credibility. Generally, the Americans seem very confused about the true nature of PR and press relations and there is the renowned example of the American Air Attache in Phnom Penh who, when questioned by reporters about the bombing of Cambodian Communists, protested: 'you always write it's bombing, bombing, bombing. It's not bombing. It's air support.'

We now arrive at the real consideration: what is news? News is information that has not been previously reported, published or read. But some news can be timeless: for instance, a manufacturer of gears had a catalogue of items that had never appeared in the technical press, twelve were selected and at monthly intervals a product story and picture was mailed, excellent coverage was gained, and the manufacturer received hundreds of reader enquiries. One does have to be careful about 'timeless' stories that journalists file and then rediscover many months later when details and even availability may have changed. Publication about a 'new' product that has been discontinued can be very embarrassing.

News is not a novel story which has no publicity content. Despite the pretended scruples of some editors, news cannot be a negation of publicity because every story in every publication – unless it is the editor's pure theory and opinion – is bound to be good or bad publicity for someone or something. This is because publicity is no more than making known, creating public knowledge, publicizing. Such publicity is informative, making no attempt to persuade, influence and induce action, that is, to make known in order to sell, which is the extension of publicity known today as advertising and formerly as puffery.

The words 'publicity' and 'advertising' are not synonymous, even though Publicity Manager is sometimes used as a job description rather superior to Advertising Manager. The title Publicity Manager is well-used in the holiday or entertainment fields where the work involves events and personalities leading to publicity. But strictly speaking, the two terms can be distinguished, publicity making known and advertising making known in order to sell. Thus news can often be good or bad publicity, because news informs and makes known and while it may carry the bias of the particular medium it will not be so biased, controlled and sales promoting as to be advertising.

The nearest one gets, perhaps, to 'free' advertising is when a critic gives an unconditional testimonial and goes so far as to say 'You must go out and buy this book' or 'This is a film you must not miss.' But this is really luck because the critic could have condemned book or the film as something not worth buying, reading or going to see. However, since people still exercise their own decisions great success or failure is usually deserved, critics or no critics.

Nevertheless, there is a great element of risk in press relations activity: the press officer should not comment on his organization or product – unless he is prepared to invite an editorial contradiction or a back-handed 'so the company claims' comment – but the editor can, and it may be favourable, unfavourable or neutral. An advertisement, subject to advertising law, the BCAP and media 'house rules', will be so biased, controlled and sales promoting that it will say exactly what the advertiser wants to say. This is not possible with product publicity which is not, therefore, free advertising.

The press officer may have to convince his employer or client of the true nature and purpose of a news release and must not be led astray by one who does not understand this. The editor will discard a news release that is written as a piece of advertisement copy. Large numbers of releases fail because their authors either do not know the difference between news release writing and advertisement copywriting, or they are unprofessional enough, or of such lowly status, that they obey managerial instructions which are nonsense instead of giving advice which will produce results.

Let us examine two examples. Example No 1 is a puff. Example No 2 is a news release. Just the opening paragraph is given.

> (1) There isn't a sunflower to beat Casius! It's the most exciting new vegetable seed ever introduced by Benson's. Casius was the greatest, the tallest and the most glorious variety to be seen at Basle's International Garden Seed Show.
> (2) Casius is a new giant variety of sunflower added to Benson's range of vegetable seeds. Growing to nearly four metres in height with a head sixty centimetres in diameter, Casius was the tallest variety with the largest bloom shown at the International Garden Seed Show in Basle.

The first is unacceptable puffery, indistinguishable from advertisement copy, while the second is factual and informative, unemotional and free of biased comment. Of course, if the editor chooses to add his comment that is his prerogative, but he may say that Casius is the greatest or the lousiest.

The purpose of a news release is to provide facts. If it expresses an opinion as well, this will be propaganda. If it contains self-praise, it will be an advertisement. While it is sensible to name the product and its maker as early in the story as possible, names should afterwards be used sparingly. The golden rule is that the name should appear only when its mention adds clarity and meaning to the report. Name plugging is an abuse of press relations, and rightly arouses the ire of editors.

The object of this discussion, and the definitions it has produced, is to arrive at the genuine newsworthiness of product publicity since the name is apt to be misleading to those whose loose usage of jargon tends to equate publicity with advertising.

Product publicity is *news* about products, and in the right journals or in the right pages or features, or appropriate programmes on radio and TV, products can be very important *news* to the particular audience attracted by these specialized items. The new machinery or fertilizer discussed by the agricultural correspondent will be *news* to the farmer. Product publicity seldom makes 'hard' news and is unlikely to be published in the general or home news columns of daily newspapers unless it is an invention, national achievement or has received a huge export order, or because there is some social, economic, legal or political angle. Stories about products and services are usually reserved for special features. The press officer should not send such stories to the editor of a newspaper but to the correct specialist journalist.

Selecting the right recipient of a news release is part of skilled press relations work. Each story requires its own individually picked mailing list, and it should be a list of individual journalists, specialist editors or correspondents rather than just a list of newspaper and magazine titles. Like anything else, a news release has to be marketed, and the acid test of a good press officer is the extent to which he knows his media. And by this is not meant the extent to which he knows a journalist personally: contacts mean little. The writing of a publishable story and its placing with the right media at the right time is everything. A contact cannot print a dud story whereas an editor you have never met will welcome a thoroughly good story. Advertisements seeking press officers 'with first-class Fleet Street contacts' reveal a sad misunderstanding of what press relations are all about. The only thing that matters to an editor is whether your story is of such value to his readers that it will help to maintain and extend sales or readership of his journal. And that is a matter of very elementary publishing economics.

Sometimes this restriction of product stories to the specialist features is a little unfair. We all know that when a product or service is in trouble the press will comment freely and names will be named. We are told very bluntly what kind of aircraft from whose airline hit the mountainside; which company has been brought to a standstill by a strike, and so on, whereas if one of these companies merits favourable comment the name is all too often omitted on the grounds that it would be advertising!

There is an indisputable need for news releases. Thousands of editors with small staffs could not possibly report all the news which is supplied to them free of charge by press officers. The city pages of our daily papers and business features and sections have grown in importance in recent years and are full of information about the financial affairs and personalities of public companies, mostly derived from press officers. Our popular gossip columns would scarcely survive but for the flow of stories and invitations to attend PR-organized events. *The Guardian* may adopt an attitude of intellectual superiority (mindful of its readership among left-wing teachers) and sneer at PR, but the *Financial Times* has become one of the best newspapers in the world because, among other things, it has cultivated PR sources of information.

The proof of this need for news releases lies in the fact that many

B

editors are by no means shy of ringing up or writing to press officers and asking to be put on mailing lists. When journalists change jobs they often make this known to press officers. And if one or two journals fail to get a story, luckless editors will ring up the press officer and complain if rival papers have printed the story. Although so many news releases are destined for the dustbin, others are professionally produced and are most welcome. The following letter bears out the contention that there is a demand for news releases:

Dear Mr. Smith,

Your agency's last Press Release did not reach us – perhaps because we are not on your mailing list. I can speak with some certainty because I make a point of looking personally at the material which our friends in Public Relations are kind enough to send us.

My concern, and the reason for writing you this letter, are simply explained: British Reader's Digest covers a broad spectrum of interest and to develop the kind of articles that hold the attention of our ten million British readers, my colleagues and I explore as many sources of information about the current scene as we can.

A number of our recent articles were sparked by Press Releases; if one of your objectives is to bring your client's activities to the notice of a mass audience, you may feel that it would be worth your while to send details to British Reader's Digest in case the subject fits our editorial requirements.

Please address your Releases to:

The Editor
British Reader's Digest
25 Berkeley Square
London W1X 6AB

As a token of our interest in your interest, I have pleasure in enclosing a copy of *our* latest Release.

Yours sincerely,
(Signed) Michael Randolph,
Editor, British Editions.

Industrial Relations

Better known as staff relations, we are here concerned with internal communications which are not to be confused with paternal efforts such as sports clubs, works outings and dowdy house journals. Industrial relations concern the changing world of relations between employer and worker which make old-world paternalism and equally old-world trade union militancy a matter of pre-Edward Heath history. Of course, such positive industrial relations cannot exist without the appropriate management policy. To repeat, PR is a management philosophy.

In the UK, worker participation is feared by the unions because it will destroy the stranglehold of narrow craft unionism while management, being mainly conservative in the narrowest sense, cannot accept such a liberal solution to the tyranny of futile strikes. Philips in Holland have prospered through the works council system and a few British companies had received the message by the middle 70's and a few house journals had appeared in which critical readers' letters were published, and there were even intelligently re-written versions of the annual report and accounts. Another splendid innovation (by an American firm) was IBM's use of wall newspapers, incentive awards recommended by staff for their colleagues, and an internal factory PRO and staff, at their factory in Greenock.

Volvo's new factory at Kalmar is a particularly interesting example of industrial relations emanating from the top. Faced with the problem of 12 per cent absenteeism and a 50 per cent labour turnover at Gothenburg, where half the labour force were Finnish or Yugoslav, Volvo created a new factory with new production methods at the fishing port of Kalmar where 65 per cent of the local people were out of work, although the managing director was criticized for announcing this on television before informing his workers.

At Kalmar only 600 people are required to build 30,000 cars a year, working in groups of 15–25 to meet a set number of cars per day. There are no noisy conveyors, no monotonous job cycles and no production foremen. With foreign labour there were inevitable communication problems which no longer exist with indigenous labour. Car shells are shipped from the parent factory and carried round the Kalmar plant on 275 low trolleys, battery operated, which are progressed manually or by a computer so that the trolleys can be made to pause in buffer zones or made to crawl at 3 m per minute. All this costs 10 per cent more than conventional methods yet this extra cost is cancelled out by the absence of stoppages. This management answer to conservative trade unionism shop-floor militancy was not only made unnecessary but impossible.

Job satisfaction is a prime factor in industrial relations. The majority of strikes result from rumours and fears of insecurity together with boring unpleasant work which could be eliminated as Volvo has done.

Monotonous labour-intensive work will never be justified as it is in over-populated developing countries. This has to be understood by UK management if people are to enjoy working for their employers. It is interesting that job satisfaction does exist in non-union companies where the staff are paid higher-than-union rates, are not restricted to certain 'trades', the work provides personal independence, or the grade of work is highly technical and beyond union standards. However, these idealistic conditions may not suit every industry and trade unions are themselves a form of communication between workers and management, with go-ahead management training shop stewards in both new technologies to be adopted by the company and in management techniques. These shop stewards then become the innovators in passing on the message to the adopters. Even this may not be enough, and the PR need may be for management to talk directly to the total organization.

This was brought out in an article by David Morgan Rees, group information officer of Bridon (formerly British Ropes) (2.1).

'It is in the area of industrial relations that I believe industrial communicators will have their most important challenges in the future. The pace of change in industrial relations will accelerate. This will mean a host of new communications problems to be dealt with wisely and imaginatively.

'The gathering momentum towards worker participation in British industry is one example. . . This new style of participative management cannot work successfully on the present low level of knowledge and understanding which exists about "the business of Business". . .

'The communication needs in such a situation are enormous. They make all previous commitment to the principles of in-company communication methods such as company newspapers and "teach-ins" seem modest in comparison . . .

'I believe that in this new situation a major emphasis in any communications programme within industry must now be on finding new and better ways of explaining basic company finance to all employees, not only those in management. Alongside this there is a need to make sure that the increasingly complicated pattern of employment conditions and benefits can be put across to employees in simple and intelligible ways to achieve maximum understanding. . .

'Because good communications people should be good all-round communicators . . . they should play a far greater part in helping to train managers to do the same. For in the end the most effective form of communications is the face-to-face briefing of employees in small groups. . .

'This is where communications people can share their expertise with colleagues in intensive training programmes to help them to do the job of briefing better. . .

'For many in-line managements this extension of the work of PR people into personal matters may seem presumptuous. Perhaps this is because they still have the impression of PR as being nothing more than wooing the press.'

These excerpts show how PR can make a contribution to industrial health that one would scarcely think possible if one listened seriously to PR's detractors. The media and techniques that can be used for industrial relations purposes are:

1. Eyeball-to-eyeball talks by directors, managers, executives and supervisors.

2. House journals produced by independent editors free of top-management interference.

3. Wall newspaper, again produced independently.

4. Own radio station (e.g. United Biscuits radio station serving factories in London, Manchester and Glasgow by landline).

5. Closed circuit TV.

6. Video cassette-recorder.

7. Documentary films.

8. Meetings: seminars, conferences, social gatherings.

9. Letters to employees.

Corporate and Financial PR

These two go together except that the investing public is not the only one to be interested in the character of the company. Years ago corporate PR was thought of in rather specious terms as prestige publicity. Now business firms are judged very critically by their behaviour towards numerous publics, this culminating in their standing on the Stock Exchange. A successful new product launch, an unwise investment overseas, a pollution scandal, a series of valuable export orders, an unsuccessful take-over bid, an unflattering report from the Monopolies Commission, connivance in unsavoury foreign politics, serious industrial conflict, will give the company the image it deserves which share prices will reflect. Poor share prices present take-over risks.

In the City there are PR consultants skilled at dealing with the financial and business press, familiar with the ways of the City and conversant with the Stock Exchange rules regarding share issues and the City Code on Take-overs and Mergers. As advisers on corporate PR they will be anxious to encourage client behaviour which will not create a bear market, and it will be seen that the image of an organization depends greatly on the PR-mindedness of the chief executive. A PR-minded chief executive is one whose sense of responsibility, ability to be frank and communicative, and thoughtfulness for others inspires confidence and wins friends so that disaster is averted or never even risked.

Success and bigness can be their own enemies, and it may be difficult to gain credit for very considerable achievement, no matter whether the organization is a nationalized industry or a multinational corporation. The modern consumerist is against big business and their let's-all-be-peasants attitude to economic rationality may be the spin-off to revelations about bribery and corruption, but it is a psychological attitude with which the PRO must contend. In the eyes of too many people, to be big is to be bad, as if it were criminal to succeed, and anything big and successful must be attacked, insulted, accused and bled white. Few international companies have suffered from this spitefulness quite so much as ITT.

Nigel Rowe, ITT Europe's assistant director of public relations in Brussels, began an article (2.2) with the words 'ITT is arguably the most vilified corporation in the Western World'.

Since the previous Autumn ITT had been publishing dramatic whole-page advertisements in answer to criticisms about their economic impact on countries like Britain. At the same time, the abuse about ITT continued in the international press. ITT were accused of financing the Nixon election campaign, and of having contributed to the downfall of the Allende regime in Chile, neither of which were true. The full story of ITT Europe's corporate PR programme will be found in the case studies in Part Four.

ITT have taken this further and on May 13, 1975 Maurice R. Valente, president of ITT Europe, said at a luncheon meeting at the American Club of Brussels:

> '. . . the present situation has already brought calls for greater government intervention and control in most of Europe. . . One of the most dangerous effects on business today results from a lack of public information about it because ignorance breeds hostility, suspicion and even fear. . . In my view, industry and

business must play a strong and appropriately assertive role in ensuring that *all* the facts are known and understood (and the myths demolished) *before* governments and other regulatory bodies take decisions that lock us all into new ground rules that are punative and in the finality counter-productive to the best interest of those they seek to protect. . . It is no longer enough for business simply to be *doing* a good job. It is also our responsibility to ensure that everyone *knows* we are doing a good job. . . But there is a "communications gap" at the moment – and this gap must be bridged. . . the job business and its articulate spokesmen have to do now is to "get out and sell".'

Mr. Valente's speech made a long overdue plea for more information from business and management, reiterating what has been said earlier in this book about management's lack of training in communication processes.

The experience is not peculiar to ITT, nor is it new. In 1962 there was the spectacular take-over battle between ICI and Courtaulds which need never have happened if Courtaulds had been more communicative in the past and looked more seriously to its corporate image. As a result, Courtaulds had to spend several hundred thousand pounds to establish the truth about itself through short-term expensive advertising instead of long-term inexpensive PR.

Is corporate advertising worthwhile? There is no easy answer except to say that by introducing advertising one is resorting to persuasive communication instead of informative. If the need is to present facts quickly and with impact, advertising has its inherent advantages – but at a price. This kind of corporate advertising has a certain air of desperation about it, and is not perhaps the best of PR tactics.

There is, of course, control over media, timing, size and position of space and the content of the message, and this can be vital in a short-term campaign. But the expensive, brash short-term campaign does imply that there was a previous failure to communicate. Courtauld's had to do it. ICI had their *Pathfinders* TV commercials which mystified some viewers who couldn't understand what they were trying to sell in spots normally taken up by hard-selling ads.

A Brussels-based American multinational conglomerate which has had its PR problems is CPC Europe (originally known as Corn Products), it has chosen to almost hide behind some obscure initials, leaving its family of famous firms to enjoy their own individual identities. These companies are very old-established ones, famous in countries like Britain, Germany and Switzerland to mention only Brown & Polson, Gerber Baby Foods, Knorr soups and Maizena. However, a conglomerate can suffer when a product failure in one company threatens to attract adverse publicity to other members of the corporation.

A nightmare situation occurred in July 1974 when a wrong computer input in one of CPC's British plants led to the production of a dangerous material that was shipped through a Dutch CPC industrial company to a Dutch cattle food compounder. As a result some calves died, and this was complicated by the fact that Dutch calves were being exported to other European countries. The Italian government closed the frontier to Dutch calves, exploiting the situation for political reasons, since it was cheaper to import from eastern countries.

CPC in Brussels, concerned about the need to protect public health and safety, immediately informed the Dutch health authorities in case people who ate the meat suffered. But CPC Europe were unable to issue a press statement because their insurance company in the States warned that coverage would be at risk if the company admitted liability. Eventually, a press statement was permitted but not before news agencies were passing the story round the world in two conflicting versions. The press were already talking of 80,000 animals which were either 'quarantined' or 'dead', this being based on a report from a Dutch 'stringer' to a news agency. Conflicting information was a problem and the main worry was that this industrial problem should reflect on the good name of CPC's consumer products, especially baby foods.

The corporation was at the mercy of a world press that was publishing horrific discrepancies. For instance, the *Wall Street Journal* published erroneous facts. The quantity of feed quoted could not have killed the number of calves claimed in the report. A retraction was refused, but when threatened with legal action a new story was printed. After this evidence of false press information, many papers dropped the story. Only a brief sketch has been given here, but throughout this trying time CPC received highly professional advice and service from Hill and Knowlton International. This experience is the reverse of ITT's: would the member companies of CPC have suffered damaging publicity had it been better known that they were part of the same organization as the Dutch industrial company with the cattle feed disaster? There can be times when a corporate image is undesirable. There is a lot to be said for the saying that a chain is as strong as its weakest link.

Before leaving the subject of corporate advertising it is important to see it in historical perspective and to note its positive value as a form of PR rather than as a class of advertising.

In the 50's there was a spate of corporate advertising which was then dubbed 'prestige' or worse still 'institutional' advertising – terms created by advertising agents who had spent the war years as government department PRO's. Their idea of post-war PR was prestige advertising which solved the problem of how to keep PR 'above-the-line', that is within the realm of the commission system. It was a purely advertising agency attitude to PR, and when the PR consultancies became established this type of beautiful advertising was seen to be a wasteful way of spending meagre PR appropriations.

In the 60's and the first half of this decade corporate advertising was resorted to only when the communication task was so urgent that advertising was the best technique in a fire-fighting situation. There is nothing wrong in using advertising for PR purposes if it works. Usually, it works best when there is not time to wait upon the whims of the news media to provide editorial or programme coverage or to do so promptly. But, if the editor does not share our enthusiasm for the reader interest in our message this could also be the measure of the likely interest in the big full-page advertisement costing hundreds and maybe thousands of pounds. Consequently, such advertising is a sledge-hammer PR device, like backing a fortune on the last race in the attempt to recoup losses on all the previous races. ITT did have the grace to admit that they had been inadequate informants in the past, although the most serious criticisms of ITT were not of the European organization but of the company's alleged skullduggery in North and South America. The European organization was caught up in a 'Watergate-CIA'type smear campaign, so easily manufactured against an American multinational.

There is also a tendency to think that if corporate advertising is decorated with *avant-garde* art forms that this will signify that the corporate body is up to date or a generous patron of the arts. We are supposed to be dealing with communication, and humour is sometimes the best way to deflate critics. Culture can go unheeded by philistines. Where possible – and this was probably not the case with ITT and its concern with statistics – corporate advertising benefits from wit and humour. Something could be learned from the wartime posters which proclaimed 'Is Your Journey Really Necessary?' and 'Be Like Dad, Keep Mum.' Moreover, we are dealing with a world in which *The Sun* is rising while *The Times* sets. What are corporate advertisements doing in *The Guardian* and *The Observer*?

We must not leave this section without a word about annual reports.

Fortunately we have out-lived the gorgeous annual reports of a decade or so ago in favour of ones that are comprehensible with the emphasis on legible typography rather than full-colour photographs. Some are also translated or digested into press advertisements that give the essential information, perhaps explained by thumb-nail sketches and charts. Confidence may be sought through press advertisements as with a half-page summary of the chairman's speech which the Rio Tinto-Zinc Corporation reproduced below the headline *Revitalizing the United Kingdom economy*. On the same day, May 23, 1975, Guest Keen and Nettlefolds (GKN) had a similar half-page advertisement with a portrait of the chairman and a quotation headline which read *We have come through with flying colours. We shall do so again.* Here we have advertising being used for the double purpose of announcing the company results and gaining confidence through achievement.

Government PR

In this section we must consider only the PR aspects of government communication and also try to avoid party politics. Senior British government PRO's are usually called chief information officers or CIO's. To some extent their work may be a mixture of propaganda, advertising and PR and these very different forms of communication need to be disentangled. Propaganda will concern the government's efforts to win acceptance at home and abroad for its policies, advertising may be used in press, poster and TV campaigns for, say, road safety campaigns. But PR is reserved for explaining Government policies, providing information about Ministerial actions and explaining to the electorate the services and benefits provided by government departments. For example, new or proposed schemes will be announced in White Papers which lobby correspondents will discuss in the news media. Ministers will meet the press at press conferences. If they give background information to aid journalists writing about the affairs of the day, Ministers will not be quoted but the information will be from non-attributable sources. Expressions such as 'from a usually reliable source' may be used in reports.

Information, such as copies of speeches or policy statements, which may be issued to the press by the different party headquarters is very different. A distinction has to be made between information about the elected government's work on behalf of the nation, and the information issued by political parties, even by the party in power. This may seem confusing to overseas readers from countries with military or one party governments where it may be difficult to differentiate between propaganda and PR.

If it is government policy in a one party state to introduce social services these have to be explained to the people and PR techniques are called for. A census may be difficult to carry out unless PR techniques have been applied to rural people of various ethnic groups and religions to show that unless a census is taken it will be impossible to plan social developments such as roads, water, power and health services. In fact, in developing countries PR has a role to play infinitely more vital and complicated than it is in western industrial countries.

The Central Office of Information acts as the official agency for the appointment of suppliers of services such as advertising agencies, PR consultants, printers, photographers, film makers and so on. The COI is also Britain's spokesman overseas, except for tourism, and operates through officials in British embassies and consulates. Thus, if a British firm has a non-advertising documentary film which demonstrates British expertise and enterprise the COI can arrange for its distribution abroad ranging from private showings to its appearance on TV. COI publicity services for exporters are described in Chapter Eleven.

Local Government PR

The creation of the new local authorities in 1974 gave a new impetus to the appointment of PR staff since it was very necessary to explain the work and services of the new authorities throughout the country. Good relations with all the news media are very important.

Different authorities have different characteristics, services, locations and information needs. Some are involved in tourism, some are interested in attracting industry to factory sites, while others have special services such as airports, sports centres, historic attractions, shopping centres and other amenities which prompt the use of information services.

At one time the public library was thought to be the only information centre that was necessary, but times have changed and many hundreds of PR personnel are now emloyed in the local government service.

The following wording from an advertisement in the *UK Press Gazette* and *Campaign* seeking PR staff for the London borough of Tower Hamlets provides an interesting interpretation of local government PR duties:

What Do The Words
Public Relations
Mean To You?

Here at Tower Hamlets they mean a group of young professional people dedicated to serving the community by acting
as a two-way communications link between residents and
the Council and by presenting a true and fair image of their
part in London's East End.

If you like the sound of this, read on.

Two job descriptions then followed.

Public and Social Service PR

Under this umbrella title must be included many specialized services,
often associated with local government, but sometimes operating
independently or through government departments. Among these are
the police, fire brigade, ambulance, hospital, probation service and the
social services that take care of the less privileged, the handicapped and
the aged. Again many hundreds of PR personnel are engaged in these
fields.

In recent years the value of PR in establishing better relations
between the police and the public has been an object lesson in the use of
PR techniques. Some excellent films have been made about the Met-
ropolitan Police, and good use of the media has been made through
TV programmes such as *Police Five* which have encouraged public
co-operation and the reports on traffic conditions given out by the
local radio stations. Awareness of the importance of good press relations was stressed by Chief Constable John Alderson of Devon and
Cornwall Constabulary when, shortly after his appointment, he
despatched a circular stating;

'The police have made unnecessary difficulties for themselves
by tending to withhold information which could safely be made
public. . .

'This tendency has been encouraged because at times openness
with the news media has resulted in incorrect or unfairly critical
reporting to which the natural reaction is to be less forthcoming
in future. . .

'It is my firm belief that the Force has a great deal more to be proud of than the public know and that a little more openness with the news media, heightening trust, confidence and co-operation, is all that is required to correct that ignorance. . .

'Provided an embargo has not been imposed at higher level and disclosure would not compromise judicial processes, factual, non-controversial information may be so supplied by any officer.

However, the last paragraph has not always been accepted by the press, and in the course of some famous investigations press relations have not been cordial. The kidnapping of Mrs. Muriel McKay and of Miss Lesley Whittle had tragic results which might have been averted if the media had been more reticent. In Britain, more sensible press relations are possible if the police take advantage of the facility to explain the facts and request an embargo. The French are tougher with the press and kidnap victims have been recovered when there has been silence during the first few days while ransom negotiations have taken place. Editors have to be dissuaded from seeking to boost circulation figures by scooping sensational news which could mean the death of a kidnap victim.

The *Croydon Advertiser,* on February 28, 1975, reported that a local reader had won a £50,000 premium bond prize, running a front page headline: *Bond winner now fears daughter's kidnap.* This was tantamount to inviting tragedy, and the semi-profile photograph and description of a '62 year old secretary of an orphanage' who lived in a terrace house in Norbury hardly supported the secrecy given to the winner's name. One wonders what the police thought of this newspaper story.

Voluntary Body and Non-Commercial PR

Here let us consider the great volume of PR that is conducted by charities, special interest societies, professional institutes, trade associations, trade unions and other bodies that depend on having members, subscriptions and donations. Some of these organizations may not have full-time PROs and PR is but one of the responsibilities of the director and members of his secretariat. The PR work is often both internal and external, addressed to members and supporters and the outside world. In some cases the PR task is to overcome misconceptions such as charities being superseded by the Welfare State. Some, such as Save the Children Fund, have moved from caring for British children to those of the Third World.

Armed Forces PR

The Army, Navy and Air Force in any country is also involved in PR, internally and externally and in peace and war. Throughout the troubles in Northern Ireland there have been frequent interviews with the Army for press, radio and TV. During the October war between Egypt and Israel in 1967 there were excellent media relations between the Israeli forces and international reporters, but President Sadat admitted afterwards that on the Egyptian side information had not been forthcoming with the same frankness and freedom.

British Forces press relations are similar to those described for the police. Even in countries where the regime may be disliked abroad it is found that military PROs have professional standards similar to our own. For instance, when a Swedish TV unit produced a film critical of South Africa and making sinister accusations about a massacre, the head of South African Military PR adopted an 'open house' policy and invited the world's press to visit the territory and to make their own unfettered investigations.

An interesting example of a well-organized professional military PR operation comes from Nigeria where, with a military government, there are military PRO's organized in a special service known as the Directorate of Military Public Relations Corps who run an internal programme which includes the publication of army newspapers and welfare services for army wives. They also publish a *Public Relations Officers' Handbook,* two quotes from which describe the role of the military PRO and how he fits into the Army's 'good neighbour' policy towards civilians. This is interesting because in peacetime the Armed Forces in most countries have to maintain community relations and may provide community services such as sea and mountain rescue units.

WHAT IS AN ARMY 'PRO'?

a. To the soldier, he is the man who suggests many of the topics a commander talks about during the commander's talk to his men.

b. To the press, he is the man to see to get the facts.

c. To the general public, he is the voice at the other end of a 'phone who is expected to answer any question about the Army.

d. To the dissident university youth, he is the purveyor of propaganda.

e. To the businessman, he is often an answer-man. . .
f. To his commanding general officer or CO, he is the staff officer who keeps him informed and advised on information matters.

Following the same professional PR approach as the Devon and Cornwall Chief Constable, see page 36, the *Handbook* says:

'Your first objective, always within bounds of security, is full and timely disclosure of the facts as they are known. The Army should be open and unafraid to admit its occasional blemishes, as well as its many accomplishments. This policy enhances the Army's credibility.'

The *Handbook* also explains that the Nigerian Army PRO can improve military–civilian relationships by friendship, promotion of good deeds in the community, disaster relief, participating in civil functions, availability of Army education for the young, informing government officials of Army activities, displays, promotional publications and protecting the environment. This supports the belief that Nigeria is the most PR-conscious country in the Third World.

In this chapter the attempt has been made to draw the broader picture of PR, but this is only a beginning. The full picture requires adoption of the practical exercises in planning press and public relations which are dealt with in the following chapters. One should remember, however, that in referring to 'press' relations use is made of a long-used expression which is perhaps misleading to the newcomer to PR. It progressed from 'handout' to 'press release' to 'news release', acknowledging that news is given to all news media, and we have in this book introduced the expression 'media relations' when wishing to embrace the press, radio, TV and newsreels. However, 'press relations' remains with us, and the press in the large western industrial countries is still the largest and most diversified communication medium in the sense that it helps us to separate and reach specialized readerships rather than the mass audience for much of radio and TV.

References

2.1 MORGAN REES, D., *Guardian*, August 28, 1974
2.2 ROWE, N., *Guardian*, February 7, 1975

CHAPTER THREE

The Publics
of PR

When a marketing campaign is being planned the market is defined and the channels of distribution are determined. The consumer advertising will be aimed at the social grade which represents the largest number of potential buyers. Media will be selected which most cheaply reaches the largest number of prospects with the least duplication. The publics are few. They may, for example, consist only of selected retailers of a certain size, and purchasers of a certain class and income level.

Such severe delineations may be necessary to a sales campaign because the sales seeking and promoting units (whether men, discounts or advertising) are large blocks of costs which together represent distribution costs. The cost of a sales force, of trade terms or of advertising are each in turn very substantial sums, and it is economic to reduce expenditure into the fewest possible units.

Today, it is more profitable to sell to supermarkets and chains or to wholesalers. The successful consumer goods company has a reducing customer list of correspondingly increasing order value. In the hardware trade there are manufacturers who will not allow their salesmen to enter a prospective outlet unless the shop is double fronted and has a staff of at least six sales assistants.

But this does not apply to PR, and this alone is one very good reason why PR should not be limited to the marketing function, and furthermore, why PR budgets should feature as an allocation quite separate from an advertising appropriation. This is why advertising managers and advertising agents should not be permitted to control expenditure on PR. This is not to say that PR should not *support* the marketing function, but the control should be at board level so that an organization's total PR budget can be apportioned to the three functions of a business: namely, finance, production, and marketing. The PRO, PR manager or, better still, communication director should control a threefold PR operation of which the marketing aspect is a part.

This point is introduced here, although it will need to be repeated elsewhere, because the PR practitioner, whether on the staff or performing an outside service, has to conduct PR activities which concern every public with which the organization has any contact or association. PR cannot conveniently restrict its activities to the largest common denominator of potential customers. This is because in order to exist, succeed, and survive an organization depends on many more people than those who ultimately consume its products. Even in the distribution of products a manufacturer has to communicate with his own salesmen, delivery staff, and servicing experts; with wholesalers, mail-order houses, agents, importers, exporters, overseas agents, and many kinds of retailer such as chain stores, department stores, supermarkets, down to the smallest of back-street shopkeepers; and with every possible buyer present, future, regular or potential. In the sphere of distribution many other publics are involved in the success or failure of the exercise to mention only printers, packaging manufacturers, transportation contractors, media owners, advertising agents, and even PR consultants. To those we can add opinion leaders and others concerned with testing, criticizing, approving or penalizing such as analysts, government departments and officials, consumer associations and the like.

On the marketing side alone the PR practitioner is responsible for communications so complex that advertising is dwarfed as a fragment – despite its great cost – of the marketing exercise. It is logical to pause here and note how illogical it is to apportion a minor part of the advertising appropriation to PR. Equally, it is wrong to regard advertising as a mere part of PR. More properly, PR is to do with many things different from and in addition to advertising.

This is not really a criticism but an inevitable accident in the historical development of two service industries which have tended to become muddled together. When one reconsiders the diversity of publics with which the PR practitioner is concerned it is not difficult to realize, perhaps with some surprise, that advertising is a much simpler communication process. Its cleverness lies in ideas and designs aimed at winning attention so that the message can be absorbed. But PR – far from being free publicity – is a concept of total communication. Advertising, important though it is, is but one specialized aspect of communication.

With what other publics does an organization have to communicate? It may not be a business organization. It could be a hospital board, a spastics society or a local authority. Only a minority of PR practitioners are engaged in consultancies, and perhaps this is a hopeful sign that management of all kinds of organizations is recognizing the need to direct its communications in a systematic and skilled manner.

Some Practical Examples

The most practical way to explain the publics of different organizations is to attempt to list them, but these lists cannot be complete or entirely accurate since variations are bound to exist between the nature and needs of individual organizations even within the same category. Publics, not media, are given, but publics may include those who express opinions through media, as in the case of politicians. Some writers include media among publics. While it is true that journalists and broadcasters also need to be informed and educated they are considered here as the means of reaching publics, not themselves publics.

Fig. 3.1   The Publics for Local Government PR

Staff
Trade unions and professional bodies
Wage tribunals
Local government associations
Government departments
Local MP's
Other local authorities
Local associations
Local industry and trade
The electorate and the ratepayers
The investment market
Suppliers of goods and materials
Potential residents
Potential industry and commerce
Visitors

Figure 3.1 shows a basic list of publics for Local Government. This list can be revised according to the kind of authority and its special responsibilities or interests.

The visitor category could embrace shoppers, commuting workers, tourists, cultural patrons, sports fans and so on.

Fig. 3.2   Typical Publics for PR of a Toy Manufacturer

Staff
Trade unions, professional bodies, trade associations
Distributors: wholesalers, retailers, mail-order traders, credit
traders, coupon/stamp gift distributors, exporters
Parents
Teachers
Children
Suppliers of raw materials, services
Potential staff, e.g. unskilled women operatives
Members of community adjacent to factory
Local authority officials and staff
Local MP's
Shareholders and investors
Opinion leaders who may either object to or praise certain toys
Government officials, e.g. Department of Trade – competitive im-
    ports

Figure 3.2 shows a typical set of publics for a toy manufacturer and
here we begin to see the pattern of publics for manufacturers in
general. Figure 3.3 shows how the pattern can be varied as the market
differs or is extended.

A basic list of publics for a voluntary organization is given in Figure
3.4. This list can be varied, but it applies in general terms to various
organizations which depend on voluntary workers and donated funds
and either conduct charitable work or seek support for their cause.

Fig 3.3   Typical Publics for the PR of a Motor Car Manufacturer

Staff
Trade unions, professional bodies, trade associations
Distributors, agents and overseas distributors
Motoring associations
Road safety organizations
Motor sport enthusiasts
Buyers and those who influence car buying – drivers, fleet owners,
    wives, driving schools, travelling salesmen
Suppliers of components and accessories
Suppliers of raw materials, e.g. steel, body finishes
Suppliers of fuel to operate plants
Potential staff (from apprentices to graduates)
Members of community adjacent to factory
Motor insurance companies

Government departments
The police
Motoring correspondents
Dissatisfied owners
Secondhand market
Opinion leaders *re* design, road safety, etc.
Holiday and travel trade
Rail, sea and air ferry operators

Fig. 3.4   Typical Publics for the PR of a Voluntary Organization

Members
Subscribers, benefactors
Users of services provided
Potential supporters – either workers or donors
Opponents and critics
MP's, councillors
Government departments
Local authorities
Other associated organizations
Opinion leaders

From the examples given already it will be seen that PR nearly always has to operate at two levels – internally and externally – and the internal operation may be as elaborate as the external, when it has to be directed to members who may become disinterested and resign unless there is sufficient communication to convince them that the organization is active and worth supporting. This activity may well involve participation which is one of the surest ways of combating the cry, 'What do I get for my subscription?'

Let us examine the possible publics of a few more examples.

Fig. 3.5   Typical Publics for the PR of a Department Store

Staff
Potential staff
Credit customers
Regular and casual customers
Customers in outlying areas
Community adjacent to store, e.g. award
    of trophies, participation in carnivals
Suppliers of services
Suppliers of own-name goods
Suppliers of branded goods
Local authority

Motorists and motoring organizations for organizing car
 parking facilities
Builders for furnishing show houses
Special interest groups, e.g. travel clubs, youth clubs,
 sports clubs.

A department store (Fig. 3.5), because of the variety of its goods and services, can make very effective use of PR if the trouble is taken to analyse buyers and potential buyers into separate publics which can be addressed by, say, a simple newsletter mailed to members of clubs and societies – especially if special discounts can be offered.

In Figure 3.6 we list PR publics for a company whose products may be unknown to the man in the street, a company which manufactures building, engineering, electrical or electronic components – anything from expanded polystyrene to transistors.

These breakdowns of the publics of different organizations are by no means exhaustive, but they indicate the market analysis which is necessary in the preparatory stages of planning a programme of PR activity.

*Fig 3.6   Typical Publics for the PR of a Technical Component
        Manufacturer*

Staff
Potential staff – apprentices, engineers
Specifiers, e.g. design engineers, architects
Contractors
Technical teachers at universities, technical colleges
Trade unions, trade associations
Community in vicinity of factory
Technical information centres, e.g. building centres
Technical writers
Government research establishments
Overseas agents

Unless the publics are defined the media cannot be selected and PR material cannot be prepared to satisfy specific interests and needs. Nor can the extent of activity be measured in manhour and other costs. In defining publics it is possible to recognize the size of the communication problem, and such may be the constraints of time, money and resources that some publics may have to be neglected, others concentrated upon. The temptation to fly in all directions – the cause of so much PR failure – is resisted when the total communication span is seen in all its impossible immensity and variation. No practical PR programme can be planned until the publics have been identified and priorities have been declared.

This is an appropriate point at which to introduce the IPR definition: Public relations practice is the deliberate, planned and sustained effort to establish and maintain mutual understanding between an organization and its public.

But since we wish to adopt a 'management by objectives' approach to PR, the next chapter opens with our own definition.

CHAPTER FOUR

Objective
PR Planning

PR consists of all forms of planned communication, outwards and inwards, between an organization and its publics for the purpose of achieving specific objectives concerning mutual understanding.

There could be no more damning condemnation of PR than that it is intangible, but it is not. However, if one plunges into PR in a haphazard fashion, failing to determine objectives, failing to define publics, failing to plan campaigns, techniques and media, failing to budget costs and control budgets, and failing to evaluate results against precise objectives, that can scarcely be described as responsible, professional PR. Unless there are objectives there is nothing against which to evaluate results.

Let us therefore borrow the formula first published in *Marketing and PR Media Planning* (4.1):

Six-Point PR Planning Model

1. Appreciation of the situation.
2. Definition of objectives.
3. Definition of publics.
4. Choice of media and techniques.
5. Budget.
6. Evaluation of results.

Separate chapters are devoted to the last four points and it will be sufficient here to comment on points 1 and 2, and to refer to the constraints that such logical planning will reveal. One important reason why some PR efforts fail is that attention has not been paid to the constraints that may be working against success. For instance, the largest budgetary item in PR campaign planning is manhours, which may be represented by either staff salaries or consultancy fees, and if sufficient manhours cannot be allocated to a particular task it is unlikely that the expected results will be achieved. Too often this is the case and management may throw 50 jobs at the PRO or PR consultant, not bother to think in terms of manhours, and then when time has been dissipated on too many tasks, accuse PR of being a waste of money, intangible and disappointing. An expenditure on PR has to be planned like anything else using labour and materials, and PR is labour intensive.

Here is a true story to illustrate the above point. An advertising agency account executive was attending a planning meeting in the client's boardroom. At the end of the meeting a formidable amount of work had been delegated to 'PR' and the account executive commented on the size of the PR department only to discover that there was no such department and that the advertising manager took care of all PR. The company concerned is an international household name.

Payment by Results

The IPR Code contains the following clause:

> *Payment Contingent upon Achievements*
>
> A member shall not negotiate or agree terms with a prospective employer or client on the basis of payment contingent upon specific future public relations achievement.

It is not intended that planning PR by objectives should be misconstrued as conflicting with the IPR Code of Professional Conduct. The clause quoted is capable of two meanings, one unethical and one professional. The 'specific future . . . achievement' stated in the clause refers to results which cannot be guaranteed such as one hundred press cuttings for £1,000 because the PR practitioner has no control over whether or not stories will be used. But if the PR objective is to achieve something measureable the PR practitioner will be judged by the results he achieves and may keep or lose his job or client according to his success or failure. In this chapter we are concerned with professionally planned PR that is very definitely aimed at achieving specific results, and the cost of so doing will be budgeted meticulously. Not to do so would be haphazard PR.

Appreciation of the Situation

Before planning can begin it is essential that the truth about attitudes to the company and its personnel, products and services is known. How can a consultant present a proposition if he has to rely on the client's opinion of the communication problems involved? The ideal method is for the client to shop around and then appoint the PR consultant he prefers to conduct an initial investigation for a fee and present his report and recommendations. This first stage would be PR counselling or *real* consultancy work since the expression PR consultant is largely a misnomer when what is really an agency is engaged in executing PR work, not providing consultations and giving advice.

It may be necessary to conduct some form of research such as an image study, an opinion poll, a discussion group or piggybacking onto a continuous omnibus survey. For example, a basic problem may be to interpret the image that is held of the organization. Strictly speaking, the image should be a true impression, but it all depends on what experience or information the impression is based. The PR task may be to present a consistent and true image based on adequate experience and full knowledge. As explained in Chapter One, there can be many different kinds of image, and part of appreciating the situation will be to discover the current image held by various publics, and the multiple image that may possibly exist within given publics as a result of contact with company representatives whether this be between staff and management or distributors and salesmen.

Or the investigation may be more direct, entailing visits to offices, branches, depots, factories and a sample of distributors in order to get a picture of the situation. Yet another form of investigation may be to visit libraries or to telephone information services (e.g. British Institute of Management library, *Financial Times* library, *Daily Telegraph* information bureau) and gain information from books, newspapers, magazines, government reports, press cuttings, and so forth. This research is discussed in detail in Chapter Twelve.

With the information so gained it is now possible to state that the organization is found to be in a certain situation. The chances are that it will be at variance with the chief executive's or the board's notion of the situation.

Definition of Objectives

Now it is possible to decide the task or tasks which PR has to undertake, the communications problems which PR is expected to solve. This is very different from seeking some favourable mentions in the press or some 'free' advertising. Let us consider possible PR objectives for a business concern:

1. Make understood a change of policy.
2. Overcome a public misunderstanding.
3. Keep public informed about the progress of a project.
4. Develop knowledge and understanding of a new product, service, material or organization.
5. Make the financial market fully aware of the company's record and prospects prior to a share issue.
6. Overcome prejudice in the community, possibly through imperfect understanding of what the organization does or how it will affect local interests.
7. Encourage recruitment of staff, or attract the right calibre of applicant.
8. Establish better distributor relations.
9. Make customer services better known and improve customer relations.
10. Make known the company's sponsorship commitments, showing the company's sense of social responsibility.
11. Make known company personnel and personalities so that the company is known for the interesting, competent or important people in it, especially if the company has suffered from a monolithic image.
12. Make known the company's contributions to conservation, recycling and protection of the environment.
13. Make the organization and its products or services known and understood in export markets, explaining their relevance to local needs and conditions.
14. Establish good relations between the organization and political agencies, consumer organizations and pressure groups.
15. Maintain the best possible industrial relations.

Under ten headings, many more kinds of results are described in Chapter Twelve: Research and Evaluating Results.

Clearly to compile a list of *possible* PR objectives becomes exhausting. This is where the constraints become operative. What are the priorities? Which are short, which are long-term objectives and how many short–term ones can be matched into a programme in the time available? How many require the services of PR staff or can be carried out as the function of other company personnel?

Let us assume that it is the Autumn and we are planning the PR programme for the following year.

The Constraints that Discipline PR Planning

The next stage will be to consider the publics which apply to each objective, publics having been discussed in the last chapter, and then to select the media and techniques in order to reach these different categories of people. How many publics are there and can they be reached? Then comes the budgeting of manhours and labour costs, materials and expenses to execute the campaign. Is it financially possible to reach all the desired publics? What are the most economical techniques for doing so? Can several publics be reached simultaneously by a blanket medium like TV? Or is it necessary to use specialized journals, or even mount an eyeball-to-eyeball personal confrontation between, say, the chief executive and an opinion leader? Finally, there are the methods of evaluating the results, that is, whether or not and with what effect the objectives have been achieved.

It is possible to begin with existing PR staff (or consultancy fee representing manhours), or to estimate the number of manhours which will be consumed by the campaign. Either method is likely to set a limit on the mumber of objectives which can be entertained. Similarly, for effective communication it may be necessary to limit the number of publics reached and to consider whether media exist which are capable of reaching our chosen publics. Or else to create media such as an external house journal, a documentary film or a travelling exhibition. But the available funds may limit us to one or the other. The PR budget will, of course, be the major restraint and is likely to be part of a larger budget which is related to forecasted income. To know how the budget is fashioned is important. One way and another there will be constraints upon doing everything.

Emphasis can be made upon the time and manpower element, the greatest item in the PR budget. There are peculiar ideas regarding the cost of PR. When one realizes how few manhours there are in a PRO's salary or a PR consultant's fee, entertainment (other than polite hospitality) must be a minor part of any serious PR programme. There are also those who think that PR is no more than news releases, envelopes and stamps, forgetting how much salaried time has to be spent in researching, writing, agreeing and revising the story before it ever gets to production and mailing.

To demonstrate the techniques of programme planning a fictitious example will be projected and discussed, calling for a comprehensive

PR programme. A problem, of course, is to show an example of universal appeal, and since PR is an activity which can be applied to any organization the reader must apply some imagination if he cannot always identify his own needs with those discussed in this chapter. Students are apt to complain if the instruction is not applicable to their immediate experience, but the fact is that a good PR man should be capable of undertaking most PR assignments in most circumstances because the principles of communication are constant. There is no mystique about PR, it is only the ability to take infinite pains.

So let us take as our example a national chain store group, examine its problems, and see how PR can be applied to them.

Planning a PR Programme for a National Chain Store Group

We are considering a retail organization whose branches are to be found throughout the country.

Let us assume that the objective of the PR exercise is to establish the company's reputation in a characteristic manner. This is not an advertising campaign to promote sales of specified goods or to promote selling events. But it is assuredly part of the marketing strategy. It is a case of selling the difference, of educating the buying public – or even special sections of it – that the goods, services, trading, purchasing, employment, and investment methods of this company have genuine merits.

We need not specify that difference for this example: it is sufficient to declare that for the purpose of this exercise there is one capable of being communicated by PR methods. So we can say, then, that this store has something different to offer purchasers in all the main towns of the country, and that advantage of this difference may be taken by the mass shopping public. This difference will also influence relations with publics other than purchasers.

Defining the Publics

Who are the publics? Let us list them and explain why they are important to the PR programme. They fall into two groups, national and local, and this has a bearing on choice of media. Some publics can be approached at both national and local levels.

    National. (a)   The buying public to which the company aims to sell
               (b)   Since the company is a public one, the shareholding

    public (this being capable of even more subtle sub-division)

(c) Suppliers of goods for resale
(d) Trade associations, research associations, and government departments concerned with standards
(e) Trade Unions to which staff belong
(f) Political parties
(g) Members of Parliament
(h) Opinion leaders such as writers, lecturers, broadcasters, dieticians, consumerists and others interested in the goods sold
(i) Centres of staff training, e.g. the College for the Distributive Trades
(j) Women's national organizations, e.g. Townswomen's Guilds, Co-operative Women's Guilds, Women's Institutes

This list can lengthen tremendously according to the diversity of goods sold.

Local. (a) The buying public to which the company aims to sell but for the purpose of stressing local advantages or special services, e.g. car parking, late closing nights
(b) Local suppliers of goods for resale such as fresh foodstuffs or garden plants
(c) Local organizations such as the Chamber of Commerce, Publicity Club, Development Association or Residents' Associations
(d) Area or branch offices of trade unions to which staff belong
(e) Local branches of political parties
(f) Local government officers, councillors, and aldermen, and local services such as police, hospitals, fire brigade
(g) Local opinion leaders such as clergy, teachers
(h) Members of Parliament representing the trading area
(i) Those who can influence recruitment of labour, e.g. Labour Exchange officials, teachers, parents
(j) Local branches of women's organizations
(k) Youth clubs, sports clubs, and applicable specialist associations such as horticultural, dramatic, musical, literary, and other societies
(l) Universities, technical colleges

This is a sophistication of the similar list given in Chapter Three.

Choosing Media

Taking the two divisions again what media are available to reach these publics?

National. (a) The *buying public* can be best reached by national media of which the most suitable are the newspaper and the magazine, either through the news columns or through specialist features. News would concern, say, the opening of the company's five hundredth branch, or about personalities connected with the company. In the features it is possible to report actual products as when a fashion feature quotes a dress available from a national chain.

What about other national media? There are possibilities on TV if company personalities are interesting enough to appear in interview-type programmes. We are now becoming selective in our choice of media, and this has a bearing on costs because trying to obtain TV coverage can be both time and money consuming with perhaps disappointing results if only that TV is fundamentally an entertainment rather than an informative or educational medium.

(b) This *investment public* is somewhat over-simplified in our list and will include many categories of financial public such as brokers, bankers and unit trust managers.

The chief medium here will be the press; business section editors and journalists, banking, insurance, investment, and economic magazines; but we must not ignore special media such as annual reports and accounts, the spoken word, the external house journal and those very attractive advertisements which give potted annual reports.

(c) It may be thought that it is sufficient to drive a hard bargain with *suppliers,* on the old principle of buying cheap and selling dear, but that is 19th century in concept, and while it may have suited the fortune makers of the industrial revolution, it does not belong to late 20th century economic philosophy.

The supplier becomes a most important public, and he must in no way be neglected. The standards of his raw materials and produce, the perfection of his workmanship, the elimination of waste to produce realistic prices, and the reliability of his deliveries depend on operation in an atmosphere of confidence and understanding of the buyer's needs. Good communication is vital. Supermarkets, for example, have set their suppliers standards for foodstuffs that customers have never previously enjoyed from traditional retailers. Because of their quantity purchasing of, say, fruit, cheese or biscuits, they are able to demand common high standards. These standards can be achieved only if the supplier has a clear idea of what is required and this affects recipes, budgeting, ingredients, production, packaging, and so on. Good PR is inherent in the dealings which firms like Marks and Spencer, Sainsbury, and Key Markets have with their suppliers, even if it does come hard when supplies are rejected if they fail to measure up to the stringent standards demanded.

Supplier relations are perhaps more subtle than most. Sometimes they blend with staff relations since staff can sell better when they understand the sources of supplies. In supplier relations there is therefore a two-way system of communication comprising mutual visits to one another's premises. It is just as important that a blanket manufacturer should know how his products are sold as that the shop assistant should know how that brand of blanket is woven. It is certainly very convincing when the salesman shows that he really is knowledgeable about the product and has even seen it made. Some cosmetics manufacturers go to the trouble of training retail sales staff in the application of their products, running beauty schools.

Customer confidence results from good supplier relations, and in modern marketing a very necessary bridge can be built between the manufacturer and the consumer of the retailer is wise enough to use PR techniques constructively. Sales staff become more interested in their work, more enthusiastic about selling the merchandise, when they can sincerely advise customers as a result of first-hand personal knowledge.

One of the reasons why Magicote paint was originally a slow seller was that the retailers – generally well informed and technically proficient – had no confidence in this new type of paint. But once this prejudice was overcome by PR techniques – demonstrations to the trade and a dealer journal – the paint sold so well that competitors had to bring out their own non-drip paints in order to retrieve lost sales. In our example, a chain of stores, there are bound to be a very large number of suppliers of all sorts of things such as delivery vehicles, overalls, stationery, cash registers, and other goods quite in addition to those for resale. Good PR can make these suppliers proud to be among the chosen and consequently very willing to add to the PR effort by letting it be known that they are regular suppliers. Mutual testimonies do no harm provided they are genuinely meaningful.

(d) Good relations with *trade associations,* research bodies, and government departments can be maintained by open-handedly contributing to all efforts to raise standards. The organization will second senior executives to serve on committees and by generally being seen to be progressive the store will enhance its reputation. This can be costly, but it is a PR exercise which cannot fail to succeed in the long run. If an organization leads in raising the standards of a trade the whole trade will benefit surely, but the leader can only be even more successful since it is in the vanguard of progress.

However, care must be taken not to acquire too dominating a role in voluntary affairs otherwise the company may be accused of enjoying too much of the limelight or of being dictatorial to the disadvantage of smaller or less generous or more inactive members. This is where the personality of the representative can be so important, and the company must nominate or second a representative who will genuinely be an asset to the council or committee on which he has to serve. This is very much a PR problem.

It is a PR duty to establish and maintain good relations with *trade union officials* so that they are as well informed as possible about the company's policies and activities. For instance, it can be a good thing to put trade union officials on the mailing list for the house journal, even for news releases. Certainly no staff story should be released without inviting the trade union official (whether full-time or shop steward) to vet it first. The mere fact that this is done can be an act of good public relations, for it is more than a courtesy and involves the trade union official in company affairs.

Some short-sighted managements may hesitate to work so closely with the trade union officials, but misunderstandings can often be avoided by frankness as the better employers know to their advantage.

An interesting example of a PR exercise which may well be appreciated by trade unionists is the documentary film. This may tell the story of the firm and help to establish better understanding, or it could be a training film aimed at providing instruction which will improve proficiency; it could be an aid to recruitment, or a means of teaching safety first drill and so reducing accidents. Any one of these films could be valuable PR exercise and there are large organizations which invest very seriously in all these films. Firms like Lyons and Costain have made good use of the recruitment film, while in the engineering and oil industries there are a number of excellent safety films. Such films need not be limited to internal showings and can have other PR uses.

(f) Good relations with *political parties* can be sensible if the organization is the kind which can suffer or benefit from party policies or from politicians and party workers being badly or well informed. Good relations with parties does not imply supporting them in any way, and it could be just as important to keep the Communist Party informed as the Conservative Party. This can be done by putting the party headquarters on the mailing list for the house journal, by arranging store visits, by distributing literature, and also by inviting party branches on visits or offering them film evenings. It is no use a party pontificating about the future of an industry unless it is familiar with its characteristics, problems, traditions, products, services, skills, and so on.

An industry which finds itself menaced by a party policy may only have itself to blame, and if in the last resort a costly advertising campaign is necessary to present a case this becomes propaganda which may have less pleasant connotations. Facts are more potent weapons than opinions which, at best, are biased. A lot of the anti-nationalization propaganda of recent years represents a panic attempt to remedy the lack of PR for decades. Philosophically and psychologically, nationalization implies the neccessity to rescue an inefficient industry in the public interest. But usually the electorate do not know the truth of the matter, and they never will when an industry has its back to the wall and is seen to be spending a lot of money in its own defence.

Our retail organization may be concerned with issues of interest to party politicians such as labelling legislation, the Shop Acts, employer's liability, fuel costs, rating systems, prices and incomes, the Trade Descriptions Act, The Fair Trading Act and many similar topics. How can politicians discuss such topics without first-hand knowledge of the implications? Sometimes these topics can be channelled through representative bodies such as the National Chamber of Trade but not always. Direct relations can be more productive.

(g) It is but a small step to establishing communication with *members of the Government* and with *Members of Parliament*, not forgetting the appropriate heads of department in the Civil Service. Outside advice is taken at the committee stage on bills, while there are various *ad hoc* Parliamentary Committees on which outsiders are invited to serve. The retail organization may well be represented on one of these committees which is considering a problem of the retail trade. But also the store PRO should ensure that MP's are kept informed about the company's activities when these are of national interest – for example, the prohibiting of smoking – about which MP's should be knowledgeable. Why not send a copy of the company house journal to the House of Commons Library?

(h) *Opinion leaders* are a motley lot and with such a variety of mass media there is an opinion leader born almost every minute. It may sometimes be the despair of management but it is nevertheless the penalty of democracy. The PRO has to tolerate, respect, and inform

C

those whose opinions influence attitudes rightly or wrongly towards his organization.

This is one of the trickiest aspects of PR practice because not all opinion leaders are sincere advisers: some are performers or entertainers but the real irony of their capers lies in their ability to damn or praise in direct proportion to the size or significance of their audience. The sheer impact of TV has become ludicrous, and opinions expressed through this medium need be of no consequence to have fantastic effect. The press – not even the women's weekly magazines – has never had such hypnotic effect.

There are, of course, opinion leaders who still count, and while it is not the task of PR to influence them it is certainly the duty of PR to make the facts readily available to them. Every writer, lecturer or broadcaster has to base his material on research, but he can use only what can be discovered. It is therefore a practical PR exercise to place one's facts where they can be found in libraries, information bureaux, annuals, and directories. This can be done by setting up an information service and making this widely known so that information is demanded of it. By this is not meant a front organization – not a Retail Trade Advisory Bureau which is actually sponsored by a retail company – but a clearly identified information service run by the company. Thus, opinion leaders would be invited to use the facilities offered, and once they found that the information was factual and unbiased the organization would be respected for its honesty.

This sort of interest can be stimulated among those who are authorities on specific subjects. They will be glad of the services of a store which will lend them samples, make photographic sessions possible, or simply answer questions, and the store will usually reap the benefit of reciprocal acknowledgement.

(i) In the previous section bare mention was made of the technical teacher, and it certainly pays to recognize the needs of *staff training colleges,* especially those which train staff in establishments of further education and prepare them for qualifying examinations. The company can help in the following ways:

(a) By encouraging staff to attend courses so that classes can be formed.
(b) By supplying teaching aids such as display materials, dummy products, or possibly donating actual products.
(c) By permitting day-release of students for part-time courses.
(d) By seconding senior staff as visiting lecturers.
(e) By offering store visits to demonstrate store management

and administration, perhaps after hours when the store is closed.

Good relations with the colleges can also be enhanced by participating in school events and management such as by sponsoring prizes or serving on the board of management. Nationally this can be done through colleges such as the College for the Distributive Trades, or by sponsoring prizes for presentation by trade associations such as the Institute of Hardware, the Grocers' Institute or the National Federation of Retail Furnishers.

(j) Finally, our list of national publics mentions the *women's national organizations* such as the Townswomen's Guilds, the Women's Institutes, Co-operative Women's Guilds, and those run by the various religious denominations. Most of these organizations have national magazines and tell their branches of the facilities, for speakers, visits, and films, which companies are offering. It is possible therefore to stimulate local interest at a national level, thus augmenting the PR efforts of the company's local branch managers.

Now, having discussed the national publics it should not be difficult for the reader to expand each of the publics listed on pages 52–53 and to realize that if properly encouraged, directed, and assisted by the PRO at head office each local branch manager can communicate with his local publics and so 'establish and maintain mutual understanding' to quote the words of the IPR definition given on page 46.

To sum up, then, in order to reach at least the 22 national and local publics we can employ the media of press, radio, TV, print and literature, films, visits, visual aids, and other PR techniques involving participation in voluntary affairs. Nationally and locally, we should add, the store may participate in the advertising medium of exhibitions which will call for PR support.

There are, however, some differences between PR at national and at local level. For one thing one branch may look very much like any other branch and each shop may sell similar lines, but localities are different and a stereotyped PR programme cannot be reproduced in each place. Even so, PR principles remain the same and the need is to train branch managers to be PR-minded and to anticipate or recognize opportunities for improving communication with the publics whose understanding and confidence is required.

All this can be programmed and budgeted. It is necessary to do so otherwise the PRO could make the mistake of doing too many things indifferently; a very easy error to make when one considers the complex range of interests which exist in the retail trade. This is, clearly, a trade where PR inspiration is required at the top so that the entire organization becomes PR-minded and the company operates at all levels to achieve good communication and thereby good relationships with all publics. This is a good example of PR being adopted as a management philosophy. Every branch manager must be his own PRO, and he will need to be trained in PR skills.

Planning a Media Relations Campaign

How do you plan a media relations campaign? What does it cost? Is it planned in isolation as a separate activity or can it be planned in concert with the overall marketing scheme? What results are likely and can any sort of target be set? Are the costs likely to be justified by the results? Can we therefore include press relations in the marketing budget in a tangible way?

These are practical questions. In PR we do not operate in a vacuum of intangibility, for while it is true that goodwill is a tangible asset of small book value the press relations aspect of PR is much more precise. We propose to issue newsworthy information which, as part of a marketing or any other communications plan, must produce either a negative or a positive response. The response has a value. It can show antipathy to an organization, product or service, and be a form of market research which warns the marketing man how he must next act. Or it can show sympathy, interest, enthusiasm, demand and so encourage the marketing man to go ahead with his promotional plans. In non-commercial organizations response to news is equally important.

Media Relations and Marketing

In these ways media relations can serve as a marketing reconnaissance. But media relations can also supplement a promotional campaign and enhance the value of all the sales, advertising and merchandising efforts, while as will be shown in a separate chapter, media relations can also enhance the value of participation in an exhibition. No doubt the term *press officer* will persist for some time, but it is more practical to refer to *media* relations rather than *press* relations. Now we are dealing with marketing realities as distinct from the mere issuing of information. A press officer is not just an information bureau clerk for while that may be a useful PR service, it is a sophistication to be dealt with later. Here we are talking about grass-roots media relations, an activity as vital to a marketing programme as the salesman in the field, the advertisements in the press, or the labels on the product. Media relations emphatically take a place in the marketing mix. Media relations belongs to the publicity armoury, and must be accounted for with results checked like those of all other resources at the marketing manager's disposal. From this we see that few if any marketing managers can afford not to employ a staff or consultancy press officer and this appointment is essential.

The best way to substantiate these claims is to describe the execution of media relations tactics in viable marketing terms. Suppose we have a product which we know to be efficacious but which invites the scepticism of those unfamiliar with its performance. Because of this barrier of prejudice, conventional advertising would serve little purpose. To advertise such a product may produce little response because readers may not believe the claimed performance to be possible. To overcome this incredulity the volume of advertising might have to be inordinately expensive. It is precisely in these circumstances that media relations techniques can help the marketing man.

By means of a press reception and demonstration, or a facility visit to the factory, associated with news releases and feature articles, not forgetting radio and TV, educational information can be published which will permit the product to be reported and discussed freely by knowledgeable people. This sort of coverage will be independent – as independent as a book review compared with a book advertisement – and the risk will have to be taken that some writers may be adversely critical. Nevertheless, being new, the product or service will have genuine news value and it will provoke reader interest. This reader interest is likely to be more receptive because the facts will be presented by the editorial columns of the journal, and the journal's integrity and value depends on this information being fair and reliable. The same remarks apply to coverage on radio and TV, with independent local radio becoming increasingly important.

Media coverage of this kind can produce several hundred enquiries from one story and new products have been launched entirely by this method. These enquiries (and many journals provide reader service cards and coupons to stimulate enquiries) can be a form of research for the marketing man, indicating the extent and type of market interest. His future advertising plans may be shaped more accurately by the results of the initial publicity and the interest it arouses.

Planning in Detail

From this general introduction to some of the tasks which media relations can perform let us look more closely at the actual planning of a media relations campaign. The press officer begins with the basic principle that if he has any information which will help an editor maintain or increase sales and readership he can find a good home for it to the advantage of his organization. It is important to emphasize this because employers of press officers may be tempted to expect free editorial mentions in the same editions that they advertise in. This may be what a number of marketing, sales, advertising and other businessmen want from press relations, but it is not what they are likely to get, and the press officer may have to begin by disillusioning these people of such misconceptions about his work.

Generally speaking media relations are likely to follow one of the following courses:

1. Preparatory advance educational information.
2. Information supplementary to an advertising campaign.
3. A continuous news service.

Let us as an example, apply these to a commercial airline. The first kind of programme – advance information – might lead up to the operation of a new route or a new aircraft. The second might be conducted during the advertising of the new route or aircraft. The third would apply to the daily mixture of news about the airline's general operations which is aimed at all the publics whose continuous understanding and goodwill is important to the airline.

With a little imagination the reader can apply those three types of programme to the organizations he knows best, noting that a media relations programme need not be associated in any way with any existing short-term promotional scheme.

We have said that the press officer must be convinced that he has news to communicate. Now, we see that he has to decide how he is to contribute to the overall operation of his organization, whatever kind it may be, commercial, voluntary or public.

A Typical Campaign

Let us assume, then, that the marketing manager of a company manufacturing convenience foods (such as foods which require no preparation and merely have to be heated ready for the table) has gone through all the preliminary research, laboratory, dietary, recipe, costing, packaging, naming, pricing and distribution stages of the marketing process and has now reached the point when a product is ready to go into production for supply to a calculated market. The marketing manager now wishes to support both his sales force and his retail distributors with a combined advertising campaign and a media relations programme. The aim is to achieve repeat sales of an all-the-year-round popular food. There are many products like this to mention only instant coffee, frozen peas and tubes of mustard.

The press officer can proceed to plan his programme along the following lines:

1. What is new, different, special, interesting about the product?
2. Who is likely to be interested – who are the publics?
3. How can he reach these publics – what media or techniques should he employ?
4. What will all this cost?
5. What will the programme achieve?

For the purpose of this exercise let us say that the product is a prepared main meat dish wrapped in foil and has merely to be heated and served with a vegetable such as peas which may have been either canned or frozen. At its simplest, it can be eaten this way but other or additional vegetables and gravy could be added. It is tasty enough to serve once a week.

The product is ideal for any busy woman who does not wish to be tied to the kitchen. Anyone can serve such a meal, and it will store for months, so possible customers are legion from girls in bed-sitters, bachelors, and old people to holidaymakers in caravans, boats and tents. There are distinct commercial possibilities ranging from canteens to cafés. And it's far more sophisticated than a can of baked beans.

All these publics can be reached through the countless people who write, talk and demonstrate on the subject of food and can be reached by the following scheme.

1. A press reception and sampling session at a hotel to which would be invited journalists who write about home and catering topics in women's magazines and the women's pages of newspapers, plus journalists from the food retailing and catering trade press, and their counterparts from radio and TV. Some of the more specialist papers can also be invited and there are a great many freelance journalists who write on this kind of topic. The advantage of a press reception is that the product can be tasted and tested, and examples of its use and usefulness can be demonstrated. You cannot achieve this physical testimony with a news release or even do it so well with a posted sample which may or may not be put to the test.

2. News release follow-ups will be necessary, with recipes and ideas to stimulate the interest of journalists.

3. Printed recipe leaflets will be valuable too.

4. Photographs of the product served with various vegetables must be available from the start.

5. It is likely that co-operative efforts can be achieved with the press officers for associated products such as frozen vegetables.

Counting the Cost

Once again we will base the exercise on an assumption, this time that we are mounting a short-term press relations programme to support a product launch. We shall, however, need to spread coverage over about three months since we are dealing with both daily and weekly newspapers, printed quickly by letterpress, web-offset-litho and weekly and monthly journals which, if printed by gravure, may go to press several weeks before publication.

The most expensive item is the press reception. The bar expenses need not be heavy if there is an active programme with a welcoming drink on arrival and a bar and buffet at the close, the reception taking place during the late morning. Other expenses may be the hire of demonstrators and possibly costumes to add gaiety. If it is run by a staff press officer his costs are probably not included but if the event is run by an outside consultant there is likely to be a time-based fee. We are concerned therefore with a total cost dependent on whether the event is organized internally or externally, the difference being the allocation of staff costs plus the consultancy profit. Other costs will include news releases, envelopes, photographs, captions, recipe leaflets and postage.

The total budget should be costed on the basis that this is a national effort and in addition to the press attending the London reception press material and samples will have to be distributed to newspapers and magazines throughout the UK.

And so we arrive at the achievement, measured beside that of the sales force, the distributors and the advertising. In a joint marketing enterprise the results are seldom separable but with the aid of such a media relations programme the results are likely to be more marked. Writers and broadcasters will have told their audiences about the new food, how it tastes, the convenience it offers. The advertising will be more meaningful, housewives will be informed, diners will recognize the item on the menu, holidaymakers and tourists will remember to pack the ready-made meal, and the idea of trusting an absentee cook will be accepted. Advertising will have its impact, securing repeat sales, directing to the point of purchase, doing its hustling job but press relations will have done the human job of overcoming hostility to a strange idea, presenting the testimony of trusted editorial, spreading knowledge of its versatile application, and establishing the confidence that must stand behind the purchase of a successful product.

Modern marketing is an integrated force of which media relations form a valuable part. To succeed in marketing a new product it is necessary to employ all communicators and all communication techniques.

Assessing Results

However, to say that the results of media relations are seldom separable may not satisfy those who have to justify budgets. There are certain results which are directly attributable to the special techniques of media relations. They will be more readily recognized in some campaigns than in others, as will be seen in the examples given in the next few pages, and more will be said on this subject in Chapter Twelve which deals more analytically with research and results.

These achievements will include press cuttings which can be evaluated against the readership of the various journals – *not* against the equivalent cost of the same volume of advertisement space – and there will be the enquiries and requests for recipe leaflets, samples or whatever may be offered. These cuttings will show, for example, how far interest has penetrated beyond the mass consumer readership of the advertising schedule media, to the canteen caterers, campers and so on. Trade press coverage of the advertising campaign will have interested distributors and helped the sales force. Stories in the catering press will have helped café proprietors with their meal-planning. General coverage in the popular press will have helped to achieve quick acceptance of the product, whether for eating at home or eating out. Press relations alone can be seen to do a worthwhile job because when people become familiar with a product – or a new idea in food – in their everyday reading they will respond more receptively to advertising. The advertising does not first have to demolish the possible barriers of ignorance, apathy and hostility.

And there are other positive results. News of the successful launch is likely to provide story material for city editors, and this will encourage stock market confidence in the company. News about the successful new product will make good reading in the local press in the vicinity of the factory, and good community relations is always worth foster-

ing for many reasons, not forgetting staff relations and staff recruitment.

The point of all this is that media relations carry the information
or message to an infinitely wider audience than is usually possible or
economical with advertising. And even though it is true that a carefully managed advertising campaign will convey the message, quickly
and persuasively, to the majority of likely buyers it is also true that the
effective demand which every manufacturer seeks will be gained even
more economically if media relations techniques have also been employed to establish the knowledge and confidence which stimulates
reader and viewer acceptance and response.

Liaison with Other Departments

It is important that the marketing manager sees that there is proper
liaison between the media relations efforts and the production programming and retail distribution. For example, new products or new
models make news and the press officer can often obtain publication of
pictures and stories. But if these new lines are not available in the shops
potential buyers, stockists, wholesalers and the manufacturer's own
sales force will all be frustrated and the media coverage will be both an
embarrassment and a waste. Yet this happens repeatedly.

When sending such releases to the consumer press it is essential for
the press officer to be armed with a list of London stockists, and better
still if he can have some provincial ones as well such as a well-known
chain of stores. This is to help the reader service departments of
journals. The writers of most shopping features are extremely careful
to avoid upsetting readers because goods described are not available.
Many such features do not name the product but do name the supplier,
so the press officer must be ready with such distribution information
before he releases a product story.

This is not always as easy as it seems. Some companies sell only
through wholesalers, others may have very mixed ranges of products,
and so neither may be able to check deliveries and guarantee available
stocks in any given shop. The most they can say is that certain big
stores are agents or stockists. The problem can be overcome by swift
co-operation between the press officer and the sales manager. If the
likely appearance of, say, a story in a provincial evening newspaper
can be relayed to area distributors, a stock of the product can be placed
in a shop whose address can then be passed on to the newspaper in
readiness for passing on to enquirers after the story has appeared. Very
properly, some feature writers will not refer to specific products

unless named stockists are supplied because it would be foolish for them to make recommendations which readers cannot take up. This shows how carefully executed press relations work must be, and how closely it needs to be linked to the marketing operation.

Some Examples of Press Campaigns

Now let us consider some actual examples which indicate both the advantages of preliminary PR launchings using media relations techniques, and the contribution they can make to marketing strategy.

A New Kind of Insurance

A company, not itself engaged in insurance, decided that a form of insurance would be a valuable service to offer in conjunction with other services. But it was an entirely new subject for insurance, and people had to be convinced that it was necessary, and that included brokers. Once again, advertising was out of the question on economic grounds because enough could not be undertaken to be effective. The company was prepared to spend a couple of years educating the market.

There was an initial press reception; special articles were published in appropriate journals read by both brokers and likely policy holders; and the subject was even discussed in a BBC radio programme which offered financial advice to listeners. It was a slow haul, but the company has since extended the insurance cover to an associated field which was considered to be an even bigger risk, and this was surely evidence that the original scheme had won acceptance, largely through a painstaking educational campaign employing media relations techniques to support field salesmen.

A Domestic Appliance

A manufacturer of a domestic appliance had three press relations objectives: (1) To reach the Christmas market; (2) To gain women's press coverage co-incidental with the *Daily Mail* Ideal Home Exhibition and (3) To achieve a write-up in the *Daily Express* women's feature since this would impress his several hundred stockists scattered throughout the UK.

The objectives were quite clear and they were achieved on a very modest budget in the following ways, although not without 'sustained effort'. Some patient follow-up work was necessary to get publication in the *Daily Express*.

The Ideal Home Exhibition is held in March. Since women's magazines are printed by photogravure it is necessary to supply them with material at least three months before publication date, whereas national and provincial newspapers can be supplied with Christmas gift stories a few weeks beforehand. To reach both a product demonstration press reception was held in early November, during which a short film was shown showing production and quality control techniques at the factory.

London evenings, provincial dailies and national Sundays printed the story which was aided by an excellent photograph; the *Daily Express* ran the story shortly before the exhibition opened; the appliance was twice awarded as a prize in ATV's *Golden Shot* TV programme and posters of the award were rapidly printed and delivered to stockists two or three days later; the women's magazines carried picture stories; and the appliance was among the equipment of the *Evening News* house in the 'village' of new houses at the Exhibition. The company experienced excellent sales of the appliance on its own stand, and women journalists were invited to attend press demonstrations on the stand between opening time and 11.30 a.m. during the run of the exhibition.

Elf Grand Prix Days

In March 1975, just before Elf was involved in petrol retail activities in the UK, and with Elf Oil Exploration and Production (UK) Ltd. concerned with oil and gas rigs in the North Sea, Celtic Sea and off the west coast of Scotland, there was a very vague Elf image among the British. A PR campaign, handled by Eoin Young of Motormedia, was set up during the 1975 racing season called Elf Grand Prix Days. It took the form of a practical and exciting photographic filming service for motoring correspondents.

It was introduced at Brands Hatch on March 14 following the Friday morning practice for Sunday's British Airways *Daily Mail* Race, and the special media relations services were also provided for the *Daily Express* International Trophy Formula One race at Silverstone on April 12–13, and the John Player Grand Prix on July 19. Elf were sponsoring the Elf-Tyrrell Ford Formula One team, but the photographic and filming service was a PR service additional to the sponsorship.

The scheme gave press and TV journalists and their photographers the opportunity to obtain first-hand experience of Grand Prix circuits, riding with Jackie Stewart and the Elf Team Tyrrell drivers Jody Scheckter and Patrick Depailler in a camera-equipped Ford Capri, a Renault 17 Gordini coupé or a Renault 1300 cc R5. The cars carried front wing mounts for three TV cameras, and were fitted up inside with a fourth TV camera and sound recording equipment.

BBC 1 took advantage of the Brands Hatch facility and during Saturday afternoon *Grandstand*-viewers were taken round the track with Jackie Stewart driving a camera car round one lap of the re-surfaced track, describing the features of the circuit, and announcing the gear changes on the bends. There were also shots of the car and the driver in profile, showing the name Elf on Stewart's crash helmet.

There were some bonus points. Stewart had retired from actual racing in 1973 after winning three World Championship titles and 27 Grand Prix races, and was now working for Elf. He co-ordinated the PR programme in his capacity as Overseas Vice President Marketing for Elf/Sternol. The film turned out to be exceptionally useful to the BBC because horse racing had been cancelled due to bad weather – which incidentally heightened the excitement of the motor racing – and the Elf film helped to fill the airtime vacated by horse-racing. Moreover, in the practice run Jody Scheckter came second so that Elf gained excellent weekend sports page coverage.

For Sunday's big Race of the Champions Jackie Stewart was one of the BBC commentators, although the Elf car had bad luck and retired from first position to the pits towards the end of the race.

On the following Monday the first of the Elf Grand Prix Days was held at Silverstone. Racing gear was supplied to men and women journalists, the track was fully marshalled, and insurance cover was arranged by Elf. Movie cameras with motor drives operated by remote control enabled passengers in the Ford or Renaults to shoot their own action pictures, the film being available as soon as the car returned to the pits. Sound recording was also provided for on-the-move interviews. An Elf photographer was available at the track, but press photographers were welcome to take their own pictures.

Thus throughout the 1975 racing season in Europe Elf offered the media both personal Grand Prix circuit experience and ability to take authentic track film or stills. Elf gained in good media relations and in extra photographic coverage, helping to familiarize the British public with the Elf name and image.

Reference

4.1 JEFKINS, F., *Marketing and PR Media Planning*, Pergamon Press, 1974

CHAPTER FIVE

Internal PR Department or Outside PR Consultancy

The Internal PR Department

The majority of PR men and women in the UK are employed in internal PR units, a minority being engaged in consultancy practice. Moreover, a very large number of 'in-house' PR departments are in non-commercial organizations ranging from government departments to voluntary bodies and not forgetting the various local authorities. This implies that the bulk of PR is unconnected with marketing organizations.

In the business organization, firms without PR departments will employ PR consultants until such time as the expenditure on PR justifies the setting up of an internal PR department. Large firms may employ both, using the consultancy for counselling or for special PR work such as corporate and financial PR.

The supreme advantage of the staff PRO and his internal unit is that he is an accepted member of the organization, sharing the confidence of colleagues and possessing loyalties which extend beyond time sheets and fee limitations. Career opportunities within the organization depend on a degree of enthusiasm which will never quite touch the hired outside help however proficient he may be. This is not meant to imply criticism of consultants, but for anything less than a fee representing at least a full week's work throughout the year for one account executive, the consultant obviously cannot give undivided attention as the staff PRO can. Consultancy fees are based on man-hours and hourly rates. Being a colleague, and not a stranger, the staff PRO has access to all members and parts of the organization. In fact it is very much his job to make himself thoroughly well known as a kind of master of ceremonies or general stage manager.

That is a first-class definition of a staff PRO, 'the man who knows more about the company than anyone else in it'. The PR consultant with the best will in the world, can never quite surmount the barrier between insider and outsider. However, as we shall see later on, the consultant can offer advantages by way of compensation.

Now let us look at the various ways in which PR is handled by organizations of all kinds, irrespective of whether they have an ideally constituted PR department.

Some companies, anxious to obtain their share of news coverage, may appoint a press officer. Since his duties are mainly associated with advertising and sales promotion, the press officer is generally a specialist member of the marketing, sales or advertising manager's staff. A journalist is usually chosen because the editorial side of the press is unknown to marketing people and to deal with the press it is assumed that one must engage someone from it. The alternative in, say, the electronics or engineering fields, might be to appoint a technical author as press officer. But the fact that an applicant is a journalist is no guarantee that he has the qualities required of a good press officer.

Much depends on how well he has been trained in media relations and the majority of press officers appointed in the past have had little opportunity to obtain very much training. This is not entirely their fault: apart from evening classes, seminars and correspondence courses there has been hardly any instruction available on the subject, and until 1968 no comprehensive textbook. There has, unfortunately, been an attitude of mind that press relations either need not or cannot be taught, which is nonsense.

The press officer's experience may quite literally be limited to having attended a number of press receptions; knowing how to organize one is quite a different matter. It is not just a question of asking a hotel to provide a private room with a bar, or of lunching editors.

From these remarks it may be read that the appointment of a press officer to the staff of an advertising department can be a half-hearted and misunderstood attempt at undertaking PR. Only the appointment of a qualified PRO is adequate as a beginning, and he can be his own press officer until such time as a specialist assistant can be placed under his command and trained by him if necessary.

Although there are first-class officers in well-organized promotional departments headed by very able advertising managers, especially where a company's promotions are linked to public events, ideally the press officer should be responsible to the PRO.

If the PRO is directly responsible to top management the press officer or officers will be concerned with more than just the sectional interests of one marketing division however important that may be. In some large organizations there is a central or group PR department, but each division or subsidiary has its own PRO within each individual advertising department. To take the argument to its logical conclusion each division should have a PR as well as an advertising department, because PR is concerned with much more than supplementing advertising. The publicity manager of a holiday resort has many responsibilities. The funds available for advertising, though, in such an organization are small and press relations and other PR techniques will probably form the main part of his duties. It is important that the resort's name appears in the press as often as possible and the simple way to achieve this is to help local correspondents find stories. News of this kind ranges from marriages to murder.

The chief officer of a voluntary organization, if it is not large enough to employ specialist staff, will also conduct PR as part of his duties. Some voluntary organizations are by their very nature almost wholly engaged in PR for a particular cause, seeking to make its members' activities, policies or beliefs better understood. It may be that the dividing line between propaganda and PR is a very delicate one if the views of the organization are controversial. He will also be engaged in internal relations with members, and to do this he may edit a newsletter or house journal, run meetings and conferences, and in every way keep the members well informed.

Organizations with widely scattered locations such as the National Coal Board with pits in nine regions in the UK, or British Airways with an international set-up, are best served by their own PR staff on the spot. In fact, it is often this type of organization which makes the best use of PR because communication internally and externally is absolutely essential. Not only that, but when the local unit is *the* unit so far as the press, radio, TV, and community of the locality is concerned it is sensible to employ a communication expert on the spot. It is seldom ever a good thing to rely on someone like a works manager or branch manager to handle PR because having his own job to do, he may not bother to initiate PR. A trained self-starter is required.

There is one kind of business which often directly operates both advertising and PR without the assistance of outside agencies, and this is the department store or store chain. The advertising is often placed direct because the advertisement copy changes frequently and is without repetition and there is no time to work through an intermediary. The same applies to PR, and this can be an essential factor in successful retailing because of the intimacy of the store's relations with its various publics – staff, services, suppliers, customers (who may be sub-divided) so that PR is a constant pre-occupation. The readiness to refund cash if not satisfied creates great goodwill, and encourages confidence in counter purchases in stores which lack fitting-room facilities. Bans on smoking and on dogs, parking bays for prams, escalators, wire shopping baskets and trolleys, and numerous other thoughtful innovations add to the ease, pleasure, and convenience of shopping.

These innovations all express a desire to create good relations. The difference between the modern store with its clean, fresh, wholesome prepacked commodities and the old-fashioned, unhygienic, badly displayed stores of the past is a triumph for public relations. When a businessman takes the trouble to think about the needs, likes, and dislikes of his customers he is engaging in public relations as distinct from buying cheap and selling dear which was once the only criterion of successful enterprise. That is why there are such close affinities between modern marketing (not just advertising) with its use of research techniques and public relations since both are concerned with communicating consumer needs and the ability to satisfy consumer needs. Nowhere is this better evidenced than in the retail trade.

In the last few pages a glimpse has been given of some of the different organizations which may find it best to have their own PR units or at least engage in PR through certain executives whose other abilities are reasonably similar to those of a PRO. As a company grows, or as the use of advertising is increased, an advertising manager is appointed. This is often the way in which a further division of labour leads to the appointment of a PRO.

Management appreciation of PR is essential if an organization is to have a comprehensive PR unit servicing all functions and departments. It is very significant that the best PR is always inspired from the top as has been seen with Sir Derek Ezra at the National Coal Board, Sir Miles Thomas when he was chairman of BOAC, Teddy Buchan and Bob Westphal at Rentokil, Sir Billy Butlin and many others. This century's prime example of PR from the top and extending right through a national enterprise has surely been that of the Marks and Sief families in their inspired management of Marks and Spencer.

PR Services Available from Outside the Company

External PR units can therefore be conveniently grouped as:

1. Freelance writers/consultants

2. PR departments of advertising agents
3. PR subsidiaries of advertising agents
4. Independent PR consultants
5. PR counsellors.

Before going into detail, though, let us first consider the place of the outside PR service. It does not only fill the gap when an organization does not already have its own PR unit, although there is a very good case for using outside services until fee expenditure equals the cost of an internal PR department. The consultant can still be engaged for *ad hoc* work or for special services which would not justify expansion of the internal department. These services might be the ones in which certain consultants specialized such as events organizing, financial PR, or advance PR for exhibitors. Again, pure consultancy – more properly described as counselling – may be required to advise an organization from an unbiased standpoint.

Although most PR people are employed outside the consultancy sphere, and although industrial, commercial, central and local government, public authority, and voluntary body PR has expanded in the 70's, it is also true that the consultancies are in an identical state of growth to the advertising agencies in the 30's, and the growth potential of consultancies through division of labour and diversification of services is such that PR could surpass advertising in profits if not turnover (since advertising billings include the high cost of media rates) in the 80's. This may well be aided by a coming together of the marketing, advertising and PR interests, especially with the breakdown of the anomalous commission system and the acceptance of the fee system, by advertising agencies, making them professional consultants instead of 15 per centers.

Advantages of the Consultancy

The two advantages of using consultancy services are similar to two of those enjoyed through using an advertising agency. They are: freedom from bias and wide experience of similar products, services or interests.

(i) *Freedom from Bias*. One of the strengths and an essential characteristic of the staff PRO is his enthusiasm towards his own organization, but it can also be an inhibiting factor producing in him a bias. The consultant is more professional in his approach, taking a broader view and he should be prepared to advise with the utmost frankness. Second opinions, outside points of view, constructive criticism – these are valuable services available from the consultant. That is why the consultant needs to have very wide knowledge and experience and be capable of earning a respected hearing in boardrooms and council chambers. This does imply that the account executive or counsellor needs to be a person of degree standard or broad experience in management. His minimum qualification should be the CAM Diploma.

(ii) *Wide Experience of Other Similar Products, Services, Interests*. The consultant, in the course of years of experience together with the cumulative experience of his staff, can draw on a wealth of knowledge and experience which the client cannot possess. He will be familiar with broad market conditions, trends and problems, and will be able to take an unprejudiced view of rival companies, products and services. A consultant may operate in a particular field such as building equipment or banking. It is not necessary to handle rival accounts to operate in these broad fields. To take building equipment, the consultant could handle accounts for every component in new private houses or commercial premises, civil engineering and the construction industry. The broad experience would be valuable to a large number of non-rival clients making, say, bricks and concrete formwork.

Now we can consider each of the five types of outside PR service.

1. *Freelance Writers/Consultants*
This is a very mixed group of individuals who are not to be despised because they perhaps operate from their own homes and do not possess the usual PR office equipment and facilities. There are freelance writers and technical authors who are skilled in producing PR feature articles, skilled PROs who prefer to operate on their own, and prematurely retired well-known PROs who are unwilling to cease practising PR and can therefore offer the benefit of years of experience. Care has to be taken, of course, to avoid the cut-price services of self-designated PR consultants who have little or no experience. Reputable freelance practitioners will be members of the IPR, CAM Society, BAIE, or other appropriate bodies.

2. *PR Departments of Advertising Agencies*
This outside service can range from a small press office handling little more than product publicity to augment advertising campaigns to a large comprehensive PR department not unlike the agency set-up itself. Evaluation of this sort of unit depends on the extent of the services and their independence from domination by the advertising agency.

Some advertising agencies have built up sizable and reputable PR departments, but in other cases the mistake was made by over-optimistic agency managements to provide free PR services as 'part of the service'. When the costs of these services were fully realized the PR departments were closed down. Independent consultants view with justified misgivings any PR services provided as part of an advertising agency service, on the grounds that unrealistic fees are charged because they can be subsidized out of the commissions which the agency obtains from the client's advertising bookings. It is very dangerous to try to over-please a client on the PR side in order to retain the much larger advertising billings on which the real profits are made.

It is hard for either an agency department or subsidiary to be wholly independent: indeed, this would be against the philosophy of providing a comprehensive campaign inclusive of PR. Unhappily advertising people have very perverse ideas about the ways in which they should be allowed to exploit PR techniques. A PR department of an advertising agency should be headed by a sufficiently tough personality who can hold his own. A real danger is that an agency thinks of PR in different terms to a PR practitioner: agency PR is either hard-selling product publicity copy in the style of a news release, or it entails handling no more than the below-the-line tasks such as running competitions and other promotional exercises. If they run a press conference the agency want it tricked out like a dealer gala.

3. PR Subsidiary of an Advertising Agency

Where there is a genuine desire to permit the subsidiary to operate as a PR consultancy it can be very similar to an independent consultancy except that in the agency it has a useful source of business. It can and should service clients independent of the agency, although the very fact that it is owned by an advertising agency may limit the consultancy's opportunities to gain independent business.

A big advantage is that the subsidiary can be departmentalized and staffed to undertake a full range of PR activities. The desire to operate independently is indicated by the use of completely different company names such as, Leedex, Lexington, Planned Public Relations, and Welbeck for the subsidiaries of well-known advertising agencies. There are also some large advertising agencies with two or three subsidiary PR companies operating independently.

When Welbeck Public Relations was set up as the PR subsidiary of Foote, Cone and Belding the managing director, Denis Inchbald, stated:

'We decided on the change because we felt that a subsidiary

Public Relations Company would be more likely to attract business from non-agency clients. Many of these prefer to be clients of a PR company under its own management rather than be clients of the PR division of a big advertising agency. We also believe that a subsidiary company will help to establish public relations in the eyes of agency clients as a function in its own right, rather than as an extra agency service, thereby making it easier to negotiate realistic fees. Finally, a subsidiary company provides senior PR personnel with greater management and promotion opportunities and helps to attract and retain good staff.'

On the whole, the subsidiary is preferable to the agency PR department. Its association with an advertising agency can have benefits through shared services such as accounts, art studio, and production, but this is less apparent if the agency has to sell its services somewhat expensively at a profit to its sister company: the PR company can probably buy elsewhere more economically. Clients tend to pay more for photography and artwork from an advertising agency than from a PR consultancy, even if the answer to that one is that advertising campaigns demand – and can afford – the services of higher-price photographers and artists! This is not to say that PR can get away with second-rate creative work.

There is a lot to be said for the subsidiary, but only provided that the PR account executive is not expected to be subservient to the advertising agency account executive. This can be achieved to a large degree if the PR proposals are divorced from the advertising scheme, and a PR programme and costings are freely produced on the basis of independent investigation of the PR requirement. This cannot be stressed enough because two things can operate against this to the disadvantage of both client and PR practitioner. One is that when there is a known association between agency and consultancy the client – who seldom understands the difference between advertising and PR – may wish to deal with but one person since 'it is all the same firm'. This has to be resisted. The other is that the agency account executive may usurp the PR side of the business-getting, and when the contract has been signed inform the PR practitioner that he has 'so much' to spend on PR. This is ridiculous. It is a good plan to engage in frankness with a client so that the ultimate budget is not exceeded by the proposals, but this is very different from having an arbitrary fraction of the advertising appropriation earmarked for a PR programme by an account executive who probably has an imperfect understanding of PR costs, and an even more imperfect knowledge of PR planning.

To achieve a truly integrated marketing plan in which both advertising and PR can successfully and economically play their respective roles, a representative from both the agency and the consultancy should be present at the initial and all succeeding meetings with the potential client at a joint plans board meeting, and at a joint presentation to the potential client.

The sort of questions asked by the PR representative will not be the same as those put by the advertising people. To take one small example, the advertising may be aimed at specific social grades during seasonal buying periods, but the PR could also take in the export market using translated news releases, and the services of the Central Office of Information and the External Services of the BBC if the PR investigation revealed scope for suitable stories. Equally, the PR could be concerned with staff, community or financial relations which were outside the advertising terms of reference. That is why it is unwise for an agency account executive to award the PR company an arbitrary sum based on no cogent reasoning, if only that the advertising and PR representatives are bound to approach the client's problems and needs from contrary standpoints.

There are, of course, some points of similarity as when a new product is to be launched and the advertising man will be aware of the possibilities for a PR back-up; the argument expounded here is that the PR programme should not be *limited* to support for immediate short-term advertising, and can include long-term projects and other PR assignments besides supplementing the advertising. This is where PR can eventually help to increase the effectiveness of the advertising if PR techniques have been employed to soften sales resistance by a process of education. It is rather like saying that a builder will produce a better house if it has been architect-designed.

These remarks are made as a guide to clients, advertising agents, and PR practitioners because very serious problems can arise from conflicts and misunderstandings occurring between members of all three groups. The combination of marketing, advertising and public relations in the syllabus of the CAM Certificate examination is a sensible, progressive and harmonizing answer to this problem.

4. *Independent PR Consultants*

After what has been said above it may be thought that the author favours the independent consultant who is clearly not involved in controversial issues with advertising colleagues. The independent consultant does have obvious advantages, but three criteria should be studied whatever the ownership of the consultancy:

(a) What is the calibre and professional status of the principals and executive staff?
(b) What is the record of the consultancy?
(c) Can it provide all the services required?

Now this pre-supposes that the client is sufficiently knowledgeable about PR to be able to buy PR services. The greatest weakness of PR today is that management is less well-informed than it should be about PR, which to a degree is the fault of consultants who adopt unnecessarily protective quasi-professional restrictions on selling their services. The IPR Code of Practice is sometimes interpreted more narrowly than even the disciplinary committee, I am sure, intends. It is wrong to tout for existing business, better to create new; it is silly to knock competitors, better to show by example your supremacy. These are questions of economics rather than ethics. Either because they do not invest in business-getting, or because they think advertising is not quite nice, consultants on the whole do not make a big enough effort to promote the numerous services that could be sold if only clients knew they existed. This applies chiefly to the independent consultants: those connected with advertising agencies do take their brothers' medicine with gusto.

With certain exceptions the majority of independent consultants are small. Most of the 600 consultants listed in *Hollis Press and Public Relations Annual* are of this order. Operating in little teams rather like solicitors and consulting engineers it is perhaps understandable why they tend not to promote themselves. Their future lies in amalgamation, realistic management, and profitable promotion. But these independent consultants have some very distinct advantages which can now be discussed:

(i) *Freedom from Advertising Bias.* We have pointed out the bias of the staff PRO, but the independent consultant owes no allegiance to an advertising agency or to an advertising campaign, and his is therefore the most impartial advice of all. However small, its sheer impartiality could be its major selling point, it is worth a fee for this alone.

(ii) *Able to Work with Advertising Agents.* Not all advertising agents can offer associated PR services, and it is possible for a client to appoint an advertising agency and PR consultancy which are independent of each other. This has the merit of providing three-part discussions, while the consultant can devote himself to a PR programme unlimited by the dictates of the advertising agency. The nature of the income tends to colour the attitude towards the client. The agency (unless operating on a fee basis) is dealing in large billings of which only a small proportion represents actual income. For example, on an advertisement space costing £1000 the agent will gain £150 whereas the consultant would earn £150 from about a day's work. The agent will also earn commissions on art and production charges, but in the main to stay in business and pay for a high salaried team of experts and all their overheads the agency requires large billings amounting to hundreds of thousands of pounds. Thus the unenviable situation can occur when disagreement with PR policy or client criticism of PR work might not only jeopardize a PR account worth a few thousand pounds p.a. but also put at risk the associated advertising campaign worth hundreds of thousands of pounds. This cannot happen when there is no relationship between agency and consultancy. The client can therefore expect the best possible service from both, knowing that each firm is anxious to retain the account on its own behalf. Also if the consultant feels strongly about some point of policy, relinquishment of the account will not be disastrous to the consultancy nor will it cause the agency to suffer loss of the account.

(iii) *Choice of Specialist Consultancy Possible.* Independent consultants are the ones which are most likely to specialize in a particular class of business, and clients can take advantage of this for *ad hoc*, short-term or full annual contract services. There are consultants specializing in almost everything.

(iv) *Financial PR Consultants.* There have been some interesting developments in the field of financial PR. It has been asserted by marketing pundits that financial PR is unnecessary, yet the more serious newspapers – *The Times, The Scotsman, Daily Telegraph*, and *Sunday Times* – make great play with their business sections while City pages exist in all the popular newspapers, and they would not exist without material from PRO's who regard these features as important news outlets.

Financial PR is a service offered by some general PR consultants, but others specialize in this activity alone.

A few quotations from a brochure produced by Fabus Financial and Business PR Limited, *Getting the Message*, will illustrate the value of the specialist independent consultancy.

'What is Financial Public Relations? Basically it is no more than a branch of business communications. But, it is that *extremely important branch concerned with relaying information and viewpoints on a company's industrial, and commercial activities* to those wider audiences termed financial and investment communities.

'No Board of Directors can suppose that it is acting in the best interests of its shareholders and employees by avoiding publicity with regard to its operations. . .

'*Financial Public Relations builds bridges and carries the good and bad company news* alike from Boardroom to the outside bustling world. . .'

In Chapter Three lists of publics are given: it is well worth noting the categories of public to which the single specialized phase of financial PR can be addressed.

The FABUS brochure continues:

'Provided the company is soundly run, has reasonable prospects and has *sensibly and widely communicated itself to the financial and investment communities* it will find that it is able to raise funds without difficulty and at the keenest rates.

'*The City will recognise merit quickly enough but that merit has first to be brought to its attention.* It is the experienced Financial Public Relations man who will ensure that this merit is brought to the attention not only of the City but also of the Investment Public at large.'

It goes on to explain how this is done, but not before he has expressed the essential function of PR, the reason why any organization needs to communicate, and that is to gain credit for achievement. No organization can continue to exist under today's competitive conditions if it is modestly uncommunicative about what it has done or can do well. That is very different from the quaint assertion made by the British Institute of Management that PR is to do with 'procuring favourable attention' which is hardly the best choice of words.

5. *PR Counsellors*
This practitioner is better understood in the USA than in the UK. It is really a misnomer to call a PR practitioner a 'consultant' because once he undertakes creative and productive work he is more nearly on a par with an advertising agent. A consultant should advise only, and it would be more sensible if we had PR agencies and PR consultants. The present set-up is confusing to clients, and encourages so-called consultants to talk about a profession which is closer to being a business. Some consultancies with a division of labour do call their account executives 'consultants' which is not a bad idea when he is not the typical jack-of-all-trades account executive found in small and medium-sized consultancies.

However, the true consultant is the PR counsellor, the practitioner who investigates, reports, advises, and recommends but does not execute the agreed proposals. This kind of PR counsellor should work quite independently of other PR units and have no interest in a consultancy or what would be better described as a PR agency.

The shape of British PR suggests, nevertheless, that unless the independent consultancies divide themselves into (a) small units which concentrate on counselling and (b) combinations which offer a variety of organizing, creative, and production services, the tendency will be towards mergers with senior practitioners using their experience to serve not as account executives but as counsellors. Whichever way consultancy practice moves, the role of the seasoned counsellor is sure to develop if only because (i) there is tremendous value in his services which are an essential feature of outside PR services, and (ii) this provides a means of recruiting young people of the right calibre to less responsible positions lower down the ladder.

One of the problems of the consultancy world today is that a consultancy can consist almost entirely of people responsible for both client liaison and the execution of PR campaigns. Clients cannot be expected to take very seriously advice on a range of complex business matters from a young man or woman in his or her twenties, nor are they likely to pay large fees for these junior services. PR counselling is not a young man's business, but once PR counselling is confined to the more experienced the opportunities for the less experienced to come in at a proper level will be increased to the advantage of all. Younger people are going to be needed for the specialist jobs in PR, but these jobs will never exist when consultants – through scarcity of clients – are obliged to advertise for account executives under 30 years of age at low salaries. If some clients were to read the situations vacant advertisements for PR staff they would wonder what services the average consultancy could possibly offer them.

The PR counsellor is therefore a practitioner who may have great influence upon the future status of the PR business, the true professional in fact.

How does one find a consultant, or know what type of business he handles? A comprehensive directory of consultants and their clients is published in *Advertiser's Annual*, and also in the *Hollis Press and Public Relations Annual*. Consultants also advertise in the trade press, and from time to time features appear in the business press. Helpful advice can be obtained from the Public Relations Consultants Association at 44 Belgrave Square, London SW1, telephone 01-235 6225. The PRCA was founded in 1969. It maintains a compulsory register covering the activities of the member companies and their clients. The register is open for inspection and includes a complete list of clients.

CHAPTER SIX

Press Officer and the Press Office

The press officer's job is not to write and distribute material as directed and authorized by his employer. If employers of press relations services merely want to say what they like when they like they should use a direct mail agency. It is the press officer's place to reason why, and that is one of his most testing responsibilities. Although the press officer is employed by the purveyor of news he can only follow that employment successfully on his employer's behalf if he recognizes that he must behave responsibly to communication media. The press officer is a professional, not a hired hack writer.

Few advertising agency people can understand this, perhaps because they work in much more prescribed circles or even because it is their experience that having booked an advertisement space they can sometimes lean heavily on the advertisement manager and induce him to obtain a write-up out of his editor. This does happen, of course, and being neither genuine editorial nor sincere press relations, they are looked upon as just another part of the advertisement.

But genuine press relations efforts are publishable on their merits, not because advertisement space has been purchased. In fact, the best PR story is generally one which appears nowhere near an advertisement for the same thing.

Ten Responsibilities of a Press Officer

The competent press officer should:

1. Establish internal lines of communication so that he has ready access to sources of information within his organization.

2. Collate information and pictures for future use, building a comprehensive fact and picture library.
3. Issue material in a form acceptable to various media so that his organization is made known and understood, its achievements are appreciated and its reputation is deservedly enhanced.
4. Maintain a press service so that all enquiries from media are dealt with quickly, efficiently and honestly.
5. Be impartial to the extent that media will trust him to supply ungarnished facts.
6. Be able to judge the news value of information supplied to him, and be prepared to reject a story which is not suitable for release.
7. Be constantly aware of the danger of issuing false or misleading information even though it may be supplied by an apparently reliable source.
8. Feed back information, such as external attitudes or news about rival organizations so that his service provides a two-day liaison.
9. Be so organized that he can provide a fully competent press relations service, on a 24-hour basis if necessary.
10. Record the results of his efforts and report accordingly to his superiors.

To some readers these ten responsibilities – the ten commandments of press relations – may come as a bracing surprise. Certainly, a good many cynics in both the advertising and the press world do not expect a press officer to be so meticulous or fastidious. But scruples are the strength of press relations and these responsibilities are taken very seriously by those who adhere to the Code of Professional Conduct of the Institute of Public Relations, not purely for moral reasons but out of economic necessity. It is only when such responsibilities are accepted that the press officer can operate effectively and deserve the respect which is accorded to any other professional practitioner.

To Whom is the Press Officer Responsible?

This is a difficult question to answer because media relations practice is seldom clearly defined as an organizational function. Strictly speaking, the press officer should be responsible either directly or through the PRO to top management. In actual practice this may not be so.

In a voluntary body he is likely to be a member of a small team of permanent officials headed by a general secretary or director. In industry, as already mentioned, his status and supervision can vary tremendously. He may be the only PR man and his chief may be a promotional executive handling marketing, sales or advertising. Again, he may be a specialist assistant to the PRO whose status will depend on the extent to which the board is PR-orientated.

This assumes that media relations are conducted by a full-time press officer, but this is not always the case and this book is intended for others as well who may have to deal with the press, having no journalistic experience or inside knowledge of publishing house operations and requirements. Marketing, sales, advertising, personnel, works and shop managers may well have to deal with the press from time to time.

Unfortunately, a good many news releases are issued by people completely unskilled in this work and often utterly unaware that any special skill is required. Since the number of organizations issuing stories is large, whereas the number employing press officers is comparatively small, it is not really surprising that so many releases received by editors are unpublishable. Only a proportion of the blame for poor news releases can therefore be directed at professional press officers.

From these remarks it will be seen that media relations are dabbled in by a large number of people, with or without ability, knowledge and experience. For successful media relations, however, a competent trained press officer is necessary.

How are Press Officers Recruited?

The answer is directly related to the quality of press relations practice. What are the methods of recruiting press officers?

They are many and diverse, and there is serious need for a more direct entry to press relations with provision for trainee facilities, day release for training, and possibly some form of specialist qualification as distinct from the all-round qualification of CAM. But at present we find press officers recruited from the following fields: newspaper and magazine journalism, advertisement copywriting, transfers from other jobs in the same organization and trainees.

The latter category is almost non-existent in any real sense of the word. There are some instances of trainee PR executives who include press relations in their training. But as yet there is very little attempt to recruit trainee press officers from among graduates as happens in the advertising world. It is a very unsatisfactory state of affairs, but undoubtedly one of the most potent reasons for the absence of trainees is the lack of employer appreciation of the need for training.

Do Journalists Make Good Press Officers?

Far too often management, needing to appoint a press officer yet knowing little about the subject, will take a short cut and appoint a journalist assuming that any journalistic experience is sufficient qualification for a good press officer. This assumption is seldom valid. The average journalist knows little about media outside his immediate and usually narrowly specialized experience and consequently has practically no knowledge of media relations from the outside.

Some of our leading PR practitioners were, of course, very fine journalists. Newspaper experience is not only writing experience, but includes familiarity with the wider aspects of life, the way in which the world earns a living, and the manner in which we are governed. It may also include managing a publication with all its business, and labour relations implications. Not every journalist, however, enjoys such broad or senior experience.

A journalist working on a paper presents his copy in a very different way from that required of an accomplished press officer. The staff journalist is often working to meet a deadline and tends to type imperfectly on small pieces of paper. His job is to complete an assignment, and he does not have to market his stories. Nor does he have to please more than one editor. A conscientious press officer, however, is aware that his release has to compete with scores of others and that he must take the extra trouble necessary to produce a release which sells itself through its clarity of heading and content, neat setting out and legible presentation.

Moreover, the press officer has to understand readership profiles, know by which process each journal is printed, and be aware of copy dates, otherwise he will irritate editors by sending them stories they cannot use. The working journalist has to understand the needs of his own paper only.

It is fairer to say that the abilities and character likely to produce a first-class journalist will equally make a first-class press officer, but that is very different from saying that ex-journalists make good press officers; a good many people other than journalists are capable of excelling as press officers provided that they can match up to the requirements listed in the next section.

What Makes a Good Press Officer?

The simple answer to this question is that anyone who can write concise, precise English; is a thorough, methodical and imaginative organizer; likes, understands and gets on with people; has wide interests and experiences; is in every way an intelligent, adaptable, broadminded person with an infinite fund of curiosity; is always willing to recognize his own limitations yet maintains a zest for learning; who above all has a tenacious, persistent nature so that he never gives up, never allows himself to be fobbed off, nor falls victim to disappointment but is always enthusiastic without being boastful about what he hopes to achieve; anyone who fits that job specification will make a first-class press officer. This is very different from the typical advertising agency idea of someone who is merely able to 'con' the press: he has to be a person of distinct attributes and integrity. This job specification may surprise some readers and suggests that the press officer has to be a miracle man, but then we are aiming at perfection, not black magic.

News Sense

There is, of course, one attribute that a trained journalist does have which is indispensable to a press officer, and that is 'news sense'. In the past journalists have been favoured recruits to PR because they alone have been expected to possess news sense, but if others can acquire this ability to detect what is certain to interest other people they will be well equipped for the job. Looked at more closely, what is this 'news sense'? Isn't it exactly the same as the marketing man's ability to produce and sell goods that will satisfy a need?

News sense is not so much creating news as recognizing what aspects of a piece of information, or what manner of presentation of this information, will most succeed in interesting the media. It is really a piece of elementary motivation research.

For example, a company may obtain an export contract for the supply of a given quantity or value of goods. This item may rate a couple of lines in a business column or magazine. Similar stories are published, practically listed, daily. Often, the two or three lines printed have been subbed down from dull, wordy releases of practically no news value.

The press officer with a nose for news will delve deeper for a real story. Call this creating news if you like, but he cannot invent what is not there to be discovered. If someone has the wit and the will to look into a contract and find out, say, that this was the first time such a contract had been awarded to a British company, and then go on to find out how this British company – his company or client – had in fact beaten foreign competition then we are approaching a story of 'hard', news importance. This story need not be just an item for the business section but possibly worth space on the front page, a story of interest to radio and TV, the COI and the External Services of the BBC at Bush House. But it all began with a dull-seeming two-line admission by an unimaginative export manager who could not really be expected to have 'news sense'.

With this introduction to the role of the press officer let us now consider his necessary qualifications and abilities.

The media are sometimes cynically disposed towards PROs and press officers because they mistake them for press agents. The whole aim of press agentry is to get pictures and stories into print by one means or another that will publicize the press agent's client, and clients are usually personalities such as entertainers – people who have to be in the news to exist. Press agents are sometimes more frankly called publicity agents. Their work is akin to advertising in effect, but the method of operation is often dubious.

The difference between press relations and press agentry is clear when the principle is accepted that the press officer aims to issue material which is first and foremost news of reader interest. Publicity must accrue from this basic value, but the news will be issued with proper regard for the integrity of the press.

This difference is reasonably well understood when the source of the news is an official information service, and now that news distribution is becoming a very important branch of marketing this commercial aspect can be more help than hindrance.

Advertised goods and services are openly advocated whereas personalities rely upon publicity gained by whatever means may be within the ingenuity, power and purse of the press agent.

Advertising takes the risk of publicly making claims, and it is nowadays so hedged about by both legislation and voluntary control that most advertising is highly trustworthy and reputable. It has to be, and companies stake reputations worth millions of pounds on their advertised claims.

Desirable Qualities of a Press Officer

Now let us be analytical and consider the four most desirable and important abilities of a press officer. These are the ability to:

1. Obtain facts
2. Write journalistically
3. Market stories
4. Time distribution of stories.

1. *Ability to Obtain Facts.* He must be able to interview people, prepare a questionnaire, or carry out either field or desk research to get the information for his news stories. In this he must be politely persistent. The ability to investigate calls for more than inquisitiveness.

It requires wide experience and catholic tastes for with these attributes points of sympathetic human contact are possible. No-one wants to talk to another who appears narrow, selfish, ignorant and unsympathetic.

But above all, in his search for facts, he must be conscious of the value of these facts from the point of view of the ultimate reader. An employer or client may wish to present facts which are important to him: the press officer must assert his unquestionable right to demand and to issue only the facts which are publishable and readable. If such facts are withheld, the press officer is bound to declare there is no story that he can release. If he is asked to decorate the facts more favourably, it is his place to dissent. And if he suspects that the information is not all that it seems, it is his duty to check the facts before editors take his material on trust and publish to their disadvantage.

Without integrity any person engaged in PR work must fail, and this applies particularly to the press officer whose stock in trade must be trust. No matter how cynically certain sections of the press may regard the press officer he must nevertheless be above suspicion. Unless his employer understands this position the press officer will be unable to perform his functions. All this may sound very purist, but would a surgeon permit the patient to direct an operation?

There is no doubt that at the present time there are PROs, PR consultants, press officers and others holding associated positions who, through fear of dismissal, permit misguided users of their services to abuse them. To enjoy respect for integrity the press officer must argue from a position of strength given him by his superior experience, training, qualifications and not least of all by his proven ability to deliver the goods on his own initiative.

When a PR consultant excuses poor work on the grounds that 'the client insists' that a story be written in such a way, or that it must be

D

embargoed, or that elaborate press packs must be put in an exhibition press room, that consultant is incompetent to the point of wasting his client's money. That such a dim state of affairs is all too common only goes to show the lowly state of our business and the ineptitude of certain practitioners. *In PR the customer is seldom right*. The PR man should be paid to be right.

2. *Ability to Write Journalistically*. As we shall discuss this in more practical detail in the chapter on how to write news releases, the subject will be but briefly touched on here. A poet or novelist might make a poor press officer. We are not writing to impress or entertain. Our words must interest and inform, briefly and clearly. Every word must count but superlatives have no place since we cannot put words of praise into editors' mouths. A news release contains no comment. We have to write as we might expect a journalist to write, given the same facts, and we cannot express his opinions for him. Thus in a news release, we do not write of a 'famous' company.

Journalistic writing is the opposite to essay writing. There is no introduction, development and conclusion. Instead, in a news story, the gist of the story is told in the first paragraph, and then expanded in the paragraphs which follow. This can be seen at once in any newspaper.

3. *Ability to Market Stories*. Once he has a story the press officer must know where to place it. This is very much a selling operation even though the stories are submitted free of charge. But more than this, he must only send releases to the editors most likely to be interested in them. The marketing of press releases requires a thorough knowledge of media, and the acquisition of this knowledge is a painstaking business. The press officer who writes a story and then does a blanket mailing of all the journals covering that subject is an amateur compared to the man who knows his media and selects the right publication for each story.

Sometimes clients ask PR consultants what mailing lists are used for their stories. A good press officer does not keep lists because there is no permanent set of publications that is suitable for every story issued by a particular organization. This point must be emphasized since it is seldom appreciated. The constant study of media is therefore imperative because changes are so frequent. The market for any given story must be known and understood.

Reference to the building up of addressing plate libraries or use of distributing services from which addresses can be selected, follows in the section on the press office, and Part Two is devoted to communication media.

Media selection is a question of knowledge, not contacts. Addresses in a press officer's plate library are only useful if he knows something of the publications they represent. There is plenty of published information to mention only *Benn's Press Directory* and the *PR Planner*.

In other words, the press officer has to be his own literary agent.

4. *Ability to Time Distribution of Stories.* This ability derives chiefly from knowing how publications are produced, printed and distributed. The printing process is the most important of the three: is it letterpress, photogravure, or lithographic including web-offset? An elementary knowledge of printing is essential to anyone engaged in PR. If the press officer understands the process by which various journals are published he will know how to time the release of his stories and will not send releases to publications which have already gone to press or have been printed already.

He will know that a morning national is printed at night, the first edition for the provinces coming off the presses about 10 p.m. and the London edition about 4 a.m. Only something dramatic like a front-page murder story will interest an editor after 10 p.m. and even a 'hard' news story from a PR source is unlikely to be of much use to such an editor after tea-time.

A woman's weekly printed by photogravure may go to the printer six weeks before publication, and its planning, writing and illustration will have been done over a period three to six months before publication. On the other hand, a monthly letterpress journal needs material before the middle of the previous month, while a weekly magazine printed by the letterpress or web-offset process may want material as early as the previous Friday if published on a Wednesday.

A provincial weekly newspaper sold on Friday is often made-up on Tuesday, set and proofed on Wednesday, printed and delivered on Thursday, which means that copy is required on Monday at the latest. Thus, stories to the provincial press should be posted on Thursday or Friday, or hand-delivered on Monday (perhaps following a telephone call to say the story is on its way).

For example certain work was to be done to the parish church, but by the time it had been completed and photographed the story would have been too late for that week's issue, and stale news for the next. A photograph of the exterior was taken on the Thursday. The story was written up from the job specification and approval obtained of the draft, and the picture, caption and release were delivered to the newspaper office on the Monday morning. By the time the story appeared in print on the following Thursday the work had been completed as reported.

But writing before the event can have its snares if plans change at the last minute after the story has been written.

The Press Office

The department run by the press officer is known as the press office, and journalists making enquiries are as likely to ask the telephone operator for the press office as the press officer. Consequently it should be organized and equipped so that it can operate efficiently and with expert understanding of how the press works and what it wants. It should have good inter-communication or direct-line facilities so that the press officer can communicate quickly within his own organization. He should be served by a first-class secretary who knows exactly what to do in his absence, and in a large organization there will be assistant press officers. In some organizations with scattered locations it may be necessary to have press officers in the field who can be instantly contacted.

Two things are essential to the successful running of a press office – first, access to information internally; and secondly, access to information externally.

Access to Information Internally

This is often very difficult to establish, and the newly appointed staff press officer will have to exercise patience, persistence and a great deal of tact if he is to succeed in creating workable lines of communication. The reason for this is simple, intriguing and very human. People either take newsworthy material for granted, or – especially if they are junior executives – they are worried about giving away company secrets and advantages to their competitors.

Ideally, the press officer should be at the receiving end of information which wide-awake PR-conscious people throughout the company are passing on to him. This wonderful state of affairs is not impossible, and actually occurs in organizations where the staff have been educated by an enlightened management, and this can be done through staff journals, training schemes and staff conferences. It can happen in companies where the staff are themselves kept well informed about company policy and activities, and where there is a PR department with press officers who visit and make themselves known and understood to the staff throughout the organization wherever they may be, at home or abroad.

The press officer has to cultivate people at all levels in the organization so that he has friendly access to informants. He must be able to correspond with, telephone or call on *anyone* in the organization from the chairman to the caretaker. This is his privilege.

He does not wait for information to come to him: he has to go out and get it.

Becoming accepted means that he must do a PR job for himself. He must make himself known throughout the organization, and the results of his work must be seen and appreciated. Copies of press releases and press cuttings should be distributed to branch managers, works managers and others, and on factory notice boards copies of selected press cuttings should be displayed to show how well the organization is reported in the press. People like to know that they are in the news, or at least that their organization is publicly reported.

The press officer has the distinct and pleasant advantage of becoming a popular personality, but he does have to be careful to avoid creating jealousies by appearing to steal the limelight. He may write much of the house journal despite the credits given to apparent contributors who may have supplied only incoherent notes. The press officer has to be a ubiquitous invisible man at times, the enthusiastic organizer hidden in the wings, the one who gets little praise for the miracles but all the blame when the smallest thing goes wrong.

Editing the staff journal can be an asset to the press officer because it provides constant contact with members of the staff everywhere, and if it is the kind of organization which has factories or offices in scattered locations a system of communication can be established by the appointment of local correspondents. Thus, the press officer can operate through a network of informants.

But equally, the press officer who works in a smaller compass will still need to make himself known to possible sources of information. For example, a seaside resort publicity manager needs material for press stories, and it pays him to keep the local press well informed about his activities so that those engaged in the local holiday industry will appreciate his activities on their behalf and support him with useful facts and news items. The work of his committee and department should therefore be regularly reported in the local press.

Access to Information Externally

The information required here consists of the journals and the journalists who will be interested in receiving his news releases, pictures and articles.

Plates are best if used often enough to warrant the expense of making them. They make possible very speedy addressing of envelopes. Equipment is available ranging from modest hand-operated addressing machines to large automatically operated systems.

In setting up an addressing system two things should be remembered. First, the chosen categories should be easy to locate when required. It is hopeless to have the addresses but never know how they have been filed, and all the plates should be numbered for accurate refiling after use. Secondly, the addresses must be kept up-to-date by watching for changes as reported in the trade press, or as indicated in the press officer's day-to-day work, while a periodic check against, say, *British Rate and Data*, is imperative. Changes of addresses and title are frequent, while some journals cease publication and others are launched. However, users of PRADS or subscribers to the *PR Planner* will be supplied with regularly updated information.

If plates are held for correspondents and other staff writers, plate changes are likely to be frequent because journalists tend to change jobs quite often. A live address library is the gold mine of an efficient press office. Editors will, of course, expect the press officer to be infallible about addresses.

Included in this library should be the addresses of freelance writers who write on subjects relative to the organization, and this category can be built up by making contact with contributors to journals and authors of books. Some press officers are impatient of freelance writers, but this is a foolish attitude because many editors call in these freelance writers to produce special sides to publishing such as readers' letters and reader enquiry services. The astute press officer will use every communication resource open to him. There are, for example, several editorial services which supply regular features to journals and all these must be included in the address library.

Starting Up an Address Plate Library

The information needed to find the titles and addresses of newspapers and magazines is published in a number of directories which are all useful for slightly different purposes, and the press officer should have a complete library of these books, making sure to buy each new edition as it comes out. We have already mentioned *BRAD* which is published monthly for the benefit of the advertising business and is best described as a directory of rate cards, but a monthly subscription may be too heavy and rather unnecessary for the press officer, although an occasional copy is useful for checking purposes. There are also *BRAD* editions covering the media of Germany, France and Italy. The following annuals are recommended:

Benn's Press Directory. This is a massive work giving information about journals published throughout the world, which even lists house journals. Its chief value is that it describes the readership of each journal or, in the case of local newspapers, it describes their area of distribution.

Willings Press Guide. While details of readership are not given, titles are listed in alphabetical order and are easily found if individual envelopes are being typed as may occur with a special mailing for which cards or plates do not yet exist. This book includes some additional titles of overseas journals not to be found in other directories.

Advertiser's Annual. Although the addresses are predominantly those of advertisement and not editorial departments, this annual often includes journals not to be found elsewhere, and its classification headings provide useful categories on which to base an address library. This annual is also valuable as a source of ancillary services and suppliers useful to the press officer.

In addition, the press officer should acquire the various official booklets which are issued from time to time by the Central Office of Information and the Department of Trade which list the facilities provided by these official means of communication with the overseas press, radio and TV. The IBA and the BBC publish informative annuals about TV and radio.

If the press officer has to mail stories to the overseas press he can obtain quite good information from the directories listed above, but more complete directories are published in the larger countries although these can be expensive to buy.

Press Cutting Services

It is important to know the results of press relations work, and since it would be impracticable to subscribe to every journal to which stories are submitted the services of a press cutting agency are necessary. In London and certain other parts of the UK there are agencies which will supply cuttings at a fee for so many cuttings per subject. Some agencies also charge a search fee irrespective of whether cuttings are actually found. Cutting agencies exist in most countries with a large press.

These agencies receive a certain amount of criticism because they seldom succeed in finding more than about 50 per cent of the cuttings which exist. There are many reasons for this failure, but they are not entirely the fault of the agencies. For example, a story might appear in only one edition of a newspaper. Moreover, cutting agencies do not necessarily search every publication issued in the country. There are also stories which refer to the organization or product without actually naming it, and such items are likely to escape the press cutting staff. On the whole, the fees charged by these agencies are not high. The most satisfactory service results when a broad subject heading can be given to the agency rather than just the name of an organization. Press cuttings as a means of recording results are fully discussed in Chapter Twelve.

The Do's and Don'ts of Good Press Relations

To conclude this chapter here are twelve points worth remembering as a guide to good press relations.

1. *Understand the Press.* Don't expect editors and reporters to be out to trick you, but remember that publishing is a highly competitive business. Be realistic. If you try to hide facts you are asking for trouble. The press can be ruthless. Don't favour one paper more than another, and don't give unfair exclusives. Let every paper have the same chance with the same story and pictures. And don't give different pictures to competing journals in the same category. However, unless syndicated, feature articles must be exclusive.

2. *Tell the Truth.* Don't issue half a story, or try to gild a story in your organization's favour. Press people will usually respect confidences. Put newsmen in the picture as much as you can.

3. *Be Always Accessible.* Make sure the press can reach you at any time. When you leave the office say where you are going. Put your address on your news release and on photo captions. Give your private telephone number as well as your office number. Respond quickly to requests for information, written or phoned.

4. *Be Prepared.* If a story is likely to break, check policy and have the facts ready. Know what you are talking about. This can be very valuable if you have to refute false statements or misunderstandings.

5. *Regard Press People as Fellow Practitioners.* Respect their calling and invite them to respect yours. Remember, you can only argue from a position of strength. Don't try to teach them their job. Don't try to tell them what is news. Be patient with the cynical reporter who sneers

at PR. Go out of your way to tip him off about a possible story. Press officers and journalists should work as a team.

6. *Show Visiting Pressmen Round.* Turn calls into memorable visits. Take visiting pressmen behind the scenes. Open their eyes. Let them meet people. Make them feel welcome. Make them feel they can drop in whenever it pleases them.

7. *Provide Facilities.* Make it easy for reporters to get their stories away. Find them a quiet room, a desk and a chair, a typewriter and a telephone, a company car if necessary. Don't begrudge them any assistance. Observe every courtesy, hospitality and respect due to a guest.

8. *Maintain a Friendly Relationship.* Keep friends with the press, but do not exploit friendship. Think of occasions when you can be nice to press people. Don't try to buy their favours with too many drinks or lunches. Try to remember names. Keep a personal book of names. You will meet hundreds of journalists and remembering all their names is not easy.

9. *Don't Get a Reputation for Stopping Stories.* Sometimes you won't want them to print a story, but always try to have a replacement story if you can. Remember, the reporter is expected to come back to the office with a story.

10. *Don't Expect a Story because your Organization Advertises.* Keep the two separate. Don't get involved in advertising. Avoid the blackmail of write-ups *if* you advertise, and vice versa. Your work must be publishable on its own merits.

11. *Be Careful over Corrections.* Errors do occur. Take them up, the editor may be genuinely unaware of the true facts. But do not antagonize editors. A tactful way of dealing with mistakes is to write to the editor, thank him for publishing the story and then mention that if he receives any readers' enquiries the correct details are so and so.

12. *Remember Dead Lines, Copy Dates, Publishing Days.* Don't waste reporters' time with stories too late to catch the right or next edition. Watch out for Saturday stories – Sunday papers carry little news and by Monday a Saturday story is cold. Don't give evening papers a story at five o'clock. Remember that monthlies need stories six weeks ahead, and that gravure-printed magazines work months ahead. If space has been promised for a feature article make sure you supply the MSS by the agreed copy date.

The twelve points offered above provide a workmanlike basis for good day-to-day press relations. They should be remembered together with the reasons for the rejection of news releases which will be found in Chapter Fifteen. The simple philosophy is good relations in all directions, within and without one's organization. Nothing is perfect. The press officer will work most efficiently when he has no illusions of the world in which he has to operate. He has to deal with people and people are irrational, exasperating and human just like himself. Moreover, the media are in business to stay in business: the best way to maximize news coverage is help the media to build and keep readerships and audiences.

CHAPTER SEVEN

The Costs
of PR

Probably because in some ill-informed quarters a strange idea exists that PR is free advertising, the reckoning of PR costs is sometimes misunderstood. The costing of PR activities is no different from the costing of anything else comprising labour and materials which are combined with the intention of carrying out a task effectively and economically and, in the case of a consultant, profitably.

Some employers of internal PR staff and a good many consultants have very little idea of the real costs of PR. It is truly amazing how many employers will turn a conveniently blind eye to overhead expenses; how users of outside services will accept a service with an arbitrarily conceived and seldom ever justified overall fee; and worse still how many PR consultants abhor time sheets and operate unprofitable consultancy services which are more like charities for selfish clients. Far too many clients literally believe that PR is free publicity, and pay extraordinarily tiny fees presumably because they cannot conceive of PR work costing much to perform.

This remarkably unrealistic state of affairs can only be ended when users of PR services understand what they are buying, what it costs, and what constitutes value for money.

There is, nevertheless, a very genuine reason why some users of PR are confused about costs. They are or were in receipt of very extensive free services from their advertising agents because of the curious commission system, although this is rapidly giving way to various kinds of fee systems. The commission system, which is convenient to the media owners, really means that the media owners subsidize the service – that is, the advisory and administrative work undertaken by account executives, space buyers, production, print buying, progress chasing and other staff. The commission system not only prevents the advertising agency from making a proper professional charge for work done, but the cost of the work is hidden from the client.

Consequently, it comes very hard to have to pay for somewhat similar services when carried out by a PR consultancy, and the different method of charging is even more perplexing when it comes from the PR department or subsidiary of the advertising agency whose services are apparently free. In fact, advertising agency owners or PR consultancies do not themselves always appreciate what they should properly charge, and there was a time when some advertising agencies tried – most unprofitably – to throw in PR services as freely as others, overlooking the fact that this required a heavy subsidy from agency resources.

So, we must start with the assumption that everything must be paid for, and that as PR personnel become better selected, trained, qualified and experienced they will be able to command salaries equivalent to those earned by advertising personnel. Inevitably, PR will cost and be worth more when performed by more competent practitioners. As with advertising, vast progress is likely to occur in a short space of time once PR recruits understand how much they need to learn.

One curiosity of PR costing needs to be disposed of right away, and that is the practice of tacking a little something on to the end of an advertising budget (or deducting it from this budget) for PR. The PR executive is then told he has a certain sum for PR before he has had any opportunity to make a study and present proposals. This practice often occurs in advertising agencies where the account executive has no understanding of PR. This is yet another reason why there should be a separate budget for PR, and separate negotiations for PR services even when they are to be carried out by a department or subsidiary of the advertising agency.

The PR Budget

Let us now examine the items which constitute a PR budget, looking at this from the points of view of both the staff PRO and the outside consultant. The four basic elements are: labour, office overheads, materials, and expenses.

Labour. Salaries of management and specialist PR staff. Salaries of secretarial, clerical and accountancy staff (including National Insurance and pension fund contributions). Fees to freelance, consultancy, and other outside staff.

Office Overheads. All rent, rates, insurance, heat, light, telephone (including switchboard), office services, client liaison.

Materials. All stationery, photography, postage, print, visual aids, exhibition stands, films and other items.

Expenses. All out-of-pocket expenses incurred by staff such as fares, hotel bills and entertainment of guests, plus catering costs for functions and events.

The consultant will expect to make a gross profit of at least 15 per cent and this means charging a service fee capable of recovering salaries and overheads, although some income may be derived from commissions or quantity concessions on certain materials such as print and photography. Expenses are charged at cost, and where these are heavy, as with catering for a press reception, they are best charged direct to the client by the contractor, otherwise they may represent interest-free loans.

There is a somewhat old-fashioned argument that it is unprofessional for a PR consultant to accept commissions from suppliers, but the consultant who handles films, house journals, and exhibitions may well depend on these commissions for a major part of his income. The amount of consulting or counselling done by the average consultant may occupy only a minor part of the time or work load with most of it occurring in the original planning stages and then at subsequent progress meetings. The bulk of the fee will be taken up by the time expended on carrying out the programme. Few consultancy fees can be regarded as retainers for PR advice, although such an item can, and should, be specifically written into a consultant's budget proposals.

The client may say he can operate a PR department and save himself the consultant's profit, but he can do this only when he would otherwise be employing a PR consultancy full-time or more than full-time, and if he is conveniently situated as a consultant. It has to be recognized that although the consultant may have to bear and charge the overhead expenses of an office in the centre of a city, compared with the lower costs of an office in a provincial factory, the cost of sharing those city facilities is a very modest investment in more efficient PR services. However, the pros and cons of internal and external PR services will be debated in the next chapter.

The false argument occurs when the client resents paying consultancy fees and thinks that for a smaller or even the same outlay he could run his own PR department. He cannot, of course, run an effective PR department on this sort of outlay for two reasons: (i) If he is paying a consultant a small fee he is using only a proportion of an executive's time, and consequently if he employed a PRO full-time he would have to indulge in extra PR activity which might well incur numerous other costs such as house journals, films, seminars, work visits and so on. This in turn would probably involve further expenditure on additional salaries. (ii) While a staff PRO and secretary may be engaged for the cost of their salaries they still have to be housed, equipped, serviced and supplied at a minimum cost of at least their salary bill again. And since the additional volume of work is bound to require additional staff such as a PR assistant and an office junior with their own overheads, it is unlikely that an internal PR department comparable with a PR consultancy service can be undertaken more economically. It may be undertaken differently or more efficiently but that is another matter associated with the intimacy of in-house PR. It can therefore be misleading to compare consultancy costs with PR department costs.

Cost of an Internal PR Department

Let us now look more closely at the costs which concern the internal PR unit, assuming that the internal unit is at least an embryo PR department consisting of a public relations officer or manager, and his secretary. Anything less than this is not a serious attempt to undertake PR, but mixed operations will be discussed in the next chapter on administration.

Labour

The staff of a PR department may consist of some or all of the following personnel.

Public relations officer	Exhibitions manager
Assistant public relations officer	Events organizer
Press officer	Librarian
House journal editor	Secretarial staff
Films and photography officer	General office staff

The budget must therefore include their salaries, pension funds, insurance, and taxes as may be appropriate under current policy or legislation, and successive budgets must allow for bonuses and salary increases.

Each organization's PR department will vary according to its particular needs, and two seemingly identical companies serving much the same market could undertake PR in very different ways. This is the great advantage of PR over advertising as a means of communication, since PR can adopt more than one method with equal effectiveness. However, in a sizable PR campaign the house journal and the documentary film will both occupy important places in the programme, but a smaller campaign could use either one or the other. (It will be seen from these remarks that already we are relegating press relations to but a place in a programme, and not the whole programme as it is sometimes regarded.)

A modest PR department will therefore consist of at least a PRO, a press officer, two secretaries, and a clerical assistant or copy typist.

Costs could be lessened if the more specialist duties were supplied by outside PR consultants, photographers, film producers, exhibition stand designers, house journal producers and others. It is by no means a case of making a distinct choice between either an internal department and a consultancy; many sensible and valuable combinations are possible, and these combinations are an important aspect of PR costing. For example, it is pointless maintaining even a two-man film unit unless at least three films a year are to be made or, again, unless the film unit can double on other duties, photographic or otherwise. There is no investment in idleness.

There is, however, one contributory aspect of PR which can seldom be budgeted accurately, although some allowance should be made when the cost would otherwise have to be met out of PR department salaries. Here we mean all the inumerable PR activities which the PRO may inspire but which may well be instigated by a PR-orientated management which recognizes that PR is something implicit in the proper management and conduct of any organization.

With this in mind it is difficult to understand the thinking of those who regard PR as a luxury. PR is like sex, it exists whether we like it or not. All that is new is the integration, planning and control of the relations which an organization inevitably has with its numerous publics. A PR department in a civic centre can be a genuine investment capable of saving ratepayers' money and making local government more efficient and better understood by the people whom it serves. The classic example for need of PR was the way in which rate rebates for those with small incomes – mainly poor, elderly folk – was totally mishandled by local authorities unwilling to use PR, so that a Labour government had to indulge in a costly series of TV commercials.

The PR-conscious organization will therefore operate through PR-minded executives or officials, and their staff, in every department. Good relations is often no more than good manners. In an industrial organization the works manager, personnel manager, purchasing officer, sales manager, production manager, maintenance engineer, warehouseman, transport manager, and other departmental heads can all contribute by creating and maintaining good relations with their respective publics. To these may be added branch, area and field managers who may be in charge of retail outlets, depots, or sales offices. Their PR costs are difficult to place in the PR budget, and the recognized cost of an organization's PR may be related only to the central, inspirational PR department whose duties must include direction and instruction through the staff house journal, internal memos, staff meetings and conferences, and possibly by means of film, videotape or slide presentations. The internal role of the staff PRO must never be overlooked, and the topic is mentioned here because time has to be allowed for it when allocating staff and salaries.

In local government this sort of thing is even more apparent because much of the success of a local authority PRO's work will depend on the co-operation he obtains from committees and committee chairmen, but especially from his fellow local government officers. A major cost of local government PR is the time spent on integrating the PR requirements of a very complex organization which has a crying need for communication with its publics. Nowhere is PR more seriously needed than in establishing communication between the local government service and the ratepayers. Since the majority of ratepayers never enter its doors, it is not enough to look upon the public library as an official information service. One good thing about the creation of new authorities in 1974 was the appointment of PR staff.

Office Overheads

A PR department requires more than just offices for executives and secretaries; it is very much a workshop needing working areas for assembling, packing, designing and making up. This is expensive.

Once again, it may be cheaper to use a consultant who has all these facilities. An organization cannot expect to undertake its own PR unless it is prepared to devote a sufficient slice of office accommodation to its PR staff.

The location of the PR office is also important, and ideally it should be in a principal city, in close proximity to communication media, and other facilities, and preferably centralized. This can mean a high office rent, but this should not be shirked as there is a serious intention to set up a fully operative PR department. However, the PR office should not be isolated from the main centre of production and employment as frequent visits may be necessary. PR staff should maintain good communication with the entire organization, even if this has scattered locations, and this could incur installing direct lines, Telex or having a press officer in each location. If an organization is based out of London, a London PRO is an asset although this is sometimes overcome by having a location-based PRO supplemented by a press information service through a London PR consultancy.

From the above argument it will be seen that office overheads should include the cost of maintaining contact with the local branches, offices, factories, mines or mills wherever they may be in the UK or overseas. The PR department cannot be fully operative unless it is a central hive of information, the eyes and ears of the organization.

Normal office overheads will also include rent, rates, heat, light, telephone, cleaning and other service charges. It is essential that these be included, and the PRO should not be housed in a couple of spare offices free of charge so that no real cost is budgeted.

Materials

PR work has its own creative and production costs. A story may be published free of charge in a magazine – as it deserves to be if it is genuine news – *but it is not produced free of cost.* As we have already said, salaries and office overheads have to be allocated. Now we must consider the materials used by the labour in the office. The following is a list of some of the items which come under this heading:

(i) Envelopes: for news releases
for photographs (card backed)
for MSS, brochures, etc.
for correspondence
(ii) Letterheadings
(iii) Printed news release headings
(iv) Photograph caption blanks, preferably printed with identification details
(v) Invitation cards for press receptions
(vi) Plastic press packs
(vii) Duplicating materials
(viii) Addressing plate blanks
(ix) Suitable binders, files, etc. for press cuttings, photographic records
plus normal office supplies.

The above list can be adapted or extended according to the special needs of the organization which may require other materials such as prints of film, all kinds of printed material, blow-ups of pictures, videotapes, slides, charts and other visual aids, and the various materials

required by specialist staff such as house journal editors, photographers, film producers, exhibition designers, and events organizers.

Expenses

This is an item which has to be realistically anticipated and rigorously
controlled. Lavish expenditure is stupid, but if staff are expected to
give up their spare time and be separated from their homes, wives, and
families they deserve the compensation of first-class travel, decent
meals, and first-class hotel accommodation. Expenses are likely to
include the following items:

> Car expenses, either supplying vehicles or paying a mileage rate.
> Fares.
> Overnight hotel expenses.
> Meals while travelling.
> Entertainment of visitors, contacts.
> Catering expenses for press receptions, seminars, other PR
> events.
> Hire charges for halls and equipment such as microphones and
> projectors.
> Hire of transport – cars, vans, caravans, coaches, trains, aircraft.
> Supply of newspapers, trade magazines, year books, directories.

The expenses will obviously vary according to whether one is
perhaps mainly producing technical articles about installations or
doing something more elaborate such as touring an exhibition.

The Costs of a PR Consultant

Having established an appreciation of the more likely costs of an
internal PR department, it now becomes a straightforward matter to
understand the costs of an outside PR unit, whether one is a consultant
or a client. The costs are basically the same in items and calculations
except for two considerations. First, the consultant has to make both a
living and a profit, and earns this by offering factors of convenience,
knowledge, skill, and facility; secondly he can offer a share of his
organization which while very economical to the client who has no
need to run a fully-fledged department is naturally proportionately
more expensive as is anything bought in small quantities. The price of
PR services has therefore to be measured within these factors.

Now it is easy to reconcile the contrasts and contradictions between
the cost of placing advertising through an advertising agency and PR

through a consultancy. If advertising were handled internally the advertiser would not enjoy the commissions granted to advertising agencies, granted because it is more convenient to account collection to deal with a minimum number of agencies instead of a maximum number of advertisers. Moreover, agencies are permitted only a month's credit whereas most clients somewhat selfishly take three months' credit if they can get it. Even where the commission system has been replaced by fees, advertising tends to be less continuous than PR so that again it can be very economical to share agency facilities. But PR department and PR consultancy are equally free of the commission system to a major extent. This is because the greatest advertising expense is usually space in the press, time on TV or radio, sites for posters and signs, or printed material, all of which produce commissions to pay the agency for giving the client free administration and other services carried out by some of the most expensive advertising agency staff such as account executives, and copywriters. The greatest PR expense, especially as far as the consultant is concerned, is *time*.

The client buys time, not so many inches or centimetres, press cuttings, interviews on TV or mentions in news bulletins. These are the consequences of using time effectively. The client does not pay by results in the physical sense. Payment is for effort expended, although clearly if the results of the effort were disappointing the client might well decide to change his consultant or stop using PR.

The trouble is that some clients tend to expect a certain monetary value of press cuttings (calculated on an advertising space rate basis) for a fee of a similar amount. They fail to understand that at an hourly rate (by the simplest computation of executive hours) a day's work costs so much, and if the consultant spends only a day a month with his client, for progress meeting and gathering material, at least a proportion of the fee is spent talking to the client. And this does not take into account the time spent on day-to-day liaison. But while this can be easily explained it is sometimes more difficult to convince clients that apart from outgoing initiated effort there is constant incoming enquiring activity which also eats into fees.

Accounting for PR Services

The consultant is wise to invoice his client under three headings:

1. *Fee*, based on an hourly rate which covers labour, overheads and profit.

2. *Materials*, which may include commissions which are accepted as customs of the trade, e.g. on photography, films, blocks and print.

3. *Expenses*, being reimbursable items for fares, hotels, catering, large sums being invoiced direct to the client since the consultant cannot afford to give extended credit on, say, a hotel account for a press reception. (Some consultants pay such bills themselves but add a percentage when charging their clients.)

It now becomes necessary to determine how the hourly rate shall be calculated. It would be simple if consultants could together agree on a minimum fee structure so that clients could know the approved scale, although there would be nothing to prevent the better qualified or more successful consultant charging a higher rate if he could get it. A minimum rate would avoid price cutting and give consultants a basis for organizing their own office economy.

A well-known way of arriving at the hourly rate is to take the joint salaries of an executive and his secretary and multiply them by three. In other words he is capable of handling accounts to this value per year. The 'three times' method, despite its seeming over-simplification, is extraordinarily accurate. However, this does tend to imply that this executive has to be a jack-of-all-trades with little if any division of labour among specialist 'backroom' staff.

At the other extreme there is the system which can be applied to a consultancy with specialist departments which enable the account executive to confine himself to advising, planning, and directing. Under this method all members of the staff are given values based on their salaries plus overheads and proportionate profit on-cost. Each employee from managing director to messenger boy has to complete a job sheet, and the client is charged the monthly sum total of all the rated time expended by various personnel. The account executive would be responsible for controlling time expenditure within the agreed fee.

A bad practice is the provision of costly competitive speculative schemes, for which no payment is made by the prospective client. If he chooses, the client calling for such presentations can appoint no-one and use the ideas himself. The best professional practice is for the client to invite a chosen consultant to carry out a pilot study and make recommendations.

The following is a summary of the methods of assessing consultancy fees. The variety is surprising and it represents the failure of either the IPR or the PRCA – in the face of so many consultants – to establish a method of charging that is generally intelligible to clients.

Methods of Assessing Fees

1. *Arbitrary all-in Annual Fee*. This is the consultant's calculated guess, usually unrelated to any objective planning as set out in Chapter Four and permitting the consultant very little opportunity to justify what he has done for the fee. It is a most unsatisfactory method of charging fees, although at one time it was almost the only one known to PR consultants. This method was just as unsatisfactory to the consultant as it was to the client. If the consultant really did a good job the chances were that he would overspend and lose money on the account. Either way, he had no means of forecasting, controlling or charging out at a profit the three types of cost that he had to incur.

2. *Retainer Plus* charges for time, materials and expenses. The term *retainer* is often confused with *fee,* but they have no connection. A retainer means that a payment has been paid to ensure that no rival client is serviced. No work can be expected for a retainer. With this method (which should be unnecessary with proper costings) the client makes a token payment, and is then invoiced for the actual work done on a proper basis of hourly fee plus the cost of materials and expenses. It is a method favoured by some of the large American-owned consultancies.

3. *Hourly Rate to cover all staff* (but based on account executive's time) plus overheads and profit, plus materials and expenses. This is a reasonable and commonly used method. The rate can be varied according to the seniority and experience of the account executive.

4. *Hourly Rate per member of consultancy staff* (salary plus percentage) plus materials and expenses. This is an excellent method which has the advantage that it calls for the estimate of labour resources when planning the budget and by means of time sheets enables budgetary control to be conducted during the progress of the campaign.

5. *Annual Fee charged and consumed monthly*. The fee may be calculated by one of the methods described in 4 and 5, but control is now exacted on the month-by-month expenditure. If no work is done in a particular month, the fee is still charged because (and this is perfectly fair) the consultancy had staff and other resources available to service the account and these had to be paid for whether or not the client made use of them. But if the client consumes more than his month's ration of the annual fee, a suitable surcharge is made according to the excess hours recorded on the time sheets.

6. *Annual Fee and Supplementary Fees*. Similar to 5, this method assumes that the time is fully taken up each month, but if the time

sheets show a danger of the allotted time being exceeded the client is asked if he wishes to incur more than the monthly instalment of the annual fee.

7. *Time Bank System*. Not very popular, this method follows the calculations outlined in the Hourly Rate methods, but spreads the time over longer periods, usually three months, so that the client is permitted to have peaks and troughs in his consumption of time, even though the fee is charged on a monthly instalment basis.

8. *Ad Hoc*. Payment by the job, based on time, materials and expenses, is a convenient way of charging for short-term PR assignments.

9. *Based on Advertisement Rate*. There are some journalists who have either set themselves up as PR consultants, or who are still working on publications and offer their services in a freelance fashion, and have no idea how consultancy work is paid for. They are capable of measuring the inches or centimetres gained in editorial columns, multiplying the total by the advertisement rate per single column centimetre and billing the client accordingly. They are oblivious to manhours and hourly rates that cover overheads and show a profit. The only reason why they get business is that their clients equate PR with journalism.

With this curious mixture of fee systems two things are essential: consultants must explain to their clients exactly what they can expect for their money and how they will be charged, and clients must take the trouble to find out how and for what they will be charged.

So not only must fees be capable of being proved against strict records, but materials must be specified, and likewise the nature of expenses must be clearly stated. There should thus be no reason for a client to dispute an invoice, because every item should be in accordance with agreed policy and programme. Moreover, if the invoice specifies how many news releases were dispatched the client knows that a job has been done, and a client has every right to be pleased to receive a busy, detailed invoice because it indicates the effort made by the consultant.

All this needs to be supported by a simple *Job Number* system which can be applied to orders for goods and services, supplier's invoices, and invoices charging out to client. If a job number is raised every time some complete job, such as a photographic session or a press reception, is set up this number can be used as the code on every document, for every agenda item at meetings, and in contact reports (minutes with a right-hand column for allocated personal responsibilities) submitted by the consultancy after meetings. Clients should never prepare minutes of such meetings, and if the responsibility is accepted by the consultant the contact report can become part of the control system of the account. Thus, long-winded verbatim reports by a client's secretary with little understanding of what is going on can be avoided, and precise reports can be produced referring only to decisions and responsibilities. The contact report can be produced quickly and circulated to the client so that any misunderstandings can be eliminated in a matter of hours.

Preparing PR Estimates

Costing thus begins for the consultant at the time of preparing his proposals. From experience he will know the time required to perform certain tasks. Figure 7.1 shows a dummy estimate which might fit a proposal for a medium-size account.

Clearly, the items mentioned can be changed to suit each potential client. No mention is made of support for exhibitions, or of general news stories about the company and its personnel, while financial PR is not listed in this example. The example does, however, indicate the 'shopping list' method of showing the client what he may expect for his money.

Fig 7.1

12 Progress meetings	12 x 0 x £0.00	000.00
3 Press Receptions	3 x 0 x £0.00	000.00
Editing 4 issues House Journal	4 x 0 x £0.00	0 000.00
12 New product stories	12 x 0 x £0.00	000.00
Information bureau service	0 x £0.00	000.00
4 Feature articles	4 x 0 x £0.00	000.00
Organizing Works visit	0 x £0.00	00.00
Script for film	0 x £0.00	000.00
		£0 000.00
Estimated Material cost		000.00
Estimated Expenses		000.00
		£00 000.00

When producing a speculative scheme, probably in competition with rival consultants, a dilemma can be estimating an acceptable total fee. It is easy to say that the client *should* spend so much, and that it is the professional task of the consultant to advise on the *right* expenditure, but in most cases the client has already worked out a total marketing budget and has *allocated a certain sum* for PR. The sensible thing for the consultant to do is to invite a sharing of confidences. The consultant can supply only as much or as little service as the client is prepared to pay for, and if the client will admit his limit the consultant can work to that figure.

An indication has been given of costings in outline. It is pointless to quote actual figures since these will vary according to time, place, quantity, and other controlling factors. But we can itemize expenses and the following chapter gives skeleton costing schemes for some specific PR exercises. If these skeletons are remembered as patterns of predictable expenditure it is possible to produce rough estimates, based on known costs by a process of quick calculation. This can be valuable when dealing with superiors, colleagues, or clients. One must adopt the habit of budgeting all costs. When doing this it is wise to err on the higher side and seek to present final accounts which are slightly under estimate. This always inspires greater confidence than when estimates are exceeded, which is what most people pessimistically expect!

CHAPTER EIGHT

Skeleton Costing Schemes

This chapter is devoted to some hypothetical budget patterns which indicate how budgets for different PR exercises may be constructed.

1. A Press Reception

Figure 8.1 shows a typical estimate for a press reception in which it is assumed that the maximum necessary expenses are incurred such as a hired venue and outside catering. Demonstrators can be engaged for the occasion, or staff at their normal rates of pay. Some costs, such as rent or hire of microphones, are fixed unless a larger hall has to be taken. Some hotels do not charge a room rent if there is a bar and catering. Rents can depend on whether the premises are required for a couple of hours, half a day, or a day, and this cost could be doubled if the room had to be prepared the day before. These costs must be discussed with the hoteliers, and comparisons made before giving a firm booking.

The same applies to menus, catering charges, and what in fact a catering quotation means. There can be an immense difference between finger buffets as a small extra payment per head could be money wisely spent since the initial preparations by caterers are costly. Drinks are much the same wherever one goes, but with catering one has to be sure what one is buying, and casual ordering can be disappointing. It is a simple matter to ask the hotelier what each item on the menu means, and the same description can mean very different things from one hotel to another! If, as is often appropriate, the buffet is served about noon, a finger buffet as served at cocktail parties is useless and it is necessary to provide either substantial well-filled sandwiches augmented by hot items, or better still, a fork buffet.

There is no need for the bar charges to be exhorbitant. If there is an initial reception, then the programme of talks and demonstrations followed by a bar and buffet, the average consumption will be three drinks per head. Excessive drink costs occur only when there is a stand-up cocktail party, that is a press reception with no programme, or when there is a surfeit of hosts who carry on drinking after the guests have gone.

Fig. 8.1   Budget

	£
Printed invitation cards and white envelopes (including means of reply)	00.00
Postage on invitations	00.00
Telephone, checking names for invitations	00.00
Telephone, following up non-replies	
Hire of room	00.00
Hire of microphone, slide and/or film projector	00.00
00 Buffets at £0.00 per head	00.00
Average 3 drinks at £0.00 per head	00.00
00 Coffees at £0.00 per head	00.00
Gratuities	00.00
Press packs, 00 at £0.00 each	00.00
News releases, 00 at £0.00 per 100	00.00
Photography of subject (new product?)	00.00
00 $\frac{1}{2}$ plate prints for display and packs	00.00
00 captions	0.00
Pegboard/hardboard for photo display	0.00
Order forms for photos	0.00
Samples, with wrappings, for guests	00.00
Visitors' Book	0.00
Lapel badges	0.00
Studio charges for displays, e.g. tent cards to identify speakers on platform	00.00
Taxi fares for transporting materials	00.00
Special effects: e.g. costumes, decorations as with a seasonal subject	00.00
Incidentals	00.00

2. A Press Facility Visit

An extra budget is given in Figure 8.2 for the costs of a facility visit. It is similar to a press reception except that it involves a more detailed tour programme at the location, travelling arrangements, and full host responsibilities for catering throughout the trip with the possibility of overnight accommodation.

The economics of transport and catering have to be carefully weighed.

Fig. 8.2   Extra Budget for Facility Visit

	£
Transport for main party	
(a) to and from location 00 at £0.00 per head	00.00
(b) to and from airport, seaport, rail terminal 00 at £0.00 per head	00.00
Transport for local or short distance parties	
(a) helicopter	
(b) private car	00.00
(c) minibus	
(d) coach	
Catering:	
(a) Breakfast 00 at £0.00 per head	00.00
(b) Lunch 00 at £0.00 per head	000.00
(c) Tea 00 at £0.00 per head	00.00
(d) Dinner 00 at £0.00 per head	000.00
(e) Coffee 00 at £0.00 per head	00.00
(f) Bar 00 at £0.00 per head	000.00
Overnight accommodation 00 at £0.00 per head	000.00
Hire of	
(a) Marquee, hall	00.00
(b) Chairs	00.00
(c) Tables	00.00
(d) Umbrellas	00.00
(e) Protective clothing	00.00
Extra staff costs for escorts, guides including rehearsals	00.00
Provision of route signs, cordons, etc.	00.00

It may be cheaper to charter an aircraft than to use a train because fewer meals and less entertaining would have to be provided. The flight might also add to the pleasure of the journey. For this budget most or all of the items listed for a press reception may be required, with the possible additions or variations shown in Figure 8.2. These are adjustable items and are given here as a guide to what may be required since so much depends on the geographical position of the venue, its accessibility, and the nature of the visit.

For example, if the location is inaccessible by rail, road transport is essential and a greater proportion of time will be occupied in travelling. It may not be feasible to make road-stops for refreshments because of the time loss, but it is possible to hire an urn with supplies and quickly serve coffee and biscuits in a lay-by.

Again, the full party may not always come from one central starting point, and various forms of short-run transport may be required to bring in, say, provincial press and regional radio and TV representatives.

It may not be practical to cater for a large party of visitors at the factory or installation, and there may not be a large enough catering establishment within handy distance. In these circumstances it is more convenient to bring the caterers to the guests, and premises such as a marquee may have to be hired and furnished or adapted.

Visitors are not allowed in some food factories, on construction sites or down mines without protective clothing such as caps, helmets, coats, boots or wellingtons, and quantities in a range of sizes must be hired or purchased for the occasion.

If the party is to make a tour, it could be a wise precaution to place directional signs or arrows along the route, and also to cordon off areas not to be visited. Items on the route may require explanatory placards. All these signs must be allowed for in the budget. We have already mentioned escorts and guides, but uniformed commissionaires may be required to man entrances and direct visitors. Scale plans may be required so that all concerned may have identical visual instructions.

A number of people in a strange place have to be managed in a discreetly disciplined manner, and the costs of achieving this have to be borne in mind. In such circumstances even the most intelligent guests behave irrationally, get worried, can panic because what is thoroughly familiar to the host is totally strange to the visitor. The imaginative PRO will anticipate what is required. Money spent on directional signs, hand-drawn instructions, and large legends explaining what is being shown, could impress by their helpfulness and be a major PR aspect of the entire operation. So allow for such costs.

From these remarks the reader will see that planning and costing are logical mental disciplines which are complementary to each other. The good PRO is a worrier about details, and the budget preparation is the time for establishing details. The budget provides a check-list for action.

3. An Industrial or Documentary Film

Now let us think about the costing of a documentary film. A typical outline form is shown in Figure 8.3 and again, it must be but an outline.

Fig. 8.3

	£
Script writing fees (treatment, shooting script)	00.00
Shooting, sound recording, processing and editing	0 000.00
Location expenses	000.00
Actors, commentators' fees	000.00
Musical score, composition of	00.00
Titling	00.00
Copyright fees (e.g. library shots)	00.00
Translations, dubbing language sound track	00.00
Print costs	00.00
Distribution costs; e.g. postage, packing, air freight, film library and bookings administration	000.00
Synopsis leaflets for audiences	00.00
Film maintenance and repairs	00.00
Distribution services, e.g. Guild Sound and Vision showings to selected audiences	000.00
Preview for industrial film critics	00.00
Advertising to attract borrowings	000.00

A big influence upon the cost of film-making may be whether it is made by a staff or an outside film unit. When filming is necessary over a protracted period the staff film unit could be more economical. Since no two films are alike, the skeleton costing scheme is probably more incomplete in this instance. There are, however, certain basic decisions to be made which have a direct bearing on cost. These are: (a) Length; (b) Recorded sound or dubbed commentary; (c) Colour or black and white; (d) Stock, whether 35 mm or 16 mm; (e) Extent of location shooting; (f) Employment of actors, commentators.

Then there is the cost of showing and distribution.

The budget is made out to allow for inside or outside production.

Among the points to be specially remembered here are whether sound is to be recorded during filming, or whether the film can be silent with music, commentary, and sound effects dubbed in afterwards; whether own staff or professional actors are to be used; whether locations will be distant, time-consuming, and dependent upon weather or seasons.

4. A House Journal or Private Magazine

Next let us look at the costs of producing and distributing a house journal. Here again there are so many variables that the skeleton is a check list for adaptation to actual needs. Determinants are as follows: (a) Frequency of issue; (b) Format; (c) Number of pages; (d) Colour or black and white; (e) Method of distribution; (f) Editorial costs; (g) Art/Photography; (h) Paid contributions; (i) Income.

To dispose of the last item first, it is possible for house journals to have income which can partially offset costs, make them self-liquidating or actually make the publication a profitable venture. There are two ways of doing this. One is the traditional method of the publishing business, that being sale of advertisement space, but as always this is possible only when the readership has value to advertisers because of quantity or speciality. The other, which is becoming more widely accepted, is the sale of copies. The willingness of staff to pay for their house journal is a measure of its excellence and success. These remarks chiefly apply to *staff magazines,* for it is less easy to charge for copies of dealer magazines and ones for external distribution to customers and others. Some externals are actually sold on bookstalls, especially in developing countries where journals are few in number. The status of the house magazine is greatly increased when readers are prepared to buy it. Putting a cover charge on a house magazine is also a means of controlling distribution in organizations with very large staffs where the enormous print order for a totally free distribution would be prohibitive and wasteful.

So we can seriously regard some house journals as having a balance sheet. The editor may be responsible for working within a cost budget, a break-even budget or a profitable budget. The majority of house journals will be regarded as part of the PR programme, with an allocation from the main PR appropriation for this medium.

The first eight determinants can now be commented upon in some detail.

Frequency. How often will the periodical be published? Weekly, fortnightly, monthly, quarterly? Most other costs will be multiplied by the frequency figure, and the number of issues has therefore a big bearing on total costs while conversely the total budget can determine the number of issues.

Format. Size of page – whether newspaper or magazine – and the volume of material to be carried as determined by the number of columns and column width (if any) will also have a bearing on paper, typesetting, make-ready, proofing, and machining costs. Size will also concern envelope costs.

Number of Pages. Printing costs (including paper) can be quoted in multiples of four pages, but the pages have also to be filled and editorial, photographic, art, and reproduction costs must be worked out according to the number of pages. The number of pages (and the quantity and weight of paper) also concerns postage rates.

Colour or Black and White? Each colour beyond the first means an extra printing plate and an extra working. Full colour requires four colours, yellow, magenta, cyan and black. Very good effects can be achieved by using black and a second colour, and very economical use of two colours can be obtained if the second colour is used on the outside front cover, outside back cover and on the two inside pages which are printed together in the four page forme, all other pages being printed one colour, usually black. Some fairly inexpensive colour work is available with web-offset printing, a process which has revolutionized British printing, and is not confined to newspaper-style work.

Method of Distribution. Handing out copies is by far the cheapest method of distributing staff journals but seldom a very satisfactory one. It depends on how and where distribution is made. If copies are taken round from office to office or bench to bench, this method may be all right. An often better but costlier method is to post copies direct to employees' homes where other members of the family have an opportunity of reading about the organization. Dealer and other external magazines generally require posting. If posted, an accurate mailing list must be maintained.

If the journal can be mailed flat it is more attractive to receive and more inviting to read. A rolled and wrapped magazine can look a mess when unwrapped, and an envelope is usually preferable. This is an important PR point. Don't put readers off before they have even opened the journal. The question of folding should be faced when planning page size and choosing paper.

Editorial Costs. Allowance has to be made for the time and profes-sional expertise which will be devoted to the work of producing the journal. This can range from a few spare hours put in by an executive to the employment of a full-time editorial staff or outside consultancy services. It can also include the services of local correspondents, and the costs of layout and design. It is advisable to keep an editorial time sheet. The editor will have to plan issues, seek material, write some of the contents, rewrite many contributions, prepare issues for the printer, and read proofs.

Art and Photography. Costs can be minimized if a typographical style is decided for text and titles so that hand lettering can be replaced by the buying of 'sorts' (typeset words in a specified type face) from a trade typesetting house or by the use of photo-typesetting which can make hand lettering unnecessary. The purely photographic 'cold set-ting' associated with offset-lithography can be both economic and efficient since each character is perfect whereas hot metal characters can be damaged. One problem with house journals is that photo-graphs are often obtained from amateur sources, and the prints are of varying quality and of different standards so that reproduction up to a good overall standard can demand retouching. The costs involved need to be severely controlled.

If the magazine is produced by a consultancy, art costs are the ones which can be high, especially if the outside service tends to be more concerned with *designing* journals than *editing* them.

Paid Contributions. Last on the list is the question of buying contribu-tions. Cartoons usually have to be bought, or reproduction fees have to be paid. Some external journals are produced like regular magazines and big-name contributors are sought. Authors may be approached through literary agents and fees agreed. If the editor of a staff journal wishes to reproduce a cartoon from, say, a national newspaper or magazine, he may be able to do so at a nominal fee agreed with the art editor or syndication department if it is a big publishing house. It is not usual to pay members of one's own organization for contributions, except as a special inducement to attract material.

From the above analysis it is clear that there is an assortment of variables making it less easy to suggest a reasonably well-defined list of items for even a skeleton annual budget, so the basic form shown in Figure 8.4 must be adapted as required.

Since printing is a major item for consideration in more respects than cost, preliminary discussions with more than one printer (and regarding more than one process, letterpress and lithography in most cases) will be necessary before any progress can be made with the budget, even before decisions can be made on format, number of pages, and frequency.

House journal costings, in the hands of the amateur, sometimes suffer from either one of two erroneous extremes. First, there is the situation where editing a house journal is regarded as a spare-time task, almost a hobby, and second there are the lush, heavy art-paper, multi-coloured art studio dreams which are excessively expensive and deserve the scorn of professional editors.

Fig. 8.4

			£
Editorial costs:	(a)	Editor	0 000.00
	(b)	Contributions	000.00
Art Costs:	(a)	Layout and design	000.00
	(b)	Art work	000.00
	(c)	Photography	000.00
	(d)	Retouching	000.00
	(e)	Reproduction fees	00.00
Printing, including blocks if letterpress			00 000.00
Envelopes:			000.00
Postage:			000.00
Other items; (e.g. Prizes in contests)			000.00
			£00 000.00

5. Support for an Exhibitor

Exhibitions are not included in these examples because so much depends on the venue, size of stand, and what is being exhibited. But it is worth while glancing at the budget for PR support for a participant in an exhibition shown in Figure 8.5. Here it should be remembered that PR support can begin between three and six *months* before the exhibition opens. For example, monthly magazines pre-viewing the exhibition will often want copy six to eight weeks in advance. Too many PROs accept the lack of 'secret new product' news as an excuse for doing nothing.

In all this there will be liaison with the Exhibition press officer from the moment of his appointment onwards.

It is necessary to bear in mind the different publics who can be interested in one's participation, at home and abroad, and to think in terms of before, during, and after the show. This can be a very exacting exercise, valuable because it enhances the influence of the exhibit quite in addition to helping to attract visitors to the stand. It can be important to the suppliers, shareholders, distributors, and potential overseas buyers that you *are* exhibiting, and your presence has PR value over and above the products themselves. These points

E

seldom seem to be fully appreciated. In this section we must not forget Overseas Trade Fairs, Joint Ventures, and Store Promotions in overseas cities, the participants in these seldom bothering to exploit PR possibilities to the full.

Fig. 8.5

	£
Feature articles to coincide with exhibit	000.00
Writing news releases for (a) local press; (b) trade press; (c) city editors; (d) COI; (e) sales staff, overseas agents, etc; (f) press room; (g) stand; (h) reception	000.00
Organization of VIP visit to stand	000.00
Attendance by interesting personalities, e.g. girls in national costume	000.00
Translation of news releases for overseas press, both for home and overseas exhibitions	000.00
Mechanical production of releases	00.00
Postage on distribution of releases, including air mail direct to overseas press	00.00
Envelopes for releases, card for photos	00.00
Invitation cards to (a) press preview, or (b) reception on stand; or (c) reception in private room or at nearby hotel; or (d) open invitation to press to visit stand	00.00
Entertainment of guests invited above	000.00
Press packs for guests (NOT for Press Room!)	00.00
Photography for (a) feature articles; (b) press previews; (c) press room; (d) press visitors as invited; (e) press material on stand. Half-plate black and white prints fully captioned	000.00
Supply of special information, facilities, photos, articles, requested by press visitors to stand, press room	00.00

From these outlines of possible budgets it will be seen how ideas, techniques, media, timing, and costs go hand-in-hand. For convenience the process is broken down into chapters, but in practice one plans with all the means in mind. Selection of the means is guided by knowledge and experience of their comparative merits in relation to costs. A good PR manager can estimate costs from experience and be able to do so mentally so that in the middle of, say, a board meeting he can answer questions and make proposals with a fair idea of financial feasibility. For the consultant, working within an agreed fee and expenses which could be financially disastrous to him to exceed, the ability to make rapid costings is essential to profitability.

There are two other sides to costing which must be emphasized. It is worth reiterating that when a consultant is making proposals to a client the fees quoted should be based on sound costings which should be set out price-list fashion so that the client knows what he is buying. Nice round-figure arbitrary fee quotations are worthless, ambiguous and unfair to both consultant and client. They do not reflect the hard work that costs the money in professional PR. A properly calculated proposition will reveal the volume of work that will be put into the account, not how many lunches or gins will be bought. Needless hospitality (which should not be confused with courtesy) is the fetish which has cursed PR. Secondly, when budgets and estimates are presented frankly at all stages no-one is able to criticize the accounts afterwards, provided costings have not been exceeded through carelessness. With an agreed budget the staff PRO or consultant is always in the position to resist extra demands from management or client unless there is a subsidiary fund to cover the new expenditure. A budget is both a discipline and a refuge.

In budgeting it pays to be conservative, and it is worth reminding ourselves that it is always psychologically sound if final costs are a little less than the original estimates. Good costings are always capable of being trimmed slightly, but this can be done only if every expense is anticipated, and even then allowance should be made for contingencies. But these do not have to be spent, and there must be strict control of all spending, suppliers being told that there is a strict budget. While it is true that in the past a great deal of money has been frittered away on needless wining and dining it has nevertheless tended to come from small budgets and has been at the expense of genuine PR activity. The majority of editors regard their entertainers as being quite mad for in the end they will publish only what is of interest and value to their readers and so keeps them in their jobs. Such antics only help to convince editors of the superficiality of the PR world. In a sense, the need to take an editor out to lunch in order to get a story published points to (a) the poverty of the story and (b) the ignorance of the PR practitioner. Consequently, entertainment should be a diminutive item in the budget.

CHAPTER NINE

Organizing
PR Events

The organizing of PR events calls for methodical and meticulous planning. Success often depends on experience and the press officer who has organized other kinds of events will find this experience useful. There is a lot of hard work in organizing a PR event.

The Three Types of PR Events

Let us first be sure of what is meant by the three main types of media event. The loose expression 'press party' is often used in a vague sense to mean any sort of media gathering whether assembled or conveyed, but by *press conference, press reception* and *facility visit* we refer to gatherings of accelerating complexity. In this order the first is a fairly simple affair, the second occupies a bigger place, more time and is consequently more elaborate, while the third invariably involves travel.

1. *Press Conference*

A press conference is organized like a meeting, the guests being seated to receive an announcement and to ask questions. It may be held in an office, a boardroom or a hotel assembly room. Hospitality is usually modest such as coffee, tea or sherry, served with biscuits, according to the time of day. A bar is not always necessary. Copies of the announcement will be available in news release form. A press conference is a fairly unpretentious occasion, capable of being called at short notice if the urgency of the news demands it.

Television viewers had the novel opportunity of actually seeing a press conference in action when Sir Francis Chichester landed at

Plymouth after his single-handed voyage round the world in *Gypsy Moth IV*.

2. *The Press Reception*

The success of this type of media event will largely depend on its being much more than a mere drinking occasion. PR has, in the past, gained a regrettable reputation for over-generous hospitality. Contrary to the impression held by some people, most journalists who attend press receptions come in search of a story, not a free drink.

A press reception depends for success on a programme and the promise of a story sufficient to attract a good response to the invitation. For this reason it pays to include a timed programme on or with the invitation although strangely enough this is rarely done. Some invitations do not even state the purpose of the press reception and it is a wonder anyone bothers to accept. A programmed invitation is more likely to attract the journalists who are seriously interested in your subject and best able to give it media coverage. However, the invitation will be dealt with in greater detail later on in this chapter.

A typical timetable would include: the initial reception (without formal announcement); initial refreshments according to the time of day; the business of the occasion; and a final period of hospitality of the bar and buffet kind. The business may require guests to be seated, and this session can be in a separate room away from the catering. It may include speeches, demonstrations, a film and an opportunity for questions to be asked and answered. Those responsible for answering questions should have anticipated the most likely questions and have their facts by them. A good question and answer period can do much to create goodwill if speakers are prepared to reply frankly and fully.

A short documentary film – not more than 20 minutes – can be a very useful part of the proceedings, and should be included if possible, but it must be relevant and recent if not actually new. It may be someone else's film, showing either production of the raw materials or use of the finished article, if the host company does not have a suitable film of its own. For example, a film showing the manufacture of laminates might be shown at a press reception for a furniture maker. The documentary or industrial film, free of advertising, is undoubtedly one of the best PR mediums we have, and guests at press receptions provide most receptive audiences. A film gives information entertainingly and most people enjoy watching films.

If the film is the first item on the programme after the reception it will create a very pleasant atmosphere for the remainder of the party.

Platform activities should be rehearsed and timed. A good 20-minute film is infinitely better than a dull 10-minute speech.

It can be a wise plan to divorce the business section from the refreshments. The catering bill is doubled when there is no separate business session, and the worst offenders can be the representatives of the host organization (who mistake the event for an opportunity to indulge in some free drinking). The organizer should restrict company representatives to essential hosts such as technical experts needed to talk authoritatively to guests.

The press officer should drink sparingly if at all at press receptions, and if the event is organized by a consultant for a client it is a very bad thing for the client to see consultancy staff consuming drinks for which he will have to pay. When the catering bill for a press reception is high it is usually because there has been a lot of drinking by people other than the press. Press drinking can be restricted to the short periods before and after the business session, which means that few guests will consume more than two or three drinks. These are points of great significance when budgets are being considered. A press reception does not have to cost a ridiculous amount of money, and it is totally wrong for press receptions to be regarded as extravagances.

3. Facility Visits

Facility visits provide the press with the opportunity, and often the privilege, of attending an official opening, visiting a factory or other premises, visiting an installation, going on board a new ship, flying in a new aircraft, or being taken abroad to an overseas exhibition. For the trip, anything from a private car to a chartered aircraft may be used. These events can be costly because the party has to be conveyed from point to point, fed and entertained, and on a long trip overnight accommodation is necessary.

There are two basic kinds of facility visit and the organizer should be clear in his own mind and in his invitation about the kind that he is holding. First, there is the visit which is purely to provide background information; second, there is the kind with a definite news story and this will require facilities for some guests to get the story back by telephone, Telex or fast transport in the case of TV news. The press will expect the visit to be of one kind or the other. It is foolish to take a plane-load of journalists from one end of the country to the other to see a jam or paint factory no different from one they could see on their own doorstep. Unfortunately, this happens all too often, and PR gets a bad name for extravagant thoughtlessness.

The facility visit has been organized so extravagantly on some occasions that the press have their own word for it – *junket* – and this joins the rest of the press world's contemptuous jargon concerning PR. Hollywood's prize press junket was in the 60's when 20th Century Fox spent a quarter of a million dollars on a week's junket for film critics. First, the party went to New York for the opening of *The Boston Strangler*, then over to Paris to watch the shooting of *The Staircase*, next to Tunis to see *Justine*, returning to Paris for *The Only Game in Town* and the première of *A Flea in Her Ear*. This was followed by a dinner party at Maxim's. The week was concluded by a flight to London to see *The Chairman* and then back to New York to see *Star*.

Radio and TV

These three events – conferences, receptions and visits – are labelled 'Press' but radio and TV should be considered separately and differently from the printed media. A common mistake is to include representatives of BBC radio and TV news, BBC programmes, ITN, TV company programmes, IRN, BBC Local Radio and IBA Independent Local Radio in the general invitation list. An even greater error is to simply invite BBC and ITV without realizing the numerous sections which now exist in radio and TV, commercial or otherwise.

Unless reporters from radio and TV are content to 'sit in' in search of material for future programmes, they should not be sent a general invitation to attend a press event. Instead, after careful selection of the appropriate programmes and stations, the respective producers, presenters or reporters should be written to or telephoned individually. This should be done in advance of the general press invitations. Broadcasters should be told of the event but asked to state their special needs in order to cover the story. They may wish to make a preliminary visit, film on a different day or at a different time, or tape interviews prior to the press reception. Television teams may take hours to produce a few minutes' screen time. Moreover, equipment and technicians have to be booked in good time. Much radio reporting and interviewing is conducted by freelance reporters who have to be booked to cover the story. Or the PRO himself may provide radio stations with taped interviews, using the services of UNS or other news agencies.

Organizing a Press Conference or Reception

The following considerations must be borne in mind when organizing these two kinds of press event.

1. *The Purpose*

There must be a good reason for the conference or reception. Wouldn't a news release suffice? Is there a big enough story to warrant taking up the time of the media let alone the expense? Are we absolutely clear what we want to tell and show the media?

2. *The Date*

What is the best date? Many factors will control this choice: the purpose of the event, the availability of the venue. Right choice of date is vital. For example, if a new central heating system is to be introduced the press reception should be held early in the year in order to achieve coverage in the autumn-published heating features and supplements in the women's and home interest monthlies. January would be preferable, February would be getting rather late. (If the product were a Christmas gift, the event should be in July.)

To make sure that the right speaker is free it may be necessary to work a long way ahead and there is not much sense in holding the event on a day when journalists you want are attending something else. It is by no means easy to avoid a clash of dates sometimes, but it does pay to check as far as possible. The *Financial Times* publishes a weekly table of forthcoming activities and *Exhibitions Bulletin* is a monthly guide to exhibitions being held at home and abroad during the current and the following year. The *Daily Telegraph* Information Bureau is always very helpful. We will deal with venue separately. Linked with the right date is also the right day of the week, and the right time of day. The time of day for a press gathering is much more important than is sometimes supposed. Businessmen are inclined to think first of their own convenience and availability, and to regard these events as cocktail parties which must commence at 6 p.m. and be held out of office hours so as not to interfere with the day's work. But the guests have homes to go to. They do not all work on national newspapers whose offices are open day and night. They, too, like to keep office hours. It is no pleasure to them, and not really a duty, to have to forsake dinner at home with their families to attend a commercial cocktail party.

If the organizer does insist on an evening affair he must expect to attract office juniors and freelance contributors to whom the invitations have been passed by more senior people who prefer to attend the other press functions which are held at more convenient times of the day.

So, generally speaking, the best time for a press conference or reception is between 11 a.m. and 1 p.m. on a Monday or Tuesday (Wednesday is bad for journalists working on weeklies) during the first or last ten days of the month (mid-month is bad for journalists working on monthlies). Newspapermen should be given their stories before lunchtime, and an evening paper reporter will want his story as early in the day as possible. If the guests are likely to be inundated with invitations a convenient venue allows them to attend more than one event during the same morning or afternoon. This is often true of women's magazine and women's page journalists who flit from one reception to another.

3. The Venue

A venue should be chosen because it suits the occasion, provides the correct facilities, is conveniently situated, has the right appeal, and makes reasonable charges for exemplary catering. That is a short list of requirements, no more.

Choosing the venues for PR events calls for knowledge of the advantages and disadvantages of a large variety of premises, and for this purpose it pays to continuously put on file information about all likely hotels, halls and other accommodation. Careful selection is necessary and usually one finds that only a limited number of establishments are worth retaining on the recommended list.

In London there is a modern skyscraper building which possesses a magnificently appointed lecture theatre which is admirable for conferences. But there is no public transport and empty taxis hardly ever pass the door. It has earned the reputation of being a place from which it is difficult to return. Quite another problem prevents one from using certain otherwise attractive venues in some provincial cities: lack of car-parking facilities. In selecting a venue outside London the organizer has to cater for guests travelling in from other towns, usually by car.

Let us summarize the eight main considerations to be borne in mind when booking venues for press gatherings:

1. Availability of a room or rooms of the required size, and whether this accommodation is also available earlier in the day or on the previous day for preparation or rehearsal purposes.

2. Does the accommodation meet the special demands of the occasion: e.g. does it black out for films; is it sound proof; is the floor strong enough for weighty exhibits (ballroom floors seldom are); are there convenient cloakroom facilities, especially for coats, hats and umbrellas during winter months?

3. Is the catering good? Are there any specialities?

4. Is the venue or its location of special interest?

5. What are the costs per head for finger buffets, fork buffets, lunches and dinners? Is there a hire charge for rooms? What is the method and rate for gratuities? (Comparative costs are more important than one might think.)

6. Has the venue special facilities such as lighting effects, staging, microphones, projectors, screens or tape-recorders? Some are extremely well equipped for PR events.

7. Is there a car-park or are the premises adjacent to one? Apart from guests' cars, space may be required for a demonstration vehicle.

8. Are transport facilities good, e.g. taxis, public transport, and is the venue easily accessible at busy times of the day? In London it pays to hold press conferences and receptions within a reasonable distance of Fleet Street, Long Acre and Gray's Inn Road, but if the event is associated with an exhibition at Earl's Court or Olympia the Kensington hotels are more convenient. Accessibility can have a critical effect on attendance figures if a number of PR events happen to be claiming the same people on the same day.

Other considerations may occur according to the needs of the occasion. A hotel may be required to provide lunch for a press party visiting a factory or an installation. What is the capacity of the dining room? Or it might be an attraction to invite the press to a brand new hotel which has novelty appeal. It may be that outside caterers can be brought in to provide for a party in an historic venue, for example a City livery hall or the Royal Pavilion at Brighton. Maybe catering can be arranged in a marquee in the factory grounds.

Few venues are suitable for every event, and if press parties are being held in various parts of the country satisfactory answers will be required to many questions. The important thing is knowing what questions to ask! It is not sufficient merely to write or telephone: venues should be inspected before making firm bookings.

So we have three major problems to resolve before anything else is decided: is there a big enough story to warrant holding the event at all; when and where do we hold the function?

4. *The Invitation List*

This should not be a big problem for the experienced press officer, and certainly not if he is dealing most of the time with a limited, specialized press. It can be more difficult for the consultancy dealing with a much bigger assortment of journals and journalists. The list should have not just the addresses of the journals but the names of the individuals who are to be invited.

To produce a reliable invitation list it is necessary to do a lot of telephoning because journalists do change their jobs with remarkable frequency. In fact, it is true to say that if the same organization held a reception twice a year there would be considerable changes in each succeeding invitation list.

Invitations, whether cards or letters, do have to be made out to individuals as they are personal communications. They cannot be sent vaguely to unidentified persons. This may come as a shock to those who run off grubby looking invitation letters on a duplicator and send them in unsealed envelopes to unnamed editors. Not surprisingly, such invitations produce little or no response and the organizer fills the reception with his own staff to make it look as if there is a good attendance. Good attendances are won by taking infinite pains.

When compiling an invitation list it must be large enough to produce a satisfactory turn out. If the aim is to have an attendance of 40 it may be necessary to invite 60, perhaps more. Clearly, the attendance will depend upon the various factors of newsworthiness, attractiveness of venue, and convenience of place, date and time, but in addition there are always other considerations such as staff shortages in the office, personal illness, and holidays which are beyond the control of the organizers and so deplete numbers even after acceptances have been received. On these occasions the press officer must never be over-optimistic and it is foolish to boast to employer or client that this and that paper will be represented. National newspapers tend to accept everything and then make their choice on the day!

5. *The Invitations*

The news may be so 'hot' that a telephoned invitation will be justified, and this is possible when the invitation list is a small one. Or the list may be extremely specialized, and all the journalists will be personally known to the press officer so that he can ring round in the friendliest way and invite them all at short notice. But these are exceptions to the usual run of PR events, possible with press conferences but unnecessary with press receptions which have to be planned over a matter of weeks so that there is ample time in which to give journalists seven to ten days' notice, sometimes longer.

The timing of the despatch of invitations is of importance to the overall organization of the event. There must be a day prior to the event when a reasonable knowledge of likely numbers is required so that catering, transport, seating and other arrangements can be confirmed with banqueting managers and contractors. This day may be three to seven days in advance of the actual date. And if, for some reason, numbers are limited, it may be necessary to stagger the despatch of invitations in order to control the total number of acceptances, further invitations being sent out to make up for refusals.

Fig. 9.1   Example of a press invitation card

BY APPOINTMENT
TO HER MAJESTY THE QUEEN
PEST CONTROL AND TIMBER PRESERVATION
SERVICES AND PRODUCTS
RENTOKIL LIMITED, EAST GRINSTEAD

"Cause for Concern"

RENTOKIL HYGIENE DIVISION

Cordially invites you to a
Press Film Show and Conference on
Health Risks, The Law, and The Nation's Toilets
at the Charter Room, Waldorf Hotel, W.C.2
(Templars Grill Entrance)
on Wednesday 16th April
Coffee at 10.30 a.m.
Conference starts 11 a.m.

Buffet Luncheon

R.S.V.P. Margot Linton
Felcourt, East Grinstead, Sussex (0342-23661)

Out of courtesy to guests the invitation must either be a well-produced letter or better still a printed invitation card. A card is always preferable, and letters should be resorted to only when there is not time to print a card or when numbers do not justify the design and print cost. A card has many advantages over a letter. It is a special piece of correspondence, arriving in an important-looking white envelope. Out of politeness it cannot be ignored. It does its job well. Invitation cards are often put on mantelpieces and window sills where other people see them. And if the design and printing is neat and distinctive it will help to make the event seem worth attending. If the host is prepared to go to some trouble to invite his guests properly he will surely go to the same trouble to make sure that the event is worth attending.

There was a time when it was thought that invitation cards had to be given the copperplate look, but the vogue of script typefaces has now been superseded by the use of neat modern typefaces.

When designing cards thought should be given to the way in which replies will be returned. The organizer needs to know the refusals as well as the acceptances, and the best way to obtain definite answers one way or the other is to provide an easy means of reply. When a means of reply is used a fairly accurate idea of acceptances will be known within 48 hours, while knowledge of refusals provides opportunity for follow-ups or despatch of fresh invitations. There are several ways of doing this: reply slips, reply cards, or addressed envelopes, but by far the best method is to incorporate an addressed reply card with the invitation card. The two cards offer four sides for printing. On the face of one card we have the invitation. On the back of the invitation, a timetable programme of the event should be set out. The reply card should repeat the basic details of the event and have space for the guest to indicate acceptance or refusal, 'I can/I cannot', and give his or her name and publication. On the reverse side the reply part must bear the organizer's full postal address and in the top right-hand corner a frame to indicate that a postage stamp is required, otherwise people will post it back in an envelope. When so many offices use franking machines a stamped addressed card is irrelevant, although advisable when writing to freelance writers and correspondents at home addresses.

The following is an example of simple, informative and effective wording:

The Directors of XYZ Ltd
have pleasure in inviting
. . . .
to attend a PRESS RECEPTION
in the Buckingham Room
Hotel Western, Park Lane, London W1
at 11.30 a.m. on Tuesday November 5
to view the XYZ models for 1976

Cocktails   RSVP John Smith, XYZ Ltd.,
Refreshments   88, Hall Street, London W1

This card does require the organizer to write in the names of each guest, and names must be neatly written in by hand and not typewritten. If there is a very large invitation list this handwriting may be too big a task and the alternative is to have a card which reads:

The Directors of XYZ Ltd
have pleasure in inviting you
to attend a PRESS RECEPTION

The wording of the invitation should clearly set out all the facts which will encourage the recipient to decide to attend if he possibly can. A press reception has to be marketed like anything else, hence the attention to detail which is emphasized throughout this chapter. This marketing attitude is vital because invitations must compete with many other claims upon a journalist's time, including rival invitations.

The invitation card should also indicate the kind of refreshments that will be provided, and the address for reply should be printed at the foot of the ticket even though a reply card is attached or enclosed.

The appearance of the card will be enhanced if it carries the organization's coat of arms, or the company logo, and it should comply with the accepted house style regarding typeface and colour.

Should there be any sort of enclosure with an invitation card? The answer is yes if it will do anything to encourage the journalist to come. It could be a personal note, or if it is a complicated or controversial subject it may be a good idea to include some preliminary information which will stimulate curiosity and questions. But it can be fatal to send out the news release in advance.

A telephone follow-up may be worthwhile. When telephoned some of the people will say they have never seen the invitation, and this may be perfectly true. There may be other reasons why the prospective guest has not replied, and a few friendly words on the telephone may very likely encourage an acceptance. One has to sell a press reception.

For the day a complete list of acceptances should be made up, and this can be checked against signatures in the visitors' book so that absentees may be sent the news releases and pictures they would have received had they attended.

6. *Identifying Guests*

It has become accepted at receptions, meetings and conferences that everyone should wear some form of identification. This practice has the distinct advantage that it makes contact and conversation so much easier. By means of badges, preferably adhesive, which name both guest and publication the press officer can move among the guests, quickly scanning badges and welcoming people by name.

Badges of a different colour, or bearing the organization's house symbol, should be worn by members of the host party.

The badges should be prepared from the acceptance list, and set out in alphabetical order on the reception table at the entrance to the room where the reception is being held.

7. *Press Kits or Packs*

It is not advisable to hand out press packs as guests arrive as it is difficult to eat, drink, talk and read at the same time. Packs can be available on the reception table for those who ask for information in advance. (Over-elaborate so-called press kits are an abomination of all kinds of PR event and are unnecessarily costly.) Often a simple news release is all that is needed with pictures and photographs numbered on a board and available for order. If press packs are absolutely necessary the best are undoubtedly the pliable plastic ones which can even be rolled and put in a jacket pocket if need be. The simplest is the transparent kind, but there are more sophisticated ones with button-down flaps which are useful and more secure when material is being collected during a prolonged visit or tour. The use of clumsy cardboard wallets is incomprehensible, and no journalist appreciates the kind with glued or even stapled flaps which always seem to burst open.

These remarks therefore refute what is so often common practice, but surely the guiding rule must be: use a wallet if it provides a service to your guests, but don't use a wallet merely to try to impress them with the importance of your organization. Journalists will not be impressed by sheer swank. They will be impressed by thoughtfulness.

8. *Catering*

When giving numbers to the caterers it is safe to work on a number slightly below that of the acceptance list, since not all the guests remain for the buffet. While it is extremely bad to have insufficient food, it is equally bad management and economics to have a lot of food over. The bar can be controlled by one of two methods: the bar tender can be given a maximum figure, at which point he asks the organizer whether the bar should remain open; or the bar can be closed at a certain time and coffee can be served.

The serving of coffee is an excellent device for bringing the proceedings to a close, and, since by coffee time numbers are sure to be depleted it is almost certain to be sufficient to order only half as many coffees as the total number of people present. These remarks are not intended to be pinch-penny but to indicate that by proper management press events can be budgeted and controlled in a sensible and responsible manner.

Food is more important than the bar. If a host really wants to impress the press, good food is by far the best method. The food should include some substantial items and not miniature sandwiches lost under a maze of mustard and cress. The organizer should insist on not only seeing a variety of menus and prices but should clearly understand from the banqueting manager what is meant by each item. It is no good hopefully accepting a banqueting manager's vague assurance that he can 'do something for so much a head sir'. It is sometimes surprising how much better one can do for less when one demands that each item be detailed.

9. *Gifts and Mementoes*

Should the press be given presents at press receptions? It depends on the suitability of the gift or memento to the subject of the reception. A gift is not vital, but if it is a sample or is related in some way to the organization running the reception, then it can be appropriate and desirable. There are some organizations from whom such a gift might well be expected, but otherwise gifts are more appropriate to facility visits where they are an accepted courtesy. A gift should not seem to be a bribe, merely a nice gesture, and if it is a matter of proving one's case by providing a sample it will, of course, be a very good tactic. The motor car industry suffered a very bad image by being too generous to journalists.

There was the famous or infamous TV programme when a motoring correspondent displayed an array of gifts he had received from manufacturers. One baby car manufacturer gave motoring correspondents a free car. On the other hand, a nice gesture was made by the sewing machine company which presented 120 guests at a press reception with a child's toy sewing machine. But a clock manufacturer, launching a new type of clock at a press reception, gave everyone a clock and was chagrined afterwards to receive complaints that it did not work.

10. *Managing the Event*

It has been stressed at the beginning of this chapter that a PR event must be planned right down to the last detail, and that there must be a properly planned programme. The press officer has to be both producer and stage manager. People have to do certain things correctly at stipulated times, and a press reception is not just 'played by ear'. Only the press officer can co-ordinate and manage the various elements, and everyone from managing director to distinguished guest must comply with his control. A good press officer will operate almost invisibly, and the event will seem to run itself, but all the same the press officer must be here, there and everywhere making sure that everything proceeds as it should.

By setting out the programme on the invitation ticket the press officer commits everyone concerned to a timetable. Speeches must be prepared so that copies may be available to the press; there must be a rehearsal, with or without the VIP speaker; and the press officer can take the chair and so make sure that the programme runs to time.

One of the controlling factors will be the accessibility of the venue. If more than one hotel exists of the same name the location of the chosen one must be clearly stated. If the hotel has more than one entrance the right one should be clearly stated also. If there is an indicator board in the foyer of the hotel the organizer must check that his event is correctly described. If there is any risk of guests losing their way along corridors, there should be directional notices. If the event occurs in the winter or on a wet day cloakroom facilities should be clearly indicated. We have already referred to the reception table at the door, adequately staffed to receive guests. The organizer should be present to welcome guests and do anything necessary to expedite their entry.

If the organization or the client has been made responsible for the supply of products or materials, the organizer must make sure that they have in fact arrived and are ready for use. The same applies to the arrival of a film, projector and projectionist.

The reception period will usually run for 20 or 30 minutes, the shorter the better. During this period drinks will be served according to the time of day, and guests will be introduced to members of the host party. The reception period must not drag and will continue only so long as a reasonable number of guests have yet to arrive. If it goes on too long the press will become restless and want to know when the programme is to begin. The organizer must therefore take the feeling of the assembly and watch how satisfactorily the attendance is building up. He must judge the right moment to go on to the next item on the programme, doing his best not to over-run the stated time.

Throughout the course of the event he must make sure that the timetable is obeyed, the showing of the film, the giving of speeches, the demonstrating and finally the invitation to enjoy the refreshments and ask questions of members of the host party. During this latter period the organizer will endeavour to meet as many of his guests as possible and see that they are satisfied with answers to their questions and are supplied with information. He should also endeavour to say goodbye to each guest on leaving and thank them for coming.

Finally he will have to agree the account for the hotel's services and his appreciation of the way in which the hotel contributed to the success of the event will establish good relations of value to the next occasion.

The old-fashioned stand-around cocktail party press reception has long been superseded by the programmed press party from which the guests take away a good story, not a fat head and a free gift. For instance, when Necchi launched an automatic sewing machine a dress was actually made during the two hours of the reception. Women journalists went away and wrote stories that began with words such as 'The other day I saw a dress made in two hours . . .'

Gimmicks are apt to have boomerang effects, and journalists are quick to deride attempts to invent stories. On the other hand if the product is somewhat mundane a little originality can succeed. There is the example of Knorr in Zurich who invited the press to review two new products, two-portion soups and gravy in a tube. The Knorr invitation read:

> As new styles of living develop our eating habits change and this leads to a constant flow of new requirements being made of the food products industry. It is the task of a modern concern in this sector to recognize and meet these new requirements. In this

connection the Knorr Food Products Co. Ltd has created two new products and is happy to have the opportunity of presenting these to you at the press information lunch. Let us surprise you at the premiere!

The above invitation is translated from the German.

The reception took place between 11.30 a.m. and 2 p.m. at the Koch-Studio, Zurich. The focal point was a performance by two cabaret artistes, well known in Switzerland. On the basis of information supplied by Knorr's PRO, Gerhard Schlatter, these artistes wrote two sketches in which the new products were highlighted. In this entertaining fashion the press were told about the soups and gravy in a tube. In addition, more fun was added to the occasion by giving the journalists a hobby cook's apron (designed by a cartoonist) and bearing the words 'I feel so soupy'. The apron had five pockets at the lower edge to hold samples of the five new Knorr soup varieties. There was also an instantaneous contest while journalists were sampling the soups: they had to write down whatever came into their heads as they tasted the soups, and prizes were awarded for the most original comments.

Eighty Swiss newspapers and magazines reported on the new products, some in the form of articles illustrated with pictures of the cabaret artistes during their performance.

Organizing a Facility Visit

While most of the items already discussed under press conferences and receptions will also apply to the preparation of a facility visit there are several additional items to consider.

In this category of facility visit can be included all those visits by parties of journalists to factories, installations, sites and so on requiring conveyance of guests, or at least the management of guests at some distant or outside location as distinct from receiving them in the head office boardroom or in a hotel in the vicinity of the publishing offices. It also includes trips on new trains, ships or in aircraft, provided by the owners as a facility to the press to gain first-hand knowledge and experience. It can involve no more than a single journalist who is being given facilities to write an article, or a party of almost any size. Such visits can be very complicated planning feats calling for patient preparation over a long period. Journalists are unwilling or unable to give up a day, perhaps two days, on a facility visit unless there is justification. Complaints are made from time to time about wonderfully arranged charter-plane trips with generous hospitality and souvenir gifts, but no story!

As we said when considering the press reception, there must be a clear and valid purpose for any PR event, but particularly so for one which will occupy so much of a journalist's time. It must add to his knowledge and experience, supply background material, show promise of future news development, or give him an immediate story. *It must be of value to a journalist in his daily work.* He must go home feeling glad that he accepted the invitation, and not feeling that it was all very nice but rather a waste of time. Some well-known organizations do spend several hundred pounds to achieve no more than that. These ill-conceived jaunts do the PR business no good at all.

Let us analyse the practical requirements of facility visits.

1. *Party numbers*

The primary consideration when planning a press visit is the number of people in the proposed party.

Capacity of the Premises. Visitors to a factory can be a nuisance to those working there, but this must never be apparent! A certain number of people can be handled comfortably, whether it be in a laboratory or factory or on an outdoor site. No more than 15 people might be acceptable in a research establishment, whereas six parties of 15 might be all right in a large factory.

On most factory visits small groups need to be arranged because production operations would be lost on a crowd, and so the usual practice is to organize parties of from six to 12 people, each with a guide. This may therefore decide how many groups can be taken round in the available time between arrival and lunchtime, or in the afternoon before the party must leave. One method of overcoming the time problem is to let these groups follow different routes, rather than have them following one behind the other. In this way all groups can complete their tour at very nearly the same time, and visitors are not left hanging about waiting for the others to catch up with them.

This clearly calls for some good planning and rehearsal. Guides must know what they are talking about, be capable of answering questions, yet all take about the same time in dealing with each section of the tour. There should be a manual for the guides to study, and rehearsals should include practice tours which are carefully timed and observed by the organizer. It is no use detailing members of the staff for guide duties and then hoping for the best on the day.

Catering and Accommodation Facilities. Party numbers may be controlled by the seating capacity of the dining room at the factory, or at a local hotel or restaurant. If there is suitable outdoor space a marquee may be the answer. Again, if a large party is desirable, seating limitations can be overcome by having a cold buffet with a minimum of tables, although a party which has been tramping round a factory will prefer an opportunity to sit down and relax at lunchtime. But these are the sorts of alternatives which need to be thought about carefully, remembering that factory canteen facilities will not be available while there are few parts of the country where large gatherings such as weddings, 21st birthday parties, annual dinners and the like are not being organized and catered for by a local hotel, baker and confectioner or brewery.

Naturally, it is pleasanter to keep a party together if an overnight stay is necessary, and a member of the host party should stay at the hotel with the guests. Local conditions may demand scattering the party among different hotels, but this should be avoided if possible. Many members of the press party will know one another and will enjoy the opportunity of staying in the same hotel. If a party does have to be split up it is a good idea to find out if any of the guests do wish to keep together, and accommodation can be organized to meet individual wishes.

Attention to small personal details can be most important to the success of an event, and if block bookings have been made the actual allocation of rooms at different hotels can be made during the coach, train or plane journey. To do this well a team of organizers is required with hosts, couriers or guides attached to each grouping of guests. The guests must never be left unattended, never expected to move from A to B unescorted once they have joined the party at the assembly point. Sometimes it is even wise to have someone detailed with a car to pick up latecomers or stragglers so that there is no danger of anyone failing to join the party.

A point worth remembering in this respect is that if guests have to travel a long way to join the transport (as when airports are some distance from city centres) it is safer to collect people in a central place and provide transport to the airport. It is comparatively simple for guests to assemble at a suitable well-known spot which is accessible by most forms of transport. Motor coach companies can usually advise on the best meeting places because they have picking-up points agreed between them and the police. Some airports are conveniently served by rail services so that transportation is easily arranged and controlled.

Capacity of Transport. Numbers may be determined by the peculiarities of the seating capacity, or the party booking arrangements, or the mode of transport. If a coach has 42 seats it is obviously impossible to accept 43 guests. The same rule applies to aircraft. It is not always possible to put on a larger coach or aircraft. Trains are more flexible up to a point, but the organizer must discuss with the railway booking staff the make-up of the train and the kind of stock being used since this differs considerably according to the region. It is essential to know how the seating will be dispersed, and it may be desirable to restrict the party to a single coach. Alternatively, the *minimum* size of the party could be the total seating of an entire coach.

When chartering aircraft there may be a choice of aircraft, and this choice will again depend on members. Similarly, if seats are being booked on a scheduled passenger service there may be an advantage in a number which secures a price reduction. These points should be discussed at the earliest possible moment with the airline.

The commercial staff of transportation operators can be exceedingly helpful, but it is wise to check everything and not rely too heavily on other people to take over one's responsibilities. On one occasion it was discovered at very short notice that railway tickets had been wrongly dated, which would have invalidated them when presented to the ticket collector at the barrier. Fortunately the wrong date was discovered in good time otherwise that press visit might have been calamitous. Tickets should not be posted to guests: it is safer to ask guests to exchange a voucher for a ticket supplied by the organizer at the place of departure.

From the last remark an important lesson can be learned: an organizer must be a born pessimist. He must literally make himself miserable trying to think of everything that could possibly go wrong so that he can then find a satisfactory solution to it. For example, in a certain town, the police insisted that coaches must unload their passengers the other side of a busy crossroads from their venue. This could have meant some of the party losing their way. So the organizer argued, and the police relented and permitted the coaches to unload outside the venue itself, returning at an agreed time which meant that the activities within the venue had to run strictly to time. But this sort of thing can be done only if the organizer has a sufficiently nimble mind to foresee trouble.

Limited Invitation List. When the topic is so specialized that there is a limited invitation list the problem is to find a date when the majority can attend. This difficulty is best overcome by offering alternative dates by telephone, and negotiating in this way until a sufficiently large party has been assembled. In this case the visit will hinge on the date acceptable by the guests.

The Budget. It may be physically possible to accommodate and to transport a hundred people but the cost may be prohibitive. Whatever facilities or limitations may exist it is essential to have the event strictly costed, and to work within an agreed figure. Every cost can be known in advance and nothing should be agreed upon without a prior quotation. 'Shopping list' budgets for press events are outlined in the previous chapter.

2. *Invitations*

For this type of operation the invitation must give specific details about the object of the visit and the facilities for transport and accommodation which will be provided, accompanied by a timetable from start to finish including the picking up and returning of guests. Depending upon how complicated the arrangements may be, an invitation ticket as already described for press receptions may be adequate or it may be safer to include a covering letter setting out the itinerary.

Because so many bookings have to be finalized when numbers are known it will be necessary to despatch invitations much earlier than in the case of a press reception. Transport contractors and caterers will want a week's notice of the final arrangements, so if time is required for sending out a second round of invitations should acceptances be unsatisfactory, the original invitation will need to go out a month before the date of the event. This means that copy must go to the printer at least a fortnight before delivery is required, and time must also be allowed either side of the printing dates for first of all the finalizing of details and the design of the card and then, when delivered, the making out and posting of the cards.

Thus, at least two months in advance of the event, we must know exactly what is going to happen. Working backwards yet again, it is not going to be too soon to begin making plans three months in advance, and no doubt some thought will have been given to the idea of a press visit much earlier than that.

It is important to see that the right people join the party. Such an expensive event merits the attendance of senior editorial personnel: it is not just a day out for juniors, free-loaders and hangers-on. This can be emphasized by pointing out that numbers are restricted and that it will be a privilege to attend. It does happen sometimes that when a very attractive press visit is learned about a number of journalists will ring up and ask to be invited. And some who were not invited will ring up and complain about this afterwards. This only goes to show yet another of the pitfalls of media relations: you can be too successful.

3. *Party Briefing*

No matter what details may have been sent at the time of invitation each person who has accepted must be sent detailed instructions three to seven days prior to the event. The instructions should not be sent too soon, otherwise they may be mislaid, not too late otherwise they may be delayed in the post or in the publishing house internal postal system. Before leaving home every guest should know exactly the programme of the visit.

It is unwise to issue only assembly instructions in advance, and then to issue the rest of the instructions during the journey or upon arrival, although it is sensible to re-issue instructions in case anyone has left them behind. Knowledge of the scheme of things will enable people to bring with them suitable clothing, accessories and equipment which might include such things as raincoats, sunglasses, cameras or field glasses. Thoughtful organizers make successful events.

Some organizers hand out elaborate press kits as soon as they meet guests, and when these kits are clumsy cardboard wallets it really is a problem to know what to do with them. A sheet of paper that will go into pocket or handbag is much better appreciated.

4. *News Story Facilities*

If journalists are likely to need working facilities so that they get stories, pictures, tapes or film back to their offices in time for use that day these facilities must not only be laid on but made known in advance. Telex, telephones, typewriters, lighting facilities, dark-rooms, and cars to station or airport may be necessary. It is useless inviting people to cover a story which they cannot communicate to their editors in good time.

5. *Timing*

Following on from this is the need to time events such as VIP visits and official openings so that they occur before lunch and there is time to communicate the story to evening papers and radio and TV news services which are broadcast from 6 p.m. onwards. This timing of press visits will be controlled by the location of the venue, and also by whether the party is staying overnight or travelling to and from the venue during the day. Day return visits present problems requiring very tight and foolproof schedules, and much will depend upon the speed of the transport. We must accept that the earliest a party may be able to leave a city centre – to which members have already travelled from their homes – is 9 a.m., and it should be back by 5.30 p.m. since some members of the party may well have to undertake a considerable additional journey to reach their homes. Add to this the fact that most factories close down for lunch at 12.30 p.m., and close for the day at 4.30 p.m., and there are very strict time limitations within which a visit has to be planned.

Every item in the programme must therefore be timed, and this does mean going over the ground and timing every movement of the party, making special allowances for the time it takes for a given number of people to leave or enter a vehicle or building, cross roads, ascend stairs or attend demonstrations. An experienced press officer can estimate these times without having to resort to a mock rehearsal, but it does pay to go over the sequence of movements where they will actually happen. Even then it is wise to insert in the timetable some extra minutes so that the programme is flexible enough to allow for losses of time through lateness of transport, unexpected weather conditions or some other minor disaster on the day.

This programming should be so expertly done that the party pro-ceeds comfortably throughout the sequence of events without anyone being conscious of being 'organized' and only that everything runs smoothly. Although a programme may be carefully planned and scrupulously rehearsed it seldom actually goes like clockwork because trains can run late, aircraft are notorious for being late, traffic does get held up, people get lost, and something always takes longer than expected. But this does not matter if the organizer has taken the unexpected into account.

As an example, the timetable for a women's press party to a south coast town permitted various delays in transport. In the event there was time to spare and the coach took a detour along the coast. It was a day of constant adaptation as there were a number of substitutes in the party which meant a change in the table plan and one member missed the train but joined the party later. However, a story was written afterwards congratulating the organizer on a visit that ran like clock-work.

But it may not be necessary, possible or advisable to take a press party to a distant location with all its costs and troubles of transport-ing, feeding and accommodating maybe a hundred people over a period of, say, 36 hours. The event could be televised, conveyed by post office landline and shown on a giant Eidophor screen to a press audience in a London hotel. Hiring the landline is expensive, but the total operation is simpler and can be economical if it is a big story capable of earning substantial coverage.

Royal Protocol

To minimize the presence of the media so that members of the Royal Family are not harrassed by a swarm of journalists and cameramen a rota system is operated by the press and information office at Buckingham Palace. The arrangements vary according to the occasion, but the following is the basic make-up of a royal rota press party:

ROYAL ROTA PRESS PARTY

REPORTING:	One court correspondent from the Press Association.
	One court correspondent from BBC Radio.
FILMING:	Two TV newsreel cameramen (filming on behalf of BBC and Independent Television News)
	Cinema newsreel cameraman (filming on behalf of Movietone News)
PHOTOGRAPHY:	Two black and white still photographers (one national newspaper and one photographic agency nominated by the Newspaper Publishers' Association)
	One colour still photographer (nominated by the Newspaper Publishers' Association).

Additionally: in places with provincial press coverage:

One to three reporters and one to three photographers from the local newspapers (nominated by the Newspaper Society).

Where a single journalist or photographer is nominated he does not work merely for his own newspaper but makes his story or pictures generally available.

Not all the above listed options are taken up while over and above these options it is sometimes possible, depending on the nature of the engagement, to have additional places for non-rota or static photographers or to make minor modifications.

For every single individual engagement carried out by the Queen, the Duke of Edinburgh, the Prince of Wales or Princess Anne, the Buckingham Palace press office gets in touch with the host and discusses the press arrangements for that visit. These arrangements are largely dictated by the nature of the programme itself, and the amount of space available for the media representatives. Circular badges are issued bearing this information:

ROYAL ROTA		ROYAL ROTA
Date	or	Date
PRESS		PRESS
CAMERAMAN		REPORTER

In the case of the Queen Mother, press arrangements are arranged by the press office at Clarence House and in the case of Princess Margaret by Kensington Palace.

CHAPTER TEN

Exhibitors and Exhibitions

There are two clear-cut sections to this chapter: media relations in support of an individual participant in an exhibition, and media relations for an exhibition as a whole, that is on behalf of the organizers but also beneficial to the individual exhibitors.

PR Support for Exhibitors

It is an expensive business to take stands in private or public, national or local, permanent or travelling exhibitions, to say nothing of overseas trade fairs, and DTI Joint Venture schemes which will be discussed in the next chapter. Space has to be rented, the stand has to be designed and built, equipment has to be made ready and transported to the hall, give-away literature has to be designed and printed, certain advertising may be advisable, and much staff time will be occupied in manning the stand. It is so costly that some companies will not exhibit at all while others exhibit only irregularly or in inexpensive Joint Venture schemes abroad. Nevertheless, on the whole, exhibitions such as those held at Olympia and Earls Court, London, and at the National Exhibition Centre, Birmingham, are well supported and attended. Throughout the year exhibitions are taking place every week, and the magazine *Exhibitions Bulletin* is packed with dates, venues and details. Exhibitions are, despite the misgivings of some firms, a major marketing medium, which suggests that the costs must be relative to results.

Exhibitions provide great opportunities for enhancing the value of an exhibit by the provision of PR support before, during and after the show.

The effect of PR support is to extend the value of the stand to people who cannot or will not attend so that the impact and cost of the exhibit is spread over an infinitely larger number of potential buyers. In addition, PR support can increase the number of visitors to the stand. These are bonuses not to be ignored.

The cost of providing this support is, relatively, very small. When preparing his estimate of time to be expended in order to arrive at an annual fee the PR consultant is unlikely to need to allocate more than three to five days time, spread over a period, to each client exhibition. Materials and expenses will not add too much to the bill if news releases are kept to a reasonable length, press packs are avoided, and the press room is not flooded with too many big photographs.

Thus we arrive at a time, materials and expenses cost which can be divided into three categories: (1) advance press relations; (2) supplying the press room; (3) attending the press preview and official opening. In the case of overseas exhibitions a further cost will be the translation of releases.

One of the largest single material costs, which does need to be rigorously controlled, is that of photographic prints, very few of which may be used because of the competition from so many exhibitors and the fact that most journals can print but two or three pictures at the most. Unless a picture has news value it has no place in the press room, and most of the pictures to be found in most exhibition press rooms have no place anywhere.

For the press officer intent on doing all within his power to enhance the value of his organization's stand at an exhibition the following plan is recommended:

1. *Advance Planning*

When the annual budget is being prepared it is important to know the details of the exhibition programme. This applies whether media relations are handled by a staff man or by a consultant. Time can then be allocated, and preparatory work can begin at once because it is often necessary to work from one annual exhibition to the next if the organization is a regular participator. The press officer will need to know names of exhibitions with venues, dates and stand numbers. He should have a plan of each exhibition so that he knows the location of the stands which have been booked. Even if there is but a tentative proposal to go in an exhibition, the press officer should know about it. This means that those responsible for exhibitions must work in close collaboration with the press officer, and vice versa. Moreover, they should understand why the press officer wants this information and what he can contribute to the success of participation.

2. *Contacting the Exhibition Promoters*

The press officer should contact the promoters of the exhibition and obtain any available literature and instructions to participants. For example, he should find out who is editing the exhibition catalogue and make sure that he, and no-one else in his organization, is responsible not only for supplying the description of the stand but for supplying it to whoever requires it by the specified copy date. He should also find out what special PR facilities are likely to exist, such as a cinema in which his firm's film can be shown, or a seminar in which his firm's personnel might be able to take part either on the platform or in the audience.

3. *Contacting the Exhibition Press Officer*

As a result of contacting the promoters, the press officer will have learned the name of the exhibition press officer and he should contact him as early as possible. He can discuss with the exhibition press officer what his organization will exhibit and supply information which can be used to publicize the show as a whole; he can discover who will officially open the event, and what VIP's are expected to visit and on what days; and he can generally work with the exhibition press officer to their mutual advantage. As a result of this collaboration he may be able to get news about his exhibit issued in advance stories from the press office, and he may be able to ensure that the official opener and VIP visitors come to his stand, not because of any arm twisting or bribery and corruption but merely because the exhibition promoters know that the stand is worth a visit. Equally, by knowing on what days VIP visitors will be attending the press officer can bring in his own VIP visitors without any risk of a clash of dates.

It is, of course, essential to work closely with exhibition press officers so that one may know exactly what arrangements are being made for a press preview or press day. Some promoters are very lax about press facilities, and others do not appoint their own press officer until two or three months before the event. But we will deal with these problems in the next section on PR for Exhibitions. The point is made here to emphasize the need for liaison between the press officers on both sides.

4. *Obtaining Advance Information about the Exhibit*

This is by far the most difficult part of the exercise, and it may be this which deters some PR consultants from doing more for their clients who exhibit. Exhibitors are notoriously indecisive about what they are going to exhibit and although they may be genuinely anxious not to reveal trade secrets about a new product to be launched at the show, quite often there are no secrets and it is just inefficiency which makes information unavailable. Yet the press officer must have some knowledge of his company's intentions if he is to gain useful coverage in the journals which are previewing the exhibition or publishing special numbers to coincide with the event.

5. *Press Previews*

Monthly magazines previewing exhibitions usually require copy six weeks before publication, and some like to work even further ahead to avoid special issues being something of a tax on their staffing resources. The exhibitor who does not know what he is exhibiting is likely to be left out, or given a bare mention which is of no consequence. But the press officer can overcome problems like this by making sure that editors are given at least a general description of what the company makes which is certainly better than a mere list of name, address and stand number.

Another problem arises in that editors often obtain lists of exhibitors from the promoters and then write to each exhibitor asking for information. They seldom write to the correct person, though, and very often letters never reach the press officer or PR consultant so that press coverage is lost.

Nevertheless, the astute press officer can circumvent the trouble caused by such careless mailings and clumsy handling of correspondence and produce an advance story six to eight weeks in front of the exhibition date. In time, that is, to distribute it to all the magazines and newspapers likely to be interested. In doing this he must be careful to head the story with the name of the exhibition, the date, the venue and the stand number because not every editor will know these details.

At this early stage the press officer may suffer from the disadvantage of having no pictures of the main exhibit, but he can usually supply a picture of a product which he is assured will be on the stand even if it is not the highlight or the secret new product.

From these remarks it must be apparent that the press officer has got to show considerable initiative to overcome the many obstacles to enhancing the value of an exhibit, but it can be done.

Some time prior to the opening of the exhibition the press officer should receive from the promoter's press officer details of press room arrangements such as the location of the press room, the number of releases and pictures recommended, and the date and time of the press preview and official opening. The exhibitor's press officer should take the precaution of telephoning the exhibition press officer a fortnight before the opening date to make sure that he receives final information and tickets to the press preview if these are necessary.

Two different kinds of preview have been mentioned and in case this is confusing it should be explained that magazines will sometimes preview an exhibition in the sense that they will publish a guide to the exhibition (as distinct from reviewing the event afterwards), while some promoters invite the press to attend a preview of the exhibition, either on the day previous to the opening, or an hour or so before the official opening on the morning of the first day. Big exhibitions like the Motor Show have a press day, but the first morning of the Boat Show is given over to the press and the official opening.

6. *The Press Room*

Owing to the physical peculiarities of exhibition halls the offices are mostly placed close to the outer walls so that the middle area is left free for exhibition purposes, and this results in cell-like press rooms often situated in obscure places.

It pays to deliver press room material personally and, if possible, to have some say in how and where it is to be displayed. In well-arranged press rooms the material is laid out on tables in alphabetical order (racks are a nuisance because the releases will droop forward, losing their identity) while a sample picture is given a number and displayed so that copies may be requested from the stock held by the press room staff. It is essential to visit the press room from time to time to see whether stocks of releases or pictures require replenishing.

To avoid repetition it is sufficient to say here that the news release supplied should be brief and provide news, not a company history or something equally irrelevant, that pictures must be captioned, and that nothing else is required.

7. *Manning the Stand*

It is rarely necessary for the press officer to be present on the stand after the first day unless the exhibit is very much a PR effort and he has work to do. The major part of PR support for an exhibit should have been completed before the exhibition opened, but a supply of news releases and pictures should be kept in the stand office, in addition to those in the press room, and the stand manager should take charge of them in the absence of the press officer. In practice, a staff press officer is likely to attend the stand more frequently than one employed by a consultant, unless the fee is large enough to cover the time expenditure.

8. *Press Visitors to the Stand*

There are several ways in which the press can be invited as guests of the exhibitor. These will be in addition to the efforts made by the promoters to attract journalists and may be on a different day to the press preview or press day. It depends on the resources of the exhibitor, the size of his stand, and what kind of show it is, indoors or out-of-doors. The latter category includes agricultural shows from the Royal to local county ones, and big events like Farnborough Air Show.

A big exhibitor may throw a press party on his stand, but only a limited number of these can be attended in any one day and it may be unwise to compete. In most exhibition halls private rooms can be hired for press parties, so size of stand is not necessarily a limiting factor. The more modest exhibitor can still invite the press by sending journalists an open invitation to call at any time, when hospitality will be available. Sometimes, despite a press day, it is a good idea to invite the press to come back on another day for a reception and demonstration on the stand.

9. *After the Exhibition*

As a result of the event many new press contacts will have been made and they can be mailed future stories or invited to PR events. Some of these interested journalists will have asked for more information, additional pictures, opportunities to visit the factory or feature articles, and all these things must be attended to before the interest is allowed to flag.

F

10. *Clearing the Press Room*

On the final afternoon a last visit should be made to the press room to collect surplus pictures and news releases. Pictures cost money and there is no point in leaving them to the press officer to throw away. If the exhibition press officer has been helpful and the press room has been well run, it is only courteous to express one's appreciation. PR is a friendly world, and it is likely that there will be future opportunities for further co-operation. One thing that is guaranteed to annoy an exhibition press officer is having to bag unwanted press kits – unless he has been wise enough to prohibit them in the first place!

PR Support for Exhibitions

An exhibition press officer should be appointed to an exhibition as soon as the event has been agreed upon, and with exhibitions which are held at regular yearly or two-yearly intervals media relations activity will be constant. Large exhibition promoters have a staff of press officers and this continuous effort is automatic, but the complaint can be made about smaller sponsors that they appoint press officers far too close to the event with the result that exhibitors do not get the PR support they deserve.

During the months leading up to the event the press officer can stimulate knowledge of the exhibition and interest in it by issuing news stories and supplying feature articles. This is, of course, done extremely well by the press officer to the Ideal Home Exhibition through the associated *Daily Mail* and *Evening News,* and the same steady build-up of news stories heralds other famous shows such as the Motor Show.

But the press officer can do very little if he does not know who is going to take part and what they will be showing because his stories will be about the interesting things that people will see. Since we have already said that finding out what is to be exhibited is no mean task for the exhibitor's press officer it is doubly difficult for someone even further removed from those responsible for exhibits. Yet he needs to be constantly filling in the picture of the eventual event so that he can talk and write about it. His job does not start and finish with the press room.

So, collating information about exhibitors is an important part of his job, but first he has to discover who can supply the information. Usually the person who signs the contract for the stand space, the only name that the promoters have, is useless to the press officer. He needs the name and address of the advertising manager, publicity manager, PRO, press officer or PR consultant. This means writing to each exhibitor as his stand booking comes in, asking for the name and address of the person who will be dealing with the PR on behalf of the exhibitor.

This request often comes as a surprise to those exhibitors who do not use PR and do not realize that PR has anything to do with exhibitions. Others respond very willingly, and are only too glad to put their PRO or PR consultant in touch with the exhibition press officer. A library of plates or cards can now be assembled so that all communications from the press officer to exhibitors go direct to the person responsible for supplying information. If it is not done much of the correspondence from the exhibition press officer to the exhibitors is liable to go astray, be mislaid, misunderstood or just not answered. And this is a pity because such a breakdown in communication may deprive both sides of valuable PR opportunities.

Ideally, the exhibition press officer should issue numbered bulletins, reporting progress to exhibitors and telling them what else may be required of them and to a greater or lesser extent this is done by the promoters of the larger exhibitions. An advantage of such a bulletin is that it does indicate that there is an active press officer and even if one issue goes astray because the exhibitor has no PR organization, or fails to act upon a request, succeeding communications must surely evoke a response.

When the press officer knows what the exhibition is going to look like, having been sent artists' impressions of stands and told about special working models and demonstrations, he can issue worthwhile advance stories to arouse the curiosity of potential visitors and encourage them to book the forthcoming event in their diaries. This is clearly of benefit to exhibitors and depends entirely upon their co-operation.

The following questions must be decided: Should there be a press reception, a press lunch, a preview on a previous day, or a preview prior to the official opening at, say, 11 a.m. on the first day? How are the press to be invited and received and what facilities will be provided? Should the official opening be made at a seated assembly, or in the hall by the main entrance? All the various factors mentioned above have to be taken into consideration and no hard and fast rule can be laid down, as many matters will be governed by the subject, location, size and news value of the event.

Another controlling factor is the day of the week on which an exhibition opens. When an exhibition opens mid-week or at the end of the week (like the Do–It-Yourself Exhibition) an afternoon given over to a press preview is a very good thing, giving the press ample time to gain interesting material which they can use next day or even at the weekend. But when an exhibition opens on a Monday morning a Sunday press preview will not be popular, and the possibilities of press coverage are more limited.

On these specially organized press previews hospitality is necessary, but a 'dry' press room is preferable, especially since there is seldom a lot of space and it can be a very busy place. Most journalists are busy people and the ones who hang about drinking in the press room are mainly correspondents and freelancers who have time to spare. In any case, there are plenty of bars and the exhibitor's club to which the press officer can take a journalist if he wishes to offer him a drink.

The biggest hazard of the press officer who is seriously concerned with providing the *press* with a service is the material which the exhibitors bring to the press room. Some of it should be banned. In the interests of exhibitors, the exhibition promoters and the press the press officer is entitled to demand that (a) news releases be brief; (b) photographs be captioned and (c) no press packs or wallets be supplied. The conscientious press officer acts as an intermediary between exhibitors and the press and this double duty has to be remembered since it can be crucial to the success of the whole operation.

Press Room Hints for Exhibitors

Who do not Employ Professional PR Services

News Releases: 1. The release (50 copies for the Press Room please, with spares for your stand) must contain news of interest to the press reviewing the Exhibition. The first paragraph should summarize the complete news story.

2. Releases should be as short as possible, the ideal being a story restricted to one side of one sheet of paper, complete with stand number and the exhibitor's full name and address.

3. In addition to supplying the Press Room, exhibitors are advised to send news releases direct to special correspondents and specialized magazines likely to report the exhibitor's participation in the Exhibition.

Photographs: 1. Please supply 25 half-plate glossy black and white prints.

2. Each picture must be fully captioned and bear the address for further information.

3. Pictures must not be stapled to news releases.
4. Colour pictures are not required.
5. The Press do *not* want:

(a) Press packs or wallets	(d) Timetables
(b) House journals	(e) Sales literature
(c) Picture postcards	(f) Company histories

During the Exhibition the staff of the Press Room will be delighted to receive new stories.

As already said in Chapter Nine, *One of the abominations of all kinds of PR event is the over-elaborate so-called press kit,* and in the press room there is even less excuse for its use than at the press reception or on the factory visit which is at least restricted to one organization. When asked why PRO's put these monstrosities in the press room the excuse is made that this is what the clients want. This is nonsense. When consultants do what clients want they should stop pretending to be consultants. Does a doctor obey his patient? A consultant's job is to advise: he is paid to know better than his client.

The point is surely that at most a journalist has a brief case (and often he does not have even that): to take away all the press packs and bulky press releases found in most press rooms he would need a suitcase. So it is a matter of plain common sense to put in the press room concise information which journalists are likely to want to take away with them.

The only way to put a stop to this, which merely helps to encourage the press in their disrespect for PR, is for exhibition press officers to agree on a form of standard procedure which can be distributed by all press officers prior to all exhibitions. The *Press Room Hints* quoted here should be universally applied.

Exhibitions in developing countries

When population is scattered and largely agricultural as in the villages of many African, Asian and South American countries, the mobile show with dancers, singers, puppet shows or films shown on a screen erected on the roof of a Land Rover, is an excellent medium. Sometimes these travelling shows seek to win the sympathy and support of the chief, headman, or elders who act as the initiators and then convert adoptors among their people. Mobile shows have been used to introduce topics like banking, husbandry, birth control, child welfare, census procedures and many other subjects, some commercial and others promoted by the government. The puppet show is a good method where there are language problems and the message may be conveyed very enterprisingly in mime. These more direct forms of communication have much greater penetration than radio. In fact, they can go to places never reached by radio for there are large areas of the world where communication is still by the traditional methods of the drum, the gong and morning and evening official court messenger.

Since Zambia gained independence in 1964 the mobile film show has been used extensively by the Zambian Information Services. One unusual problem was how to reach isolated communities living on islands on the rivers and lakes. A survey showed that there were no fewer than 18,500 people living on 26 islands beyond the reach of the media. Other rural areas are served by 100 Land Rover film units which attract audiences of some 500 people at a time. These units are stationed at strategic points throughout this large but not densely populated country. The islanders are reached by four motor boats (fitted with cutting and clearing devices) which force a passage through the rapidly growing weeds to bring film shows to the islanders. Copies of the vernacular newspapers published by ZIS are brought to the islanders by speedboat, and journalists visit the islands in this way.

However, there are problems. In Moslem communities the women may not be permitted to see the shows and exhibitions, while there is seldom anyone more resistant to new ideas than an ill or uneducated villager who follows traditional lifestyles. One of the basic obstacles to education in illiterate populations is the lack of parental literacy. This is a handicap little known in Western society. Moreover, in developing countries lost literacy occurs among teenagers after they leave school and cannot find employment requiring literacy. Media that involve demonstration and presentation are therefore very important among these millions of people.

CHAPTER ELEVEN

Overseas PR

Overseas PR – no matter which is the PROs home country or operating base – offers attractions concerning exports and problems concerning comprehension and the physical ability to communicate. It can be a total waste of time to undertake a blind mailing to overseas publications whose addresses have been taken from a directory, especially if the story is sent out untranslated on the assumption that everybody speaks English. If the exporter has no overseas subsidiaries or selling agents with PR staff, it will be wise to appoint overseas PR consultants who are either nationals operating in their own countries or ones who are familiar with the media and the methods in a particular area such as the Common Market. Such people will not merely translate: they will re-write stories in the necessary languages.

Before examining the various ways in which the press officer can extend his efforts overseas let us first begin with the PRO whose main task is to do with the home market. The chances are that with very little extra effort his present work can be made to gain greater recognition for his organization. First, he must discuss with the sales department whether overseas sales are wanted, or whether because of restricted franchises or because of import restrictions in certain countries it is not desired that effort be squandered where it can do no good. Policies must be clearly understood by the press office.

A few examples of these problems may be helpful to the reader. A company selling chemical products found it wise to avoid the South American markets because home production was encouraged in those countries. A UK company, marketing a German-made machine, had to avoid press coverage in the German-speaking parts of Europe. A British company producing a very specialized machine for the printing industry was faced with the problem that there was only a handful of potential buyers in the UK and that sales could only be made on a world basis. Consequently, when a machine was sold to Brazil, and then another to Greece, these sales made ideal stories for overseas distribution, and both the COI and the External Services of the BBC at Bush House made good use of this information.

To quote N. H. Alexander of Engineering in Britain Information Services will be of special interest to the press officer concerned with export PR (11.1)

> 'It should be recognized first of all that journals (except those few devoted specifically to news from overseas) are primarily concerned with the activities of their home industries. The amount of space an editor can allocate to industrial information from other countries is limited. In smaller countries, such as Austria or Finland, which are accustomed to looking abroad for technical advances, it may be a quarter of the whole; in the major technical countries, such as Germany or the USA, it will be less.'

One way to overcome this is the picture-and-caption story which is not only attractive and concise but has the advantage of explaining the story pictorially and thus helping to overcome many language and dialect problems.

It is well worth looking at overseas newspapers to see how little news is published in them about the UK. For that matter there is little foreign news in most British papers.

Next Mr. Alexander wrote about the 'publishable news release' which this book is at pains to expound (11.2)

> 'For the common run of industrial news a story that can be used straight away will take precedence over one that requires extensive re-writing. . . He (*the editor*) is interested in British products and activities only if they are likely to interest his readers . . . the export of pumps from Britain is of no interest to anyone outside Britain: the import of pumps into France may be of some slight interest to French journals; but the use of British pumps by a French refinery to solve a tricky corrosion problem will interest chemical industry journals all over the world. . . It is simple politeness to anticipate the editor's difficulties and include brief explanations of geography. . . It is not self-evident that the German Post Office runs the national telephone system.'

This means that in writing releases for overseas distribution it is even more imperative to take nothing for granted. Again the press officer has to be a pessimist, anticipating trouble which in this case can be misunderstanding or perhaps complete lack of understanding because the story lacks essential if elementary facts. In all press relations work it is fatal to imagine that anyone is as familiar about one's special subject or organization as one is oneself. Addresses must say *England* – there are Brightons and Croydons and also English counties all over the globe; it is wise to refer to people as Mr. Mrs. or Miss because Christian names are not necessarily revealing of correct sex; and special care must be taken to use uncomplicated words which are not likely to translate into something absurd.

The following list which takes into consideration even the most casual of overseas press relations is intended for all press officers who wish to carry out press publicity overseas.

1. *British Journals with Overseas Circulations*

In many industries, trades and professions American and British journals have international circulations, partly because they are accepted as world authorities, partly because it would not be economic to produce similar journals in some countries, but also because it would be uneconomic to produce such journals in America and especially Britain unless there was a circulation beyond that possible in the country of origin. One effect of the Common Market has been the acquisition of European publishing houses by British firms such as IPC and the launching of journals with substantial circulations.

2. *Overseas News Agencies*

In addition to Reuters, Belgian, French, West German, Italian, Spanish, Swiss, Bulgarian, Czechoslovakian, Hungarian, Polish, Rumanian, Russian; Canadian, United States; Egyptian, Israeli; Ghanaian; Pakistani, Chinese; and Australian news agencies are located in London, and their addresses will be found in the *Hollis Press and Public Relations Annual* and *Benn's Press Directory*.

3. *Overseas Press Correspondents*

There are also London representatives of leading foreign and Commonwealth newspapers and magazines, some being full-time staff but others part-time correspondents who probably have a full-time job elsewhere and so are rarely free to attend press receptions.

4. *Freelance Writers, Press Services*

According to the country or the topic there are many freelance writers and news services which specialize in supplying certain types of material. Once the press officer begins to send material overseas he is bound to be approached by them, but a number are well known in certain fields, and most of them prepare reports on British exhibitions for overseas journals. Since they operate permanently in Britain and do their own translating they are very useful to know.

5. *Overseas Press Mailing Lists*

Just as a plate library has to be created for UK journals so will it be necessary to create one for appropriate categories of the overseas press. It is, of course, less easy to maintain these addresses. Many are published in British year books such as *Advertiser's Annual, Benn's Press Directory* and *Willings Press Guide*. Press year books are also published in most large countries but it is expensive to buy them all, while the information is naturally given in the language of the country. No one book published in the UK gives a comprehensive list of overseas publications, and it is usually necessary to work from them all. PRADS provide an overseas news release mailing service.

Generally speaking, it pays to send a story direct to a journal in its own country, preferably by airmail.

One of the best ways to build a reliable press list is to seek the advice of the company's overseas branch managers and agents, asking them for the names and addresses of appropriate journals and to send copies to the press officer so that he may study their contents and see whether they are likely to accept his stories. Yet another method favoured by the agents themselves of British companies which operate entirely through agents is to send them copies of news releases in English which they will translate and send direct to journals in their own countries. Obviously, this has a mixture of advantages and disadvantages, not least being that the press officer relinquishes all control of what is said and where the stories are sent. It is difficult enough letting a local works manager deal direct with the provincial press, but working through overseas agents whom one seldom if ever meets is full of pitfalls. Nevertheless, it is a method used by the smaller industrial companies anxious to support their agents but not having big PR budgets. It certainly shows an appreciation by these companies that overseas press relations are important. The large organization, how-ever, can employ overseas PR services as already recommended.

6. *External House Journals*

This may be one of the most practical methods of communicating direct with overseas government buyers, importers, agents and so on. In some cases, as when the market is mostly among English-speaking countries, an English language magazine will be adequate, but other-wise it will be necessary to print in at least French, German, Italian, Spanish and Portuguese if the journal is to go to Europe, South America and parts of the Middle East and Africa. The Dutch and the Scandinavians will accept English, but elsewhere other languages may be necessary. One advantage of an international house journal is that the contents can be taken from overseas sources, pictures and articles showing the products in use by different nationalities. The French, German and Italian house journal could be an excellent means to develop good relations in the Common Market. To avoid unnecessary bulk, it is better to print separate language versions.

We are extremely fortunate in having printers who are highly skilled at this type of work, with special design, translation and foreign typesetting facilities. For example, a house journal could have its illustrated areas printed in bulk by offset-litho, the different language versions being overprinted by letterpress.

7. *EIBIS International Ltd.* (11.3)

During the past 17 years EIBIS has established direct connections with the editors of more than 23,000 newspapers and trade journals throughout the world. Typically, a publishable PR story sent in three or four languages may secure publication in some 25 journals in 10 or more countries. This is a service well used by British firms and consultancies. Its success is based on a very thorough Seven Stage Checking System:

(i) English texts are carefully edited to eliminate vague or ambigu-ous phrases, or verbal play which might confuse or mislead the translator.

(ii) Wherever a difficult phrase or expression cannot be simplified, an explanatory note, or perhaps diagrams and illustrations, are pro-vided for translators.

(iii) The initial translation of the edited and annotated copy is carried out by a national of the country where the story is to be distributed.

(iv) The first translation is independently revised by another translator, either abroad or in London.

(v) A third check is made by linguists at EIBIS, to ensure that nothing has been omitted or a meaning misunderstood.

(vi) When the story has been stencilled in the foreign language, it is checked a fourth time by EIBIS staff.

(vii) So as to provide editors with a final line of defence against inaccuracies or misinterpretations, a copy of the English version accompanies every foreign language version. A press cutting service is also provided although the total number of appearances may be far greater than the cuttings indicate. The address of EIBIS International Ltd., is 3 Johnson's Court, Fleet Street, London EC4A 3EA.

8. *External Services of the BBC*

Provided the story is up-to-date and is fully documented, the External Services of the BBC at Bush House, Aldwych, London WC2 (*not* Broadcasting House) will be interested in including it in one of their many English and foreign language programmes, most of which are of an industrial or technical nature. If, for instance, the story is about a large export order being despatched from London Docks it is necessary to give full details of the product, the order value, the date of despatch and the name of the ship and the dock. Such a story needs to be supplied several days in advance, not on the day of sailing and certainly not after the goods have left our shores, otherwise the story will be dead and there will not be time to prepare it for the appropriate programmes.

9. *The Central Office of Information* (11.4)

Externally, the COI with branches in provincial cities offers exporters a worldwide publicity service. This is a free service which should be ignored by no-one engaged in export PR. The services embrace press, radio, TV, newsreel, photographic, exhibition, film and other services. The COI uses every means of communication to maintain and increase Britain's industrial prestige abroad. If the PR story is good for Britain, the COI will handle it.

The COI seeks news leads, pictures, publications or films about the launching of a new product, the improvement of an old product, a new or improved process, a notable success in research, a novel design to meet a new or old need or a large, or a first or unusual export order. Stories about the opening of a new factory, uses of imported raw materials from developing countries, or about an interesting personality going on an overseas sales tour may also be suitable.

The following are the overseas services offered by the COI:

Press. News and information is sent daily by radio, teletype, Telex and airmail to Information Officers overseas. There is an annual output of 15,000 news stories about British industry and research. In addition, illustrated feature articles are supplied to overseas specialized journals. Printed bulletins on single subjects are produced in many languages and submitted to potential buyers as well as to the trade and technical press.

Radio. Several thousand programme items are recorded every year for broadcast by overseas radio stations. The fast *Newsline* service transmits urgent stories to major capitals.

Photography. Each year about 3000 industrial photographs, involving the despatch of 300,000 prints and 50,000 printing blocks, are distributed abroad. The supply of a block often helps to obtain publication. If the COI decides to distribute a picture it requests either the required number of prints or the loan of the negative.

TV and Newsreels. More than 1000 industrial stories are included annually in regular COI TV and cinema newsreel services. A monthly film magazine is supplied for showing in cinemas in Africa, the Caribbean, South America, South-East Asia and Australasia. The London Television Service supplies short filmed items – including industrial stories – to TV stations throughout the world. There are also special series such as science and technology programmes, a weekly series covering events in Britain, and a programme specially produced for Africa. For all these programmes industrial stories are welcomed.

Exhibitions. The COI is responsible for the design, production and management of official exhibitions overseas including the preparation of British Pavilions at Expo's, and seeks information on new developments and products and the loan of models, especially working models, for inclusion in these events.

Films. This is one of the best examples of the COI's worldwide publicity service for exporters. Industrial films, provided they are free of advertising and are of international interest, can gain overseas showings through the COI film service. Foreign language versions are made, the films are catalogued, and they may be obtained through British Government Information and Commercial Officers throughout the world. In fact, it is a sensible idea when making such a film to discuss it at the treatment stage with the COI. The COI acquire the copyright for overseas TV purposes for many of these films make excellent TV material. Some 2000 British industrial films have received overseas distribution through the COI during the past 15 years.

10. *Translations*

This is a constant problem and if the press officer wants to see a practical example of how oddly some translations can read he should collect some of the horticultural literature mailed to this country by Dutch firms who sincerely believe they have correctly translated their Dutch into English. For example, instead of saying that a tulip is *short* they will say *low*. It is this difficulty in choosing the correct foreign counterparts of English technical jargon, and even current colloquialisms and slang, that make it essential to use only the best possible translators who have *current* knowledge of the language. The ideal is to use a national living in his or her country, but sometimes time is against this. When British-based translators are used it is necessary to first of all make sure that they are familiar with the subject matter. Overseas embassies and consulates in this country can often recommend good translators and advice can be obtained from the Foreign Languages Section of the COI.

Peculiarities of Overseas Media Relations

In Britain, the press officer is almost spoilt for choice in his opportunities to communicate nationally, regionally or locally through press, radio and TV. Britain enjoys a media situation that is not to be found anywhere eise in the world. In many large industrial countries the press tends to be regional with numerous press centres. The use of wire services may be more practical and common in countries like Germany whereas in Britain the Press Association is more interested in 'hard' news stories for distribution to regional dailies.

Large circulations do not always exist in other countries, journals are more dependent on advertisement revenue, and PR material may be regarded with suspicion. Lineage rates may be charged when releases are printed. Hosting is not uncommon, especially in France, when a charge will be made for printing an article written for the client by a member of the newspaper staff. In Belgian newspapers, appearing among the ordinary news items, are sometimes stories bearing a number in the bottom right-hand corner which indicates that it was paid for. Similarly, Spanish newspapers may add the word 'remitted' to a story from a PR source absolving the editor from responsibility! Dutch papers tend to give two to three times more space to PR stories than do the Belgian. Nevertheless, normal press relations activities do take place in most countries, and the general journalistic rule of 'interest and value to readers' does apply to the acceptance of PR material.

In some European countries public relations tends to have a more academic meaning than it does in Britain, having a sociological emphasis quite distinct from our use of the term. It is puzzling sometimes to find European colleges and Universities running courses in public relations when very little academic interest is taken in the subject in Britain, but they are not teaching the sort of thing to be found in the CAM syllabus. Consequently, the output of a press officer is often regarded in a somewhat derogatory fashion as 'company news' as if it were disguised advertising.

However, changes are taking place in the European acceptance of PR even if big countries like Germany are a long way behind Britain in accepting PR as a profession and having an Institute like the IPR. Organized PR is comparatively recent with both the British Institute of Public Relations and the Public Relations Society of America being founded in 1948. Quaint attitudes to public relations in other countries need to be understood in this historical light.

Collation of practices and international harmonization is going on through such organizations as CERP (Centre European de Ralaciones Publiques) and the IPRA (International Public Relations Association), both of which admit experienced PR practitioners as individual members.

Overseas public relations societies are listed in the IPR *Register of Members* and the *Hollis Press and Public Relations Annual* (11.5), but it should be remembered that in many countries these voluntary bodies are small with no offices or full-time secretariat. However, some of them initiate courses of instruction at technical colleges, have their own codes of practice and publish journals. The problem with all such Institutes, including the British, is that they rely on the subscriptions of a comparatively small number of individuals and this limits their activities and influence. Overseas PR consultants are also listed, country-by-country, in the *Hollis Press and Public Relations Annual.*

Readers interested in mounting PR exercises in Europe will find good advice in Philip Currah's book *Setting Up A European Public Relations Operation*, which is one of the series of books sponsored by the Institute of Public Relations and published by Business Books.

References

11.1 ALEXANDER, N. H., 'Writing for Export' *Public Relations*, IPR, Spring 1967
11.2 *Ibid*
11.3 EIBIS International Ltd., 3 Johnson's Court, Fleet Street, London EC4A 3EA
11.4 The Central Office of Information, Hercules Road, London SE1 7DU
11.5 *Hollis Press and Public Relations Annual*, Contact House, Lower Hampton Road, Sunbury-on-Thames, Middlesex TW6 5HG

CHAPTER TWELVE

Feedback, Research and Evaluating Results

Evaluation is the conclusion of objective planning. Either the objectives have been achieved, or they have not. There may be degrees of achievement or failure. An inquest may point to good or bad use of techniques, sufficient or insufficient effort and money. But essentially it is idle to expect results unless there were precise objectives in the first place. It is impossible for PR to work wonders if it is not decided at the outset what wonders it should perform.

In Chapter Four fifteen typical PR objectives were suggested. Now the question is, did the deliberate, planned and sustained PR effort succeed in achieving these results? In what ways can this achievement – or failure – be measured? This is not necessarily a pounds and pence, dollars and cents, assessment, although job satisfaction and staff stability can be measured in terms of training costs, better workmanship, and fewer rejects and customer complaints. Many evaluations will be qualitative rather than quantitative, and sometimes negative rather than positive.

How can success or failure be assessed in these cases? The following is a check list of the main methods of recording results of PR activity. Results can be checked on an *ad hoc*, continuous or end-of-campaign basis. When regular meetings are held to consider the progress of the campaign it is of course possible to have a continuous assessment. A number of periodic studies can be made to measure the trend or change brought about by PR activity but businessmen are apt to be sceptical about the feasibility of such evaluations.

Market Research Techniques

1. *Opinion, attitude or shift research.* Questionnaires seeking *Yes, No,*

Don't Know answers are designed and selected categories of people are interviewed. Thus, if the PR assignment is to correct a misunderstanding about a corporate image an opinion survey could be conducted initially to establish a base position. Further surveys can then be conducted at, say, three or six monthly intervals, to record the shift of opinion or extent of understanding. These results can be shown in percentages and graphically. It could then be reckoned that an expenditure of so much had resulted in an improvement of so much percent. Was this worth the expenditure or not – would a higher expenditure have produced a better result – was too much, too little or the right amount spent on the exercise? Such shifts of opinion could be critical if the company had plans for expansion, take-over, staff recruitment, fund raising or needed political support, local, national or international, in order to further its aims.

2. *Postal Questionnaires* can also be used to measure either opinions or preferences where specific publics are known, and can be used to discover what readers think of a house magazine, or to assess dealer attitudes. There is, unfortunately, the weakness and the inherent bias in a small return from those originally contacted. It is, however, a very inexpensive form of research and can be profitable when the recipients are interested in co-operating.

3. *Discussion Groups* are a mild form of motivational research since open-ended questions from the chairman can produce spontaneous responses that might not be provoked by a structured interview with a fixed questionnaire. This method could be very revealing concerning the current image.

4. *Piggy backing* has become a very economical way of conducting short-term studies, using existing omnibus consumer surveys. There are research firms which carry out regular consumer surveys, the questionnaire being made up of sets of questions from a number of subscribers. Thus, a subscriber might insert a number of questions for a number of months. He does not have to pay for the total survey operation, only for his portion of it.

5. *Telephone questionnaires* or interviews are also possible. This type of research is useful when the respondents are scattered and difficult or expensive to visit, or when specific people need to be contacted at their place of work.

6. *Desk research* consists of studying existing data such as reports published by government departments, trade associations and research units, or statistics which exist within the organization such as production, stock, sales and employment figures. It can also take in the monitoring of comment and coverage in the press and on radio and

TV. This coverage can be monitored in the following ways, and it will be noted that evaluation is *not* made on an advertisement rate card basis:

(a) Total number of inches or centimetres. This is a mathematical volume count which fails to take into consideration the value of the publications from which the press cuttings have been clipped.

(b) Names of publications. This can be related to the volume of coverage, revealing the kind and extent of press interest, including note of the publications which have not printed stories and need attention.

(c) In addition to the totting up of inches or centimetres it is possible to make an interesting calculation of the circulation and readership figures based on those issued by the Audit Bureau of Circulations (ABC) and the Joint Industry Committee for National Readership Surveys (JICNARS). These figures are more impressive and realistic than rate-card evaluations, showing how many people bought or read the publications from which the cuttings were extracted. This, again, can be broken down into social grades for the British press represents the class divisions of A, B, C1, C2, D and E classifications, nowadays based on occupation and not income.

(d) Coverage gained by competitors may be a valuable intelligence service, gained by asking a press cutting agency to supply such cuttings. This can also reveal whether competitors are receiving better or poorer attention, or making a larger or smaller PR effort. This could require a review of expenditure and tactics in order to beat the competition.

(e) Evaluation of improvement in editorial knowledge and understanding, or awareness of sources of information. This can be seen from the pieces written about the organization as distinct from the publication of issued stories and is perhaps where the supply of background information, meetings with VIP personnel, and facility visits can be seen to have paid off in more understanding and better informed comments. The ITT corporate image campaign described in Part Four could be evaluated like this, and some newspapers like the *Financial Times* published articles showing their new appreciation of the facts.

(f) Extent to which pictures have been published. Such a check can be very important because pictures are expensive and easily wasted when issued too liberally. Was the expenditure justified, should pictures be limited to certain publications, or would it be better to state on news releases that pictures are available?

(g) Monitored scripts. Broadcast material can also be recorded,

scripts being obtained from firms who monitor radio and TV programmes to order. Tape recordings can be made of both sound and
vision, provided copyright restrictions are observed concerning
commercial usage, tape-recorders or VCR's being used for evaluation
purposes.

Assessing Results of PR as a Corporate Activity

In addition more specific information may be required about the effect
of PR activity on certain publics. Thus, if PR is conducted in the
interests of the entire organization we can probe deeper and assess the
following:

1. The extent to which the community understands and
   respects our organization.
2. The willingness with which potential staff respond to our
   recruitment efforts and the demand for employment.
3. The degree of permanence of the staff.
4. How well the staff understand the organization.
5. The standard of personal relations among the staff and between staff and management.
6. The degree of sympathetic understanding which exists between suppliers of services, raw materials, packaging materials, and other goods and the organization.
7. The interest shown in the company's financial affairs by the
   various investment publics.
8. The accuracy and extent of knowledge about the organization which is possessed by opinion leaders.
9. The attitudes expressed by distributors such as wholesalers,
   mail-order traders, retailers, agents, exports, and importers.
10. The reputation of the organization, its goods and services in
    the minds of various categories of consumer.

The above list is a very broad one which can be adapted, condensed
or expanded to suit the needs of different organizations, but it will
serve to provide a simplified example of how results can be assessed in
a realistic manner. Let us look more closely at each one in turn and
consider how these assessments may be made.

1. *Community Relations*

There may be special reasons why it is important that the people in the
vicinity of the organization have a clear understanding of what it is,

does, aims to do and why it is an asset to the locality as, for instance, an employer, producer, innovator or exporter. This will depend on how far PR techniques have been put to work to gain credit for achievement. The winning of a Queen's Award for Industry should be known as widely as possible in a community – so widely that the town will regard the award as its *own* achievement.

The measure of successful community relations will be indicated by the regard which people have for an organization, that is, regard based on their knowledge and understanding. Ask any fifty people in the street and their answers will soon reveal the truth of the matter. The organization which cares about its reputation usually becomes one with a reputation worth caring about – like Cadbury's, Marks and Spencer, Rolls-Royce or Harrods. All the advertising in the world would have been useless if the fame of those names had not been earned by quality of product or service. And in its own locality an organization should have a reputation second to none for PR should begin on the doorstep, and the organization which bothers about local relations is more likely to be concerned about its good relations with every other public.

Here are some ways in which the affect of community relations can be measured:

1. The number of requests for party visits.
2. The number of invitations which the company or its directors and executives receive to take part in local affairs.
3. How frequently the organization is invited to donate important prizes such as sports trophies.
4. The interest expressed by schools and colleges.
5. Whether the organization is regularly included in guidebooks, directories, articles, and other publications describing the town.
6. Whether public services such as the police, hospitals, fire brigade, water board, gas and electricity boards, and local authority departments are well informed about the needs and activities of the organization so that when called upon for assistance they are properly sympathetic.

PR is systematic communication and it has to do with every aspect of an organization's activities whether they are directly related to profitability or not. Local problems arising from noise, smell, dirt, smoke, effluent, traffic, and highway hazards, all require good communication if public understanding, tolerance, and acceptance is to be achieved. A responsible company does not make a profit at the expense and inconvenience of the community. It does have social obligations.

Good community relations should never be underestimated. Visitors to an organization so often judge by first impressions, and a lot may depend on how policemen, taxi-drivers, bus conductors, and local residents may regard the organization and have a sound knowledge of it. Bad impressions have a habit of sticking, and yet they need never exist if an organization cares about its public relations.

Here we see a prime example of public relations, bearing out the adage that *PR is what other people think about us*. In a community it is very difficult to foster false impressions, but all too easy to encourage hostile ones simply by default. When people don't know they fill the gaps in their knowledge with fancies fed on prejudices.

Some firms go so far as to take a column of advertisement space in the local newspaper and use it as a regular newsletter or house magazine. This is less expensive than running and distributing an actual company journal and carries the company message far and wide among the community. In this column the PRO can present news about the firm's activities, and the bulletin will come to be accepted as a regular contact with the organization. But it must contain only legitimate editorial material presented in newspaper style, and must certainly not become either advertising or propaganda.

Whatever the PR techniques employed, if a conscious effort is made to achieve mutual understanding within the community results should be noticeable and even measurable. Community relations are far from being intangible when an organization is known, understood, respected, trusted, and liked by the people who have to tolerate its presence, service its needs, and accept it as a good or bad neighbour.

2. Recruitment

PR efforts in this direction can be judged by whether the demand for jobs tends to exceed the supply. This is, of course, best judged in a period of labour shortage. If the organization has a bad reputation as an employer it becomes a PR task to investigate and make proposals for eradicating the causes of disrepute.

What sort of response is there to Situations Vacant ads?

Does the Labour Exchange supply the best and the right candidates for interview? Does it clearly understand what kind of staff are required?

Are the trade unions co-operative in finding new recruits?

Do existing staff introduce friends and relatives as potential staff?

Is there a waiting list for jobs?

Do university and school employment advisers recommend the organization?

Is there an increasing demand for information about employment prospects with the organization?

Do schools and youth clubs invite the organization to supply speakers on career prospects?

What is the demand for the recruitment film, if one exists?

From this short list it is apparent that PR has a major part to play in staff recruitment, and its results should be extremely simple to measure.

3. *Permanence of Staff*

This quality of employment is dependent on the success of both community and staff relations, and so it is closely linked to the foregoing two sections and the succeeding one regarding appreciation of policy. In an organization where staff relations are excellent and when unemployment is not great, a good deal of recruitment results from staff recommendations to and of friends, which marks the success of PR influence upon staff relations. This is also important in the case of career prospects and the advice made by career advisers, or the choice made by graduates seeking trainee opportunities.

The permanence of staff is desirable when the benefits of expenditure on training cannot be enjoyed until an employee has been fully operative for some time. Some staff are bound to be transitory and some trades require wide experience gained by changing jobs, but the overall stability of the staff records satisfaction and this is indeed a measure of good staff relations. There are forms of specialized employment such as the railways where there is no alternative employer of the same skill, and here it is tremendously important to establish good staff relations despite problems of automation and redundancy. The results are all too easy to assess. Sometimes the PR techniques are lacking to such a degree that the assessment is a revelation of mismanagement: PR does work both ways.

4. *Personal Relations*

Another test of good internal relationships is the way in which staff join together to run voluntary enterprises such as netball, cricket and football teams; photographic, dramatic or musical societies; flower shows, sports days and outings; charitable activities on behalf of old people's homes or Oxfam; or discount facilities for gardeners, motorists or hobbyists.

These enterprises usually call for managerial aid from time to time, but not managerial interference. Some firms do provide theatres, meeting rooms, recreation rooms, sports grounds, and often quite lavish facilities, but particularly valuable from a PR point of view are the truly uninspired or unsponsored activities which denote a friendly staff wishing to extend personal associations among themselves.

The author can quote the examples of two almost identical rival companies: One had many such societies and was notable for its permanency of staff: the other had no staff societies, relied on the lure of high rates of pay for executives, but failed to keep its staff. Eventually, the second company – which had reckoned itself to be the market leader – was taken over by the first and was virtually dismantled by management consultants.

In a sense, many of these staff society activities can be reckoned as fringe benefits which materially and psychologically add to the normal pay packet. Management which discreetly encourages the formation of societies, and maybe finances facilities on a 50–50 basis (never 100 per cent), is very sensible of its internal PR functions.

The result of such a policy can be measured by counting the number of employees who take part, and also by the solvency of the enterprises. The author knows of one company where a measure of the excellence of its staff relations is the fact that staff socials and dances have produced surplus funds sufficient to provide television sets for numerous old people's homes. There is a waiting list of potential staff at this factory, which is yet another indication of the excellence of the staff relations.

5. *Staff Appreciation of Policy*

This can be a difficult area for PR, the more so if many of the staff are perhaps unskilled and therefore less involved in or committed to their work so that they might do a similarly unskilled job in the factory next door if attracted there by better pay or conditions. Or, again, there may be numbers of fairly junior clerical and secretarial staff who are mainly interested in their own affairs and the size of their pay packet or cheque. It is therefore all the more important that management should communicate with its staff.

In these circumstances, internal communication can be infectious, creating curiosity, interest, sympathy, and enthusiasm, all of which can improve the chain of control and make management far more efficient than is possible when an ignorant staff works in an atmosphere of indifference beyond their personal affairs. Many a strike has occurred through sheer boredom.

PR should be welcomed by trade union leaders because a well-informed staff is likely to be more productive and more capable of substantiating trade union claims. Good industrial relations are derived from employers and employees being satisfied with their rewards. Outside Britain much has been achieved by participation through works councils.

Therefore to some extent, a staff which knows what it is doing and why, and equally what management is doing and why, is more likely to increase its productivity – and thereby its earning power – so that the effect of PR techniques can be measured in terms of decreased absenteeism, higher earnings, increased production and more profitable sales. It could even go so far as to help ease restrictive practices if workers became genuinely convinced that such practices restricted their earning power. The British trade unionist is organized to better his lot, and his best chance of doing this is when he can trust the management to be efficient and successful in the realms of research and development, production planning, staff training and recruitment, finance, and above all, marketing. There is a distinct division of labour between the doers and the planners. Nowadays in industry there can be no such thing as an aristocracy of management, but neither is syndicalism feasible, whereas good communication and frank staff relations can produce a successful partnership which is free of contemptuous discipline from management and surly reluctance from employees. Industrial relations are primary PR.

This is not intended to be a political dissertation but an attempt to demonstrate why, in the latter part of the 20th century, PR has, as never before, a superb opportunity to contribute to productivity and to the nation's economic rebound from its economic disappointments.

Significantly, some of the companies with the most admirable staff relations (e.g. Marks and Spencer) have an open-handed promotion system whereby every employee is made aware of the opportunities if he or she cares to take them. This method encourages the person of initiative to gain promotion and puts paid to putting mediocre time-serving people in higher positions irrespective of merit, which is totally discouraging to those with greater ability and qualifications. A PR-conscious management places the onus of promotion upon the shoulders of the individual while at the same time providing equality of opportunity to be prepared for promotion. All this requires first-class communication, using trade union channels whenever possible.

To achieve these basically economic results a special staff relations campaign needs to be devised to suit the industry, and this should be freely conducted with the full participation of the personnel department, the training officer, and the shop stewards, right from the start.

House magazines, wall newspapers, and standardized notice boards are essential but should not be regarded as the only means of communication. All new employees should certainly receive a booklet describing the company, its history, products or services, departmental structure, and personnel. The people who run the organization should be known through house journals, films, photographs and personal visits, tours, and functions, ranging from business meetings to social occasions.

Sometimes, what is also needed is activity which stimulates and instils pride, such as visits by film and television producers and camera-crews; press visits; tours by overseas trade commissions; or participation by a works team in a quiz programme on TV. Staff like to feel recognized by the outside world.

Some space has been devoted to this topic for four reasons:

1. The idealistic view of PR as a means of creating a cosy family relationship in industry is unrealistic and merely blurs the edges of capitalism. Management and workers will never be blood brothers but the masters and men relationship can be converted into a practical partnership of abilities and talents, provided there is proper two-way communications and real opportunities for participation.

2. In far too many organizations no staff relation techniques are employed *at all* such as Fleet Street.

3. PR is one of the most practical aids to productivity.

4. Staff relations provide PR practitioners with a vast, largely unexplored sector for greater endeavour. This will depend on whether management becomes sufficiently adult in its thinking to acknowledge that PR is both initially and ultimately a management function and that its contribution to marketing is but a third of PR's allocation of activity.

Finally, and the results here are easy to assess, internal PR should make the house journal democratic to the extent that it provides a platform for staff problems, opinions, and ideas. The staff must have the means of communicating with one another and with management, but only management can meet the cost of this including the provision of a professional industrial editor acceptable to the staff and completely free of managerial control. Most managements would find this a revolutionary concept of staff journal editorship, but how magnificently they would become aware of uninhibited staff attitudes, wishes, and possibly doubts and fears as in the case of redundancy threats. The company PRO could provide material on a normal contributor basis.

6. Supplier Relations

Here is an area of PR activity that is universally neglected. Yet PR techniques can be valuable to production managers, store-keepers, stationary and print buyers, purchasing officers, and others dependent upon the goodwill of suppliers. For it can often be a matter of clear understanding, sympathy, and goodwill which results in the right goods being supplied in perfect condition at the proper time.

This happy situation can be brought about as a result of mutual factory visits, receptions and functions for suppliers, reciprocal publicity, house magazines or films made with joint facilities. It all boils down to taking suppliers into one's confidence, showing them how their products or services are used, and encouraging them to feel proud of their contribution. And it doesn't matter whether the supplier is a public utility or the manufacturer of specified materials or components.

The results of supplier relations PR can be assessed by the efficiency and reliability of the supplier, by his anxiety to please and by his appreciation of what is required of him. Again, it is a matter of communication, and the PRO – by means of house journal or some other medium – can supplement the instructions of the purchasing officer.

The PRO can do much to win the confidence and support of suppliers by naming suppliers whenever possible in news releases, feature articles, film credits, and on exhibition stands. These hospitable and generous mentions can be much more than due acknowledgements, and they will be repaid in assessable dividends such as prompt deliveries and perhaps even price concessions when these are possible.

7. Financial Relations

Today, financial relations extend beyond the Stock Exchange and the City page. Insurance companies, banks and unit trusts, pension fund chiefs, accountants, and company directors, are all big sections of the investment market. The articles and features by City editors have become comparatively popular reading, and these journalists are often invited to appear on TV to state expert opinions on economic trends. Despite socialist governments there has never been such widespread interest in capitalism nor so many ardent capitalists! The investment public includes every child with a piggy bank, and if that is a mild exaggeration at least everyone with a premium bond or a building society account.

The assessment of successful financial PR may take the following forms:

1. Coverage in the financial press including City pages of general newspapers.
2. Shareholder response to: (a) press coverage (b) stock market flotations (c) annual reports, including summaries in press ad form.
3. Press treatment of take-over bids.
4. Extent to which press (and other commentators) are knowledgeable about the company when writing about or discussing its financial affairs.
5. Extent to which the various investment publics are knowledgeable about the company's results, policies, products, services, board of directors, and place in the economy.

This last point is of greater importance than those solely concerned with PR as a marketing aid are sometimes willing to admit.

8. *Understanding of Opinion Leaders*

Opinion leaders can vary from the opinionated performers on TV to the consultants, advisers, teachers, lecturers, authors, and others who are paid for their expert knowledge. In between we have various people who are called upon to express opinions and these can include Members of Parliament, town councillors, ministers of religion, and others whose status implies ability to make judgements and pontificate on the basis of often very slight and imperfect knowledge.

Consequently, this is a wide-open, open-ended territory requiring endless and painstaking PR activity to present facts where and when most needed.

Success can be judged by the accuracy of information dispensed by the opinion leaders relative to our organization. Much depends here on the volume of PR material distributed and the funds available for PR work. Again, it is a form of PR activity frequently neglected by those who limit PR to promotional activities, but it is that most seriously conducted by those presenting facts about causes and countries.

As a supreme example of the lack of knowledge, and the lack of funds to improve that knowledge, we have only to point to the ignorance and prejudice concerning PR itself. The IPR does not have sufficient funds to perform the required but gigantic task of establishing an accurate image of PR in the minds of opinion leaders of every kind.

Measuring the effectiveness of PR activity in the field of opinion leaders depends on whether the opinion leaders are primarily entertainers or primarily authorities. It may not matter very much about trying to correct the misleading opinions of those who make a business of manufacturing them for the amusement of gullible readers and viewers who have no means of challenging or verifying what they are told. We are all the victims of the media merchants. But it does matter if they are serious, responsible people whose views are valued. Sometimes employers, clients and even PRO's are too sensitive to the ephemeral comments of unimportant critics.

9. *Distributor Attitudes*

It is easy to measure a shift in the attitude of dealers who baulk sales by their indifference, outright scepticism or hostility. The case of Magicote paint is worth mentioning. Paint dealers are usually very practical people whose advice is important to customers, and when at the time of its introduction they had no confidence in Magicote they were a hindrance to sales. But PR convinced them about the product, and sales shot up so fast that rival manufacturers had to introduce non-drip paints.

The attitudes of wholesalers, mail-order traders, retailers, agents, exporters, and importers are vital to effective distribution, and the results of PR can be measured by the following:

(a) The reception given to the company's sales representatives, which should feed itself back through their individual reports.

(b) The tone of correspondence from distributors.

(c) 'Shares of the market' figures in dealer audit survey reports.

(d) Response to advertising, merchandising schemes. (PR should help to make distributors more responsive since they are better informed about the advertiser, his product and his promotion schemes.)

(e) Response to invitations to visit the factory, or attend dealer conferences perhaps on a regional basis.

(f) The preference traders give to displaying the company's goods in shops, literature, advertisements since this indicates the traders' desire to associate themselves with the manufacturer's good name.

(g) The willingness of distributors to communicate their own wishes and ideas to the company, indicating their interest and desire for involvement.

(h) Response to the dealer magazine (if there is one), and willingness to contribute to it, or to enter window dressing and other competitions.

(i) The demand for dealer aids ranging from display material to stock blocks for insertion in dealer advertising.

(j) The willingness to be included in promotional schemes which list the names and addresses of traders.

(k) The response to invitations to dealers to visit the company's stand at exhibitions.

Because PR can be so helpful in dealer relations this list can be a very long one, and it would seem that this is a section of PR activity which can scarcely fail to be successful if the organization is recognized by distributors as seriously helping them to earn a living. And it does not matter whether the distributor is a sole agent or a trader with a very small sale for the product: what matters is that he is proud to stock the goods and acts accordingly.

10. Consumer Relations

This final group is capable of being sub-divided into many specialist groups, and ultimately the success of PR as a marketing aid will be measured by sales. But sales alone are not the only criterion: it can be important to a cigarette firm that it is well regarded even by non-smokers. Non-smokers can be shareholders, employers, distributors or local townspeople in the factory town, and they may well be reached by the PR efforts aimed chiefly at smokers.

On the whole, consumer relations can be measured by the volume of goodwill, and opinion surveys conducted in the field are one of the most convincing ways of registering what people really think about the organization, product or service.

It may be required to know what *sort* of reputation is held, and this could be a vital aid to marketing. Motivation research, if funds permitted, could indicate the most likely reasons why people have their particular likes or dislikes, and these motives may be quite foreign to the ones accepted by the organization. Thus, the reputation of a company may depend on something which PR techniques could establish still further if the motivations behind the goodwill were properly understood.

Assessment of reputation is therefore an intriguing study, and one rather better related to PR as a professional practice than the counting up and evaluating of column inches or centimetres.

What people think and believe about an organization, and why they hold such views is surely the essence of consumer relations.

Nevertheless, the marketing man, if he is to make use of PR throughout his chain of activities from product concept to after-sales service will be more interested in the external aspects of PR, the ones which affect distribution and final purchase. It is difficult to put a monetary assessment on the wisdom of introducing a striking livery for the company's fleet of vehicles, or of using an ingeniously designed company symbol. The significance can seldom be isolated and has to be related to the total marketing success. But without any doubt at all it can be seen in those growth companies which have never neglected PR.

A major result of successful PR activity should be that sales resistance has been lessened by the knowledge and understanding achieved by PR so that advertising (and salesmanship) can operate more effectively. It is the job of PR to familiarize people with the facts. Therefore, it is a measure of the success of PR that people are well informed about advertisers and advertisers' products and services, and being well informed react to advertisements without suspicion, hostility, ignorance, apathy or any other cause of unwarranted sales resistance.

Returning once again to Chapter Four and the Six-Point PR Planning Model, in discussing the means of evaluating results a great many more possible results have been suggested here as promised at the end of the examples of fifteen typical PR objectives. This expanded range of results may, of course, be subject to the constraints of money, time and other resources also mentioned in Chapter Four. These two chapters are therefore complementary since objectives must be forecast results.

Part Two
Media of Communication

CHAPTER THIRTEEN

Media Analysis and Planning

PR media have to be considered very differently from media for advertising purposes. Let us now analyse the classes of media and evaluate them for different PR programmes:

1. Press	7. Books
2. Audio visuals	8. Direct mail
3. Radio	9. The spoken word
4. Television	10. Sponsorship
5. Exhibitions	11. House journals
6. Literature	12. Other PR media

In the following sections we will investigate this array of media of communication which will show the versatility of possible PR activity. When planning a PR programme each medium deserves individual consideration, and although it is unlikely that in any one campaign the whole range will be used it is likely that an imaginative PR programme will contain a greater variety of media than would be economic in an advertising campaign.

Advertising

Although we have differentiated between PR and advertising, we can also buy space, time or rent sites for PR purposes.

There is, for example, that class of advertising known as corporate, prestige, institutional advertising. The objects of these advertisements is to tell the story of an organization and so establish its reputation. ICI, Tate and Lyle and ITT have used institutional advertising. Such advertisements usually appear in the more serious newspapers. They are usually designed in a dignified style, although this could not be said of the ITT corporate identity campaign begun in 1974, and the copy has a more literary character than is usual in promotional advertisements. The PR effect of these advertisements is hard to judge, although in some cases the object is to establish the company's reputation in the minds of future staff, graduates especially.

It would be mistaken, however, to include in this category those advertisements issued by industries and governments such as steel in its fight against nationalization, or the advertisements inserted by the South African government, which are purely propaganda. If advertising is used for PR purposes it should advocate nothing, merely state facts. The ITT ads were excellent in their factual presentation.

A valid use of advertisement space or time could be when the message is an urgent one and there is not time to wait upon the vagaries of editors who may print the story too late. Yet another issue is when a firm takes a column in a local newspaper and uses it as a house magazine addressed to the community.

Again, normal use of advertising may, of course, be used to announce a PR event such as a public meeting, film show, exhibition, demonstration, sports meeting or any other sponsored event to which it is desired to attract an attendance. This is really no different from any other kind of advertising except that the product is a PR event.

The Press

Britain has a highly centralized national press based in London which is unique among the major countries of the world but reflects the compact nature of a heavily populated industrialized country with good physical communications. Most other countries – especially the USA – have a multiplicity of magazine publishing centres and no national newspapers. In the UK a strong national press also exists in Scotland, and to a lesser extent in Wales and Northern Ireland. There is also a very strong provincial press comprised of Sunday, morning, weekly and bi-weekly newspapers together with a flourishing array of local magazines of many different kinds. The London evening papers are sometimes mistakenly believed to be national, but within 40 or 50 miles of London they begin to compete with provincial evening papers, with new ones emerging in recent years in the home counties. Britain therefore has a highly diversified newspaper world.

It is versatility that makes the press the primary medium for PR programmes even though it is threatened by the rivalry of electronic media and such devices as the BBC's CEEFAX and the IBA's ORACLE systems of televising the written word, not to mention the future prospect of TV sets being able to receive news and print newspapers in the home. But for the moment, and taking the world as a whole which includes countries that have yet to introduce TV, the press is unlikely to vanish or even lose its primary position for a few decades. It is even possible that radio may prove more of a menace to the press than TV, British independent local radio having large audiences among people who can accept radio news when they can neither read newspapers nor watch TV, e.g. housewives working about the house, factory and other workers, and motorists.

It is often difficult for the non-British-born to believe that *The Times* is not the most popular and successful paper in Britain and to appreciate that it has a tiny circulation and operates at a financial loss, being subsidized out of the profits of the Thomson Organization. The phenomenon of the *Sun*'s rise from under one million to about four millions is perhaps a good indication of the literary accomplishment of the British common reader, his small interest in hard news and his disregard for politics and world affairs. It may be that readers of the popular press have a surfeit of news on TV. The parochialness of newspaper readers is commonplace throughout the world, and when in another country it is easy to lose touch with what is happening in one's own.

The modern content of newspapers is to the advantage of the PRO, and a very large part of that content is PR derived. People want to read news about things that are important to *them* such as their cars and gardens. A readership survey of the *Financial Times* showed that the most popular feature was the front page news digest, and that the arts page was extremely popular. It has become such an interesting newspaper that its financial tradition has become a disadvantage and thought has been given to changing its title.

The following are the social grades used on the national readership survey undertaken by JICNARS:

Grade A (3%) Upper middle class
Grade B (12%) Middle class
Grade C1 (22%) Lower middle class ('white collar' and 'white blouse' workers)
Grade C2 (32%) Skilled working class ('blue collar' workers)
Grade D (23%) Semi-skilled and unskilled working class
Grade E (9%) Those at the lowest levels of subsistence (pensioners, widows, etc.)

Although most newspapers are read by more than one grade, a

rough breakdown of the class circulation of British national newspapers is something like this:

Upper middle class:	*The Times, Financial Times, Sunday Times*
Liberal-intellectual-teacher:	*The Guardian, The Observer*
Middle class:	*Daily Telegraph, Sunday Telegraph*
Lower middle class:	*Daily Express, Daily Mail, Sunday Express*
Working class:	*Daily Mirror, The Sun, Sunday People, News of the World, Sunday Mirror*

The largest circulations are among the newspapers read by the working class, and this corresponds to the peak viewing audience figures for TV. It will be seen from the percentage figures against the social grades that the C1, C2 and D grades form 77 per cent of the whole, this being the mass market reached by the mass media.

To give some idea of the number and variety of British publications in addition to the national papers mentioned above, and the two London evenings, there are (according to *Benn's Press Directory*):

Provincial UK mornings	22
,, ,, evenings	79
,, ,, Sundays	6
Greater London weeklies	155
Other UK weeklies	1003
UK periodicals various	4000
Directories, yearbooks	1074

With more than 6000 newspapers and magazines (not counting free sheets, free magazines and house journals) the British press represents a huge and varied outlet for PR information. A more careful breakdown of the UK press can now be made as follows:

National mornings
London evenings
National Sundays
National consumer and specialized interest magazines
National trade, technical and professional magazines
Directories, yearbooks, diaries, etc.
Regional mornings
Regional evenings

Regional Sundays
Town, suburban and regional weeklies
Regional magazines such as county, local interest and Chamber
   of Trade and Commerce journals
Local directories, guide books, maps
Free sheet weeklies
Free magazines

The British press is divisible into the following categories:

Newspapers

Outside London there are more than 100 daily newspapers, most of which have special correspondents and special interest features which will welcome material of interest and value to their readers. They are well worth cultivating and to some degree they correspond to the daily newspapers found in large cities abroad where only these and no nationals exist. Britain is unique in having both types of daily, although the further one gets away from London the more influential becomes the local daily and vice versa.

The future of the London dailies depends on the extent to which the publishers are able to introduce more economic production, installing web-offset-litho printing machines, photo-typesetting and computerized print shops which would of course mean using a quarter of the staff. Many provincial newspapers have been using these more economic methods for many years to the advantage of sister-nationals which they have subsidized. In South Africa full colour newspapers were enjoyed years before they had TV, thanks to web-offset-litho printing. In the early 1970's irregular publication of ill-printed, late-delivered national dailies was a headache for the PRO who worked hard to produce stories that failed to appear. It was in these circumstances that independent local radio, with the special services of firms like Univeral News Services, began to seriously compete with the national press.

A comparison of the number of stages involved in letterpress printing compared with web-offset-litho is made in Figure 13.1.

The *free sheet* newspaper has existed for as long as it has been possible to finance a newspaper solely from advertising revenue. Free sheets have usually been locally distributed and hand-delivered to every house in the distribution area. Although editorial space is limited and there are many classified advertisements, some free sheets run domestic advice features and welcome PR material.

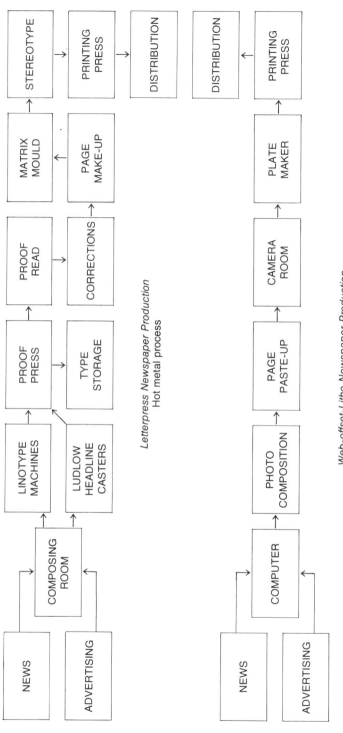

Fig. 13.1   Letterpress and Web-offset-Litho printing stages compared

Letterpress Newspaper Production
Hot metal process

Web-offset-Litho Newspaper Production
Photographic process

Another form of free sheet which has been given an impetus by the reorganizing of Britain's local authorities is the civic newspaper. This came about largely because the local press was failing to adequately report local government affairs.

The *alternative* or *community* newspaper has become an interesting development of the 70's with some one hundred of these radical papers being either sold or distributed door-to-door. Income is seldom derived from advertising and comes from sales, donations or in some cases from local authority grants. The alternative newspaper is a kind of ground-roots consumerist paper, sometimes the class counterpart of the ratepayer's association magazine, with a circulation area no larger than a housing estate. It should not be ignored in community relations campaigns.

Magazines

It is in this publishing sphere that Britain has a diversity of titles second only to the USA, and they range from popular weeklies to technical journals which are read all over the world. In many overseas countries the British and American press are the only journals available on their particular subjects since it would not be an economic proposition to publish such specialist journals in that country. Conversely, some subjects are so specialized that they are an economic proposition in Britain only provided there is a substantial overseas circulation. There is, therefore, an English language magazine covering almost every subject one can think of.

Magazines can be divided into certain broad categories and a useful indication of them can be found in directories such as *Advertiser's Annual*, *British Rate and Data*, and *Benn's Press Directory*. The following sections contain only a selection of the main categories.

Women's Magazines. These extend from multi-million circulation weeklies such as *Woman* and *Woman's Own* to more specialized women's journals dealing with childcare, dressmaking, home interests or certain age groups. There are women's magazines catering for readers as different as factory girls and the wives of tycoons, and their contents will range from romantic strip cartoons to room-by-room descriptions of stately homes. In the middle are the cheaply produced colour gravure weeklies with their regular output of knitting patterns, recipes, romantic serials, make-up advice, and coloured advertisements appealing to the mass women's market. They may, however, suffer from the competition of colour TV advertisements just as the popular daily newspapers suffered from black and white commercial TV.

Children's Magazines. In this group we find few titles of long standing and this ever-changing readership obviously demands new fashions in reading matter.

Specialized Magazines. It would be invidious to analyse all the specialized interest groups, but most interests and hobbies have their own journals to mention only gardening, motoring, philately, politics, religion and sports. Sometimes these publications are described as 'class' magazines. They can generally be bought from retail newsagents.

Trade, Technical and Professional. These three are often lumped together perhaps because they are not usually sold over the counter – unless specially ordered – and may be distributed on a postal subscription, or mailed free of charge to 'request' readers under what is known as 'controlled circulation'. These magazines may have bigger circulations than purchased ones, and since they are thus able to attract more advertising they can afford to be bigger magazines. Their format is often different from traditional journals with advertisements and editorial side by side, often accommodated on broad pages, and resembling catalogues of new products, materials and services to prospective buyers.

There are some magazines which cover all three fields, but generally speaking a trade magazine covers the distribution of goods, the technical magazine appeals to technicians, while the professional journal is typified by the legal and medical press. Subtle distinctions should be noted carefully. In compiling mailing lists it is easy to be misled by the similarity of titles and important to select those which are relevant to the story. A good PRO knows his media intimately.

One of the great problems about media selection in the sphere of trade, technical and professional journals is how to select the right ones for the mailing list for a particular story. It is rare indeed that stories can be mailed to standard lists: most stories require a tailor-made list to suit the content of the story.

Local Magazines. In recent years there has been a growth of county and glossy magazines. These can be general interest magazines dealing with local history, etc., glossy journals covering local social life, industrial journals, agricultural or Chamber of Trade and Commerce journals.

In addition to the publications themselves there are groups of journalists who specialize in certain subjects. There are also home page editors, and the specialist correspondents. These journalists are sometimes editors of specialist magazines as well as being columnists in newspapers. Sometimes they write in a great many different newspapers and magazines, also broadcasting and appearing on TV. Allied to these are the freelance writers who again generally keep to particular subjects.

House Journals. In this category we have internal and external private magazines. They sometimes accept outside contributions, the larger ones sell advertising space, and while the majority are issued free of charge, some are sold. Most house journal editors are members of the British Association of Industrial Editors which holds an annual contest and presents awards to encourage high standards of editing and production. More than 600 house journals are listed in *Benn's Press Directory*.

House journals or private magazines are another PR medium and are dealt with separately later on in this chapter.

There is also an untidy group of general interest magazines which suit no other heading.

Year Books, Annuals

These reference books divide into two kinds, those which merely list members or provide a directory of names and addresses, and those which contain informative articles and technical recommendations such as standard specifications.

Audio Visuals – Films, Slides, Video Cassettes and Discs

While the press may remain the primary *news* medium, audio visuals possess versatility, flexibility and controllability plus splendid value for money. With such attributes that lend themselves so well to *planned* PR exercises, audio visuals must surely rank as the most important of all communication media. A hindrance to the individual though, is its cost and size for portability. Audio visuals such as films, slides, videotapes and video discs together with house journals are excellent media for reaching specific publics, often fairly intimately in small localized groups. Moreover, whereas the mass media provide hit-or-miss coverage, audio visuals can usually be directed at influential innovators and adopters of PR messages.

Documentary, Sponsored and Industrial Films

Under this heading are included private non-advertising films. Because they will succeed best if they are entertaining, informative and educational rather than persuasive, it is wise to avoid blatant company or product name displays. A good many otherwise excellent films have been destroyed as PR media because there has been too little PR direction and too much dominance and interference by management, marketing, sales and advertising people. Commercial references should be ones that fit naturally. Usually, the content of the film and the occasion of its showing will identify the sponsor without need for close-ups of packages, factory signs or vehicles bearing the company name and livery.

Reliance should be placed on the special characteristics of the film rather than on its opportunity to put over some extra advertising. It is one of the most pleasant forms of communication, entertaining and generally viewed in pleasant circumstances. It has movement, sound and colour and the PR message can be conveyed realistically. The audience is captive for perhaps twenty or thirty minutes so that this form of PR message has greater memorability than most others.

The first thing to decide is the *potential audience* for the particular *message* that is to be communicated through this medium. This can be turned round to fit our Six-Point Planning Model.

A cost benefit basis of comparison with other media should be carried out to ensure the right medium is chosen. Another advantage of the film is that it can contribute to other PR activities such as press receptions, facility visits, exhibitions, seminars, dealer conferences and overseas PR. Film can also be transferred on to tape for further use in the form of video cassettes.

Before a film is made it is usual for the film makers to present a *treatment* or synopsis of the proposed film, as a successful film cannot be made unless the sponsor is absolutely certain why he wants the film and what he wants it to do. Anyone who has viewed a lot of documentary films will know that a good many sponsors have simply wanted a nice film about their organization, and *purpose* and *potential audience* had never been considered at the treatment stage. This is a waste of a supreme PR medium.

A film will usually have a working life of at least five years. Some films (e.g. John Laing's *Coventry Cathedral*) are timeless, the Shell film of Croydon Airport, made in the 30's, has become a classic. Thus a PR film becomes an investment.

This leads us to the question of cost and the PR budget. The cost of film making depends on factors already discussed in example number three in Chapter Eight which deals with skeleton costing schemes. A point to remember is that the costs of making and distributing a film may be spread over several annual budgets, so that its cost can work out very economically bearing in mind its long working life. To the cost must be added the costs of prints, distribution and maintenance. Some films are expensive because of the use of professional actors and distant locations but a lot of inexpensive films are made on one location using company staff as actors.

Distribution is vital to the success of documentary films.

Large organizations such as Bowater have private cinemas and these have the advantage of entertaining on the premises and can also be used for staff training programmes and conferences. A film can also provide the means of taking the organization to the client. 8 mm film is ideal for this as there are portable devices for projecting it. Clubs and organizations which meet regularly, such as women's societies, can be given film programmes at their meeting places. Private showings can also be organized for films. Because cinema going is less popular today, there are few opportunities for the acceptance of a documentary film at public cinemas. There are countless clubs, schools and other organizations which borrow films through film libraries, and this is a bonus distribution which can be additional to the planned distribution.

Subject to the approval of the Foreign and Commonwealth Office, the Central Office of Information will acquire films free of advertising for overseas distribution if they satisfy their standards and help to promote Britain overseas. Various forms of agreement can be reached, and distribution can be extended if the sponsor is co-operative, but the COI contribution can include the production of foreign language versions, worldwide distribution, and showings on overseas TV.

From these brief comments it will be seen that the film is capable of very extensive use, and its importance should never be under-estimated. Further use of films will be considered under TV.

Organizations which make regular use of films for PR purposes have their own libraries, publish catalogues and advertise the availability of films. Well-known libraries are those of BP, ICI, National Benzole, Shell and Rentokil, while the Central Film Library has an industrial film service. The films are mostly on free loan in the UK, but the same films may be available overseas through the library of the Central Office of Information, its catalogue being held in British embassies and consulates throughout the world.

The Industrial Film Guide (Kogan Page) is a comprehensive guide to industrial films, film distributors, film libraries, and hirers and suppliers of equipment. Film companies, studios and libraries are also listed in the *Hollis Press and Public Relations Annual.*

Mention is made above of advertising to attract borrowers. This usually applies to films of wide general or educational interest, as implied by the wording of the following advertisement which appeared in the *Times Higher Education Supplement*:

> I C I
> films
> Educational catalysts
>
> Two new films from ICI.
> Catalysts in the educational reaction.
> Crucibles of interest for students
> of all ages.
>
> 1. Catalysis
> An introduction to the theory and
> practice of catalysis
>
> 2. Ammonia
> Basis of plant growth and life.
> How it works and why it is essential.
>
> Memorable and instructive,
> these 16 mm films are free to schools,
> clubs and other non-paying audiences.
>
> For a copy of ICI's film catalogue
> write to:
>
> ICI Film Library,
> Thames House, Millbank,
> London SW1

Films produce publicity for themselves and for their sponsors. A sponsored film should be properly launched with its own première attended by industrial film critics who will review in the trade and business press. It can also be entered for contests such as the annual one run by British Industrial and Scientific Film Association, while many other film festivals are held overseas. Success in these contests produces further publicity for the film and its sponsor. Premières and festivals can result in a film achieving very useful press coverage.

If the sponsor has a subject which is likely to be useful to film and TV producers it will pay him to produce short filmclips which can be made available or placed in a library. In this way, film of aircraft, ships, trains and well-known places can be introduced into studio-made films to give the illusion of the actors travelling or being on location.

Synchronized Slide Presentation

It is possible to use two projectors linked in such a way that the picture from the second can immediately replace the picture from the first.

It is also possible to arrange that the light is dimmed progressively on the first projector as it is increased on the second while both pictures are on the screen. This gives the effect of a dissolve. This basic principle has permitted the development of what has come to be called 'multi-screen' presentation, where banks of dual projectors, as described above, can be set up each one covering a portion of the total screen area. By this method, each bank can project part of the total unified image on the screen or the total picture area can be broken up into separate images. This sort of presentation suits permanent exhibits, and a good example is the *News At Ten* presentation at the IBA Television and Radio Gallery.

The whole system, either of one single pair or of a multi-screen group, can be linked in synchronization to a sound track.

The equipment required for such a presentation is necessary on each occasion and thus what may be saved in production is usually spent in presentation. One answer to this problem, making simpler presentations possible, is to re-record the total slide programme on film, thus permitting convenient presentation with a 16 mm projector. These projectors are available almost anywhere. This process is known as filmagraph.

Videotape, Cassettes and Video Discs

Under studio conditions videotape can be cheaper to produce than film, for one does not have to wait for film to be processed. Editing is quick because the tape can be displayed on a TV receiver, shots retaken and the complete tape produced in one session. While it is possible to project VCR onto a large screen, film is usually best for showing to large audiences. Film can be transferred to tape, and preference may be given to making a film in the first place either because of the superior quality of the film or because until VCR's are commonplace normal film projection is more universally convenient. However, 5 cm tape can also be transferred to film.

Videotape is especially useful for PR purposes when supplied in cassettes for playing on a Philips or Sony video cassette-recorder in conjunction with a TV receiver. This method is excellent for training purposes and for conveying PR messages to staff, dealers or consumers visiting showrooms.

There is also the video disc or audio visual long-playing record which is to video what the long-playing record is to audio. It has 50,000 frames, runs as 25 frames per second and has a playing time of 30 minutes, and can be pressed very quickly in large quantities in PVC. It will appeal almost entirely to the domestic market and will not replace video cassettes in industry and commerce nor in the home where recordings are made off air. Like the LP record it will need long production runs to make it an economic proposition, but there are nevertheless some possible PR uses. Could, for instance, a video disc replace a house magazine, especially with the introduction of a combined VCR VLP machine?

Radio

The transistorized radio has created not only a huge increase in numbers of listeners but also in kinds of listener and in listening hours.

Some of the advantages of radio are:

1. Radio is listened to at all times of the day, but especially outside peak TV viewing hours such as in the morning.

2. It has the power of immediacy.

3. It is simple to deal with – by post, telephone or personal visit to the studio.

4. It can reach illiterates, either by transistor or Rediffusion.

5. Professional services are available, and these will be detailed below.

6. It is easily monitored by tape-recorder.

7. With such a large network of stations which are more localized than TV it is possible to use radio locally, nationally and (through the BBC External Services) internationally. Overseas listeners (including British people living abroad) also listen to broadcasts from British stations.

In addition to instantaneous broadcasts there are talks, magazines, series and serials which can incorporate PR material if it suits the programme. *Today, The World At One, The Archers* and *Woman's Hour* offer scope for PR stories, background information, themes and interviews.

Britain's first audio news and feature service was launched by Universal News Services, offering both an audio *news* service and an audio *feature* service. The first gives prompt radio coverage over direct private audio circuits of any suitable news story, while the second gives complete coverage of local radio stations and other suitable media for non-spot news and feature material. Since this is very different from writing and mailing news releases, or publishing feature articles, it is worth looking more closely at the UNS techniques.

The *UNS audio news service* works like this. First, the story material is structured and then a radio reporter and the interviewee are briefed. A three-minute recording is made, either in the studio or outside with portable equipment. The recorded tape is edited and cue material is prepared and recorded. The recording and cue are distributed by direct audio circuits to the BBC news room, BBC general news service desk (serving TV and all local BBC local radio stations), BBC world service, Independent Radio News (serving all commercial radio stations), and Independent Television News. All the appropriate broadcasting outlets are alerted by UNS teleprinter. The client receives a file copy on either cassette or open spool.

The *UNS audio features service* begins with the discussing and planning of the feature with the client, followed by the briefing of the radio reporter and the interviewee. A three-minute recording is made, either in the studio or outside with portable equipment. Then the recorded tape is edited and copies are made for each local station. A cue sheet is prepared for each station. Tapes and cue sheets are then despatched to the selected programme producers in every local radio area.

The above are package deals but variations and additional services are available such as monitoring, producing series or full-length programmes, installing sound booths at exhibitions and conferences for continuous radio coverage, land-line interviews to save travel time and expense, and foreign language broadcasts.

An interesting example of the practical use of radio as a PR medium comes from the Ministry of Rural Development in Zambia. The task was to increase agricultural productivity by educating farmers in the regions. Radio was the chosen medium and the Radio Farm Forum was the technique applied. It was found that where radios were owned at all in the more distant parts of the country they were capable of receiving broadcasts only from the neighbouring countries of Angola and Tanzania. So, some 500 more powerful sets were supplied free to local centres and other sets were supplied at cost price to individuals. More than 1000 sets are now being used in the rural areas to receive the programmes.

The local Forums are led by an agricultural officer who recruits 15 members who in turn may bring relatives and friends to form a regular listening group with a maximum attendance of forty men and women. The year's programme is drawn up from topics suggested by the agricultural officers and members. Each weekly programme takes the form of a play with five or six characters, and is devised with the assistance of technical experts and farmers.

The dramatic content of the programme is ingenious, and the dramatization of one play about late planting had the following plot: indifference of a farmer towards planting in time – postponing – beer drinking – first rain – last minute efforts to procure fertilizers, tractors, etc. – faith in witchcraft's help – poor crop – repentance.

Discussion on the content of the programme is followed up by practical exercises when the listening group is given a demonstration by an instructor which requires the farmers to put into practice what they have learned.

The questions received from these programmes have been so valuable that booklets containing questions and answers on each broadcast topic have been produced and distributed to the farmers. These Radio Farm Forum books are complete self-help training manuals.

The broadcasts are in seven vernacular versions and also in English. The Radio Farm Forum is supplemented by or associated with other information which includes a farmer's diary and a calender setting out the monthly farming tasks throughout the year. News releases giving advice on current topics are also sent to the Zambian Information Service for publication in vernacular newspapers. The Rural Information Services department has also made several films. It is a comprehensive PR programme.

Zambia's Radio Farm Forum was initiated through a UNESCO Mission in 1966 which surveyed the prospects, and a UNESCO expert gave initial advice.

This is an example of the way in which PR techniques and media are being applied to the development of Third World countries.

Television

This is the greatest snare and delusion among PR media. The temptation to use TV as a PR medium must often be resisted because it has to be recognized that TV is primarily an entertainment medium and personalities and subjects will be presented to please audiences, not people who would like to express their point of view to a large audience. It is very easy to suffer from the effects of editing and the juxtapositioning of material, which were not expected during individual sessions.

TV is unlike any other medium. It has many of the attributes and characteristics of the film yet it is viewed on a small screen and in domestic circumstances so that the captivity of the cinema is missing. In some countries of the Third World TV is state controlled for the purposes of propaganda or education, but although Britain has a public service TV it is really the modern escapist medium of the masses. However, people will watch things they would not read about, and there is the magic difference that TV commands over every other medium. People watch it: it has the original appeal of the silent cinema. To the PRO TV means that if your managing director looks like an unpopular politician you keep him off the box, although he might be excellent in a radio interview.

There are ways in which TV can be used successfully in PR programmes but it is a medium to consider with caution. It is a visual medium with many pitfalls for the individual who may be interviewed and it is also a tedious medium which can consume a large amount of budgeted manhours. Is the large expenditure of time and money justified by the small amount of eventual screen time, the way in which the subject will be treated, and the kind of audience who will watch it? The biggest danger of TV is its appeal to client's or employer's vanity although the net PR value may be nil.

Even if an organization lends a premises free for filming, often when the scenes appear on the screen there is nothing that could possibly be of PR value to the provider of the facilities.

However, there are certain ways in which the PR practitioner can achieve good media relations with this medium and they fall under the following headings:

1. *News* for regional and national bulletins. This usually requires advance notice and provision of independent facilities quite different from those of a press reception or press facility visit.

2. *Discussion programmes* if the organization can produce a personality who televises well.

3. *Series* in which the organization can feature on its own merits, as when it provides a topic for the series.

4. *Give-away programmes* which are prepared to purchase one's products for use as prizes, provided the product can be identified by viewers.

5. *Documentary films* which may be used in whole or part as programme material.

6. *Properties* for use in sets or products which actors may use such as cars in crime series.

7. *Library shots* (e.g. pictures of aircraft specifically taken by airlines for use in films and TV series). Visnews (13.1) is a particularly useful supplier of all kinds of news and location material to the TV companies.

Just as there is the PRADS service in press relations, and the UNS press and radio services so there is the Visnews sponsored filmclip service for TV.

However, TV programmes are planned and sometimes 'canned' a long time in advance, and it may be useless to propose an idea for next week's show when the series is half-way through. It is best to keep in touch with producers and their staff and try to anticipate future possibilities, as when a series comes off and it is announced that it will be returning in a few months' time.

Another possibility is coverage on BBC TV News or Independent Television News. The best advice here is to tell TV news editors well in advance about your event so that a camera can be booked. Studio interviews are also possible if the subject is of sufficiently wide interest. This topic is also discussed in Chapter Nine which deals with organizing PR events.

Exhibitions

There is a tendency nowadays, especially in advertising agencies, to regard all forms of exhibition as PR. Public and trade exhibitions consist of stands which are just as much a form of advertising as a TV commercial.

PR concerns the exhibition in two interesting but separate ways. There can be PR activities in addition to the exhibit itself such as advance media relations, invitations to visit the stand, press receptions and associated film shows or seminars. There is also the purely PR exhibit when the exhibition medium is used as part of a PR programme. The police make good use of this technique to create public understanding of their services with exhibits mounted at large gatherings where there is a ready-made audience.

Having made these distinctions about the PR aspects of exhibitions there are, of course, occasions when a stand at a public or trade exhibition might be taken for PR purposes but this really applies to organizations such as voluntary bodies which choose to use advertising media as part of their PR programme. A large public exhibition may be just the place to promote the work of a charitable institution and to seek support by explaining its work.

The exhibition has the virtue of reality. Things can be actually seen, handled, sampled, compared, and questioned. These are irrevocable tests, inviting criticism, and consequently having great power to create and establish knowledge, understanding, and goodwill. The best way to overcome doubts is to invite people to convince themselves, and an exhibition provides exactly this opportunity. But again, the difference between an exhibition stand for advertising purposes and one for PR has to be stressed. The demonstrators and salesmen on the former may use slick, high-pressure salesmanship methods, whereas those staffing a PR stand will be more restrained and informative. Sometimes this is mistaken to be the contrast between 'hard sell' and 'soft sell', but it is wrong to describe the first as advertising and the second as PR when they are both advertising.

The merit of the exhibition for PR purposes is that there can be personal confrontation – one of the finest forms of PR – and the willingness to invite comment.

The private exhibition can be combined with other PR media already and about to be discussed, and we must not overlook the small, portable exhibition arranged on hardboard, peg-board or Marler-Hayley display stands, or even simply laid out on tables.

Literature

PR literature is explanatory and educational reading matter which tells a story rather than sales literature which seeks to persuade and sell. Typical examples are factual accounts of the history and activities of an organization, cookery recipe leaflets, or handyman's guides to decorating and household tasks. The PR effect of this literature can be to inspire confidence in an organization, to encourage a housewife to extend her range of cookery skill by showing her what can be produced, or to make the husband wish to improve his home by teaching him how to do it.

PR literature may consist of leaflets, folders, booklets, books, and other pieces of print including wall charts, diaries, postcards, and pictures for exhibiting and framing. A leaflet is a single sheet printed one or both sides; a folder is a larger piece of print which folds down to a convenient size; a booklet consists of more than four pages, the binding being perhaps a wire stitch, saddle-stitched. Larger booklets may require side-stitched, sewn, and/or glued bindings with drawn-on covers until we come to the book which consists of 8- or 16-page sections or signatures bound together.

Books

Sponsored Books is an area well worth considering when one has something substantial and authoritative to say. For example, a manufacturer of insecticides and herbicides might sponsor a book on gardening, or a manufacturer of radar equipment might sponsor one on yachting. Several publishers offer sponsored book schemes. There are books distributed through the normal bookselling channels, but financially guaranteed by the sponsor while some are sold very profitably by mail order. The essential thing about a sponsored book is that it should not be a dull company history but a book of practical value which enhances the sponsor's reputation. The Rentokil Library is a good example.

This medium is not suitable for every PR campaign but where it can be used it has the advantage of permanence or at least very long life, making the investment extremely economical.

First, there is the authoritative work on a technical subject, in which the sponsor is acknowledged, and agrees to meet production costs by purchasing an agreed number of copies. The publisher will list and distribute the book which will carry his regular imprint and to all intents and purposes be a normal speculatively produced book. There are such books on glass, aluminium, packaging, and pest control.

Second, there is the popular book produced for a sponsor by a specialist publisher and sold in very large quantities by direct mail. Superbly designed and printed in colour, these books have been issued on topics such as power tools and food products.

Third, there is the privately produced book which can suffer from unprofessional production and the bias of its author and sponsor. Some terribly dull company histories have been produced in this way. To be accepted as a genuine book there should really be an independent publisher. A private book implies one that no-one considers worth risking money on publishing because it is unlikely to sell.

Fourth, there is the specialist semi-popular book whose sponsorship may actually aid sales. Guide books are a good example, being sponsored by well-known names in the motoring trade. There are also some well-known miscellanies which make good Christmas gifts such as the *Guinness Book of Records* and the Rothman's book on tennis and football.

Direct Mail

Here we come to a medium which some marketing people tend to regard lock-stock-and-barrel as a form of PR. It is a term which is apt to cause considerable misunderstanding, and some explanations are offered here.

Direct mail is usually taken to mean the advertising medium whereby goods or services are made known by post, whether or not an immediate sale is urged. A book publisher may use this medium, including an order form for a mail-order sale, but a department store may distribute a sale catalogue by post and seek to encourage personal shoppers. Moreover, there is no such thing as mail-order advertising in the sense of a medium. Mail-order trading may be achieved by the use of the media of press or direct mail.

Direct mail advertising, or postal publicity as it is sometimes called, is a medium which enjoys the advantages of privacy and selectivity, and the ability to send a comprehensive message in the form of supporting literature.

It is particularly interesting, then, that while the advertising tactics of direct mail may not be applicable to PR (other than as an advertising medium as in the case of a charity appeal), the mechanics of direct mail are frequently used by the PR practitioner. The simplest example is the news release which is clearly best distributed by direct mail techniques. For instance: some measure of personalization can be most desirable so that stories are not sent to 'The Editor' but to the 'Home Page Editor' or the 'Science Correspondent' although it helps if the mailing list can be so up-to-date that the envelope can be personally addressed by actual name.

Similarly direct mail is implied when despatching a house magazine to the home addresses of employees, or direct to distributors, customers or other external readers. But here we are only using the technique of *direct* distribution, and the need for maintaining a reliable list. A folded and wrapped journal can be less attractive to receive and read than one which arrives flat and in a natural condition as when an envelope is used.

Again, a brochure describing an organization, its history and facilities, range of services, equipment, techniques, and qualified or skilled staff, might well be direct mailed to clients and potential clients.

In the same way, invitations to an exhibition stand, film show, seminar, demonstration, dealer conference, works visit, press conference or press reception require the direct mail techniques of accurate mailing list, planned contents, correct timing, and reply facilities.

There are certain occasions when direct mail can be selected as the best means of conveying a PR message, as when the PRO wishes to distribute a message to opinion leaders such as Members of Parliament, teachers, and others who can be personally addressed by letter. The information can be presented in a personal style and bear the signature of someone influential such as the president of the organization. The letter's value would depend on its ability to improve the recipient's knowledge of the subject, and it should therefore avoid pressing a case too vehemently. The same tactics can be approached by a voluntary organization seeking new members, donors or other supporters.

Direct mail is therefore a very versatile medium suitable for either advertising or PR.

The Spoken Word

Mention has already been made of the importance of personal confrontation. The spoken word is a PR technique which can be applied to an individual conversation just as much as to the addressing of an audience which may or may not be visible. The skills of public speaking cannot be enumerated here, but ability to express himself clearly, intelligently, and interestingly is fundamental to a well-trained PR practitioner. Whether he has to converse on the telephone, address a press reception, face a TV interview or speak at a public meeting, the PR practitioner should be an expert in the use of this medium which is particularly suitable for PR purposes. Few PR media can be more convincing, because we are right down to basic human contact and communication, and it can be very difficult to project a message through a human personality which is not readily acceptable to the majority in the audience. This is the great test of TV, which can be disastrous to those who, however sincere, are unable to project themselves sympathetically.

By introducing TV we have perhaps complicated the spoken word by associating it with the visual impression created by sight of the speaker. Nevertheless, it is only on the telephone or radio that the speaker cannot be observed, and so when talking the speaker does have to learn to present himself at his best and with the fewest possible distractions. When considering the spoken word as part of a PR programme it is therefore essential to decide whether the organization has people of the right ability, or whether they may have to be specially engaged for the occasion.

Exactitude is of paramount importance in PR planning, and where the element to be planned and managed is as unreliable as the human personality in circumstances where rigid discipline is probably impossible, the PRO or consultant has to direct operations in an inoffensive yet persuasive manner. The chairman or managing director who will not prepare advance notes, attend a rehearsal, take well-meant advice or use a microphone is a menace to a PR operation, and may well turn the occasion into a disaster. The VIP who sensibly places himself in the hands of his PRO, and co-operates in every way, is an asset of tremendous value to his organization.

It is not that the PRO will present a favourable but false image, but that he will extract from often very rough material a personality which does not irritate listeners or viewers by its faults. There are several habits that the PR practitioner must seek to eradicate from his speakers such as: hands in pocket jingling money, rocking on one's heels, taking off and putting on spectacles repeatedly, gesticulating with the hands, walking up and down, running hands through hair, scratching one's nose, loosening one's collar, pulling one's ear and hitching up one's trousers. These mannerisms are, of course, indications of nervousness and all the PRO really does in preparing a speaker is to help him to relax and help him to do nothing else except speak clearly and pleasantly so that his message is conveyed convincingly. The spontaneous quips from newsreaders indicate the relaxed speaker. By way of contradiction, it must be acknowledged that there are speakers whose mannerisms are characteristic, such as those of certain conductors of symphony orchestras.

Sponsorship

Sponsorship has PR and anti-PR connotations. To be acceptable as a sponsor an organization must be well known. The commercial sponsor makes a valuable contribution to society, probably supporting interests which could not survive or exist otherwise in a capitalist society where there is no state support. English cricket, for instance, owes much to the generosity of Gillette (an American company!), an incongruous situation compared to that in other countries where a national sport would be state financed in the national interest. The tobacco firms sponsor the bulk of British-sponsored outdoor sport, and with the increasing clamour against cigarette smoking the reputation of these firms becomes ambiguous. Sponsorship can have a boomerang effect.

There may be many and often combined reasons for sponsorship – marketing, advertising, corporate image, press relations and philanthropic to name but a few. Coca-Cola, selling to young people, have associated themselves with youthful sports, especially swimming, but also with athletics and football in developing countries.

An interesting example of how to develop a sponsorship in a fairly simple way comes from Ireland. D. E. Williams Ltd., of Tullamore promote the Czar Vodka Steeplechase at Kilbeggan. In addition to a cash prize the winning owner receives a painting of the horse and jockey. This picture is then reproduced as the full-colour centrepiece of a one-sheet Czar Vodka calendar for the following year.

John Haig, the distillers, are very satisfied with the local press, radio and TV coverage they receive from their sponsorship of the Haig National Village Cricket Championship, a knock-out competition with a £35,000 budget which has done much to encourage cricket at village level. The genesis of 'The Haig' is interesting.

The idea was first conceived in the winter of 1970 when the National Cricket Association and *The Cricketer* magazine conducted a joint survey of club cricket and from this decided that village cricket deserved and would benefit from some form of encouragement. A sponsor was sought to back a competition at village level. This co-incided with John Haig's investigation of the question of sports spon-sorship, during which they looked at more than 50 different sporting activities. Michael Henderson, managing director of Haig, heard an interview with Ben Brocklehurst, managing director of *The Cricketer*, on the Jack de Manio *Today* programme on BBC Radio 4, during which the subject of finding a sponsor for village cricket was discussed. Mr. Henderson decided that village cricket was the sport for Haig.

A committee was formed consisting of Aidan Crawley, president of the MCC and chairman of London Weekend Television as chairman, Jim Dunbar, secretary of the National Cricket Association, Ben Brocklehurst and Michael Henderson. Rules were drawn up stating that 'the object of the competition shall be to promote the best in village cricket and give an opportunity to village cricketers to compete in a national event'. It was agreed that *The Cricketer* would organize the Championship and that the Laws of Cricket would apply, with the addendum that each side should bat for 40 overs unless their innings was completed earlier, or unless the captains agreed to a lesser number of overs before the start of the match.

A village was deemed a rural community of not more than 2500 inhabitants; players had to be paid-up members of their club who had played an aggregate of eight games in less than three years, although players did not have to live in the village; but players were ineligible if they had ever played first-class cricket (unless they were over 60), if they were competing in the National Club Knock Out during the same year, or if they received a fee for playing cricket. At the request of the Minor Counties a rule was added to the effect that 'Players will not be eligible if they have played County 2nd XI or Minor County cricket within the previous three years.'

There was an entry of 795 clubs when the Championship was first held in 1972, the winner being Troon from Cornwall. It was also the year when village cricket was played at Lords, and this was one of the main attractions of the competition. Troon won again in 1973 when there was an entry of 750 teams, and the entry has remained around this figure in subsequent years.

The winners receive a silver Haig trophy, plus miniature, and a cheque for £500 for club funds. Runners-up receive a silver dimple decanter and a cheque for £250, and the two losing semi-finalists get a cheque for £125. *The Cricketer* publishes *The Haig Village Cricket Annual* which may be purchased as a souvenir of the year's event. A number of other awards are made throughout the course of the Championship such as one for a Throwing the Cricket Ball competition.

But there has been considerable hostility (e.g. anti-smoking TV documentary programmes seen by millions of viewers) to the sponsoring of motor racing teams (e.g. John Player Special) which have 'stolen' publicity on both BBC and ITV channels during the coverage of international motor racing despite the fact that cigarette advertising is banned from commercial TV. The tobacco firms – Players, Rothmans, Wills – have also sponsored a great many sports and other interests such as golf, tennis, cricket, private flying, art exhibitions, symphony orchestras and annuals.

It is important to consider the PR value of sponsorship. Will it enhance the reputation of the company, or help to establish better understanding of its activities? Will it show that the company is socially responsible, not merely profiting from sales but contributing to the society in which its customers live? Judicious sponsorship can increase the quality of life and standards of living. There can be an anti-PR reaction if a sponsor is seen to be unduly exploiting a situation for publicity purposes. Yet the award of a trophy may result in perfectly justifiable publicity when the event is fully named by the media. When the *Daily Mail* sponsored an aircraft to save Vietnamese refugee children this was a responsible action which did not deserve the criticism by some people that it was merely a publicity stunt.

Sponsorship can be divided into certain areas of interest, the following being a simple breakdown:

1. Books – e.g. *Pears Encyclopaedia*, *Guinness Book of Records*, *Michelin Guides*, the *Rentokil Library* and the Rothmans sporting annuals.

2. Exhibitions – e.g. sponsorship by newspapers, magazines, and trade associations.

3. Education – such as bursaries, exhibitions, fellowships and travelling scholarships.

4. Expeditions and Adventures – as when explorations and mountaineering feats are supported financially or provided with supplies.

5. Sport – probably the most popular field of sponsorship.

6. Culture – such as naming the sponsors as with the Midland Bank's opera proms at the Covent Garden Opera House, posters being displayed in branches of the bank.

7. Causes and Charities – as when an industrial firm provides a film to promote the interests of a voluntary body.

8. Local Events – this being an opportunity to further community relations.

9. Films – documentary films produced to further interest in a subject such as conservation.

10. Professional Awards – such as the *Financial Times Architecture Award*, the *Conoco Jet Awards* for motoring journalists and broadcasters and many others for journalists, photographers, actors, variety artists and so forth.

Whether sponsorship is undertaken for purely PR reasons or not there is clearly a PR aspect to all such financial patronage. It is therefore essential that the PRO or PR consultant should co-operate in all such ventures. There may be times when the PR practitioner has to advise against sponsorship, perhaps because the cost is not justified by communication advantages or because the organization is simply being exploited by fund-seekers who are irrelevant to the organization or undesirable associates. For instance, at a time of financial crisis a well-known bank was heavily criticized for subscribing a large sum of money to an expedition that seemed to many people, including the bank's customers, to be unnecessary and extravagant.

House Journals

These are sometimes called house organs, house magazines or private magazines, they may be internal or external and it is unwise to make one journal serve both purposes since the reading interests and the PR purposes are entirely different. In large organizations a number of house journals may be produced for different readerships, even for different categories of staff.

This, like the industrial film, is a medium conceived by PR for PR. It is a primary PR medium, and one that may be superior to press relations. The importance of the house journal can be seen in the ITT Europe case study in Part Four.

In recent years this medium has matured beyond the patronizing staff magazine to one that permits reader participation, and from the glossy prestige external to one that has to do a realistic communication job with particular publics.

The external house magazine calls for the highest PR skills and can be one of the most economical means of conveying specific messages to well-defined publics. A few years ago only 15 per cent of house magazines in the UK were external but the percentage is rapidly increasing as the value of direct communication is appreciated. An external should not be a piece of sales literature dressed up in the guise of a magazine. Both are legitimate PR media for which the PRO should be responsible.

There are other kinds of house journal which might be described as semi-externals which are distributed by voluntary bodies to their members, charities to their subscribers, and local authorities to their ratepayers, such as *Marketing* and *The World's Children*. Some of them will be found listed under 'periodicals' rather than under 'house magazines' in *Benn's Press Directory*, which really signifies the recognition given to them. *Benn's Press Directory* defines a house journal as 'a publication produced by an industrial undertaking, a business house or a public service for the benefit of its employees and/or consumers'. This is rather restrictive since it excludes membership magazines and the numerous civic newspapers published by local authorities. The word 'house' is a misnomer as it tends to confine the idea of a private magazine to business houses when the greater part of PR is outside the sphere of industry and commerce.

Seven-Point Formula for Planning a House Journal

1. The readers – who will they be?
2. The quantity.
3. The frequency – weekly, monthly, quarterly.
4. Title – something distinctive and in character but not too clever.
5. The printing process – probably letterpress or some form of lithography.
6. Style – magazine or newspaper format, black and white or colour, etc.

7. Cost – how many pages, how many copies, how frequently, black and white or colour, etc.

Industrial editors, as house journal editors are generally called, have their own very active organization, the British Association of Industrial Editors (13.2), which is linked with many similar organizations throughout the world.

In an opinion poll appearing in *BAIE The First Twenty-Five Years* 56 per cent expected newspapers to be replaced by electronic media but only 29 per cent expected the same to happen to house journals. It was expected, though, that more attention would be paid to cost effectiveness and it was thought probable that some organizations would adopt the visual techniques of the TV screen.

No doubt developments, as indicated in the section on visual aids, will have its impact on internal house journals, perhaps less so on externals. The wall newspaper, by no means a new idea, is a compromise with its display at numerous points throughout a factory or office block. It was used by London Transport for progress reports on the building of the Victoria Line in the form of posters at underground stations. The two big advantages of a publication are its portability and longevity. Electronic media have immediacy but are transient.

Bound up with these considerations is the king-pin of success: distribution. Nothing can kill the effectiveness of a house journal more than bad distribution. It is usually best to mail copies direct to readers; high cost of envelopes and postage may be met by cheaper paper, fewer pages or reducing the frequency of issue. In some cases – dependent on the value placed by readers on the publication – a cover charge is justified.

To produce a journal and then issue it haphazardly to whoever might possibly be interested can only happen when PR is unplanned, when objectives have not been determined, and certain results are not desired and forecast. In the ITT Europe case study in Part Four we see the external *Profile* being produced for a definite corporate PR purpose, and a mailing list of 50,000 readers being created over a period of five months.

Other PR Media

There are certain other techniques which may be used independently or which impinge on what has been said already.

House style means the adoption of a uniform appearance, colour scheme, typography, symbol or some other means of identifying the character of the organization. This applies particularly to all forms of print from stationery to advertisements and can also extend to signs and notices, staff uniforms, badges, ties, ash trays and cuff-links.

Another form of house style is the *livery* that distinguishes vehicles, ships and aircraft which is well represented by road tankers, ships' funnels and the decoration of aircraft. Identity is an important part of communication and an excellent example is the house styling and livery of Thomson Holidays and their Britannia Airways which is apparent in their TV advertising, brochures, travel agency publicity, aircraft, baggage labels, air hostess uniforms and courier scarves. The completeness of the Thomson Holidays styling creates an air of confidence.

Flags are another form of identification and a company flag can do much to assist in good neighbour relations, helping to break down the anonominity that can create an unnecessary barrier.

Airships have been Goodyear's very practical way of identifying themselves in America and Europe by means of goodwill flights and they have also been used to display illuminated public service announcements at night. Goodyear have four non-rigid airships, the *America*, *Columbia* and *Mayflower* operating in the States, and the *Europa* being based in Europe.

The smallest of the four is the *Mayflower*, being 160 ft (49 m) long, carrying a pilot and six passengers, having two six-cylinder pusher type 175 hp engines, a cruising speed of 35 mph (56 km/h) and a maximum speed of 53 mph (85 km/h), a maximum altitude of 10,000 ft (3048 m) and a range of 500 miles (805 km).

The other three airships are 192 ft (58 m) long, carry a pilot and six passengers, have a pair of 210 hp engines, cruise at 35 mph (56 km/h) and have a top speed of 50 mph (80 km/h), with a maximum altitude of 8500 ft (2590 m) and a range of 500 miles (805 km). Both types have a normal altitude of 1000–3000 ft (305–914 m). The combination of graceful speed, large appearance and low altitude make them considerable attention-getters.

Europa was assembled at Cardington. The construction programme commenced in November 1971, and the airship first flew in March 1972. Because she needs to have a crew of 22 including five pilots and a ground crew of 16 plus a PR representative, it is a very expensive operation and initially it was announced that the exercise was costing Goodyear £1¼ million not counting operating costs. The airship was constructed solely as a PR vehicle to help make Goodyear better known in European countries. She operates for a six-month period throughout Europe, and then spends the winter at her base at Capena near Rome. Goodyear do not hire the airship to any other company, but in countries where this is permitted – not the UK! – the night sign is used for public service messages.

The night sign is a piece of social service work which has been well used in the USA to remind people to conserve water during droughts, and to appeal to motorists to drive safely and to wear safety belts. In the USA Goodyear have two kinds of night sign, the *Mayflower*'s Skytacular and the Super Skytacular full-colour animated night sign which is used on the larger airships *America* and *Columbia*.

The Super Skytacular signs are 105 ft (32 m) long and 24.5 ft (7.5 m) high, and are on both sides of the airship, using a total of 7560 lamps. Messages to be run on the sign are born on exotic electronic equipment. A technician 'draws' the animation and copy on a cathode ray tube with a light gun. From there the computer takes over, the process resulting in a magnetic data tape. A six-minute tape consists of 40 million pieces or bits of 'on-off' information which, when run through electronic readers on board, control lamp and colour selection and message speed.

On the *Mayflower* the Skytacular night sign is smaller – 105 ft (32 m) long and 14 ft (4.3 m) high. There are 3080 lights in all, controlled by pre-punched plastic-based tapes fed into an electronic reader.

This is clearly a costly PR activity that could only be mounted by a firm such as a large international tyre manufacturer, but it is introduced here because it shows an imaginative approach to international corporate and product PR, it is another example of electronic media, and it is an unusual instance of sponsorship since the night signs (also used for Goodyear's own messages) are used on behalf of service organizations, non-profit charities and other good causes.

References

13.1 Visnews, Cumberland Avenue, London NW10 7EH
13.2 British Association of Industrial Editors (BAIE), 2a Elm Bank Gardens, London SW13 0NT

Part Three
Creativity

CHAPTER FOURTEEN

Presentation of the News Release

There are two important aspects to the production of a successful news release. One is the way it is presented and the other is the way it is written. Although the presentation is largely a matter of designing and duplicating what has been written by hand or on a typewriter the author should have the final appearance in mind at the creative stage. He will then discipline himself to apply techniques which are logical, and therefore essential, if a publishable news release is to be produced. He will restrict capital letters to proper names and eliminate full points from abbreviations for practical and not pedantic reasons. He will also know that what may be good secretarial practice is not necessarily good media relations practice, and he will be able to instruct secretarial staff in what, to them, may well be strange typing techniques and styling. A news release (or an article) has to be set out as a manuscript and not like a business letter. Judging by the appearance of many news releases this is unknown to most secretaries and typists.

Therefore, in this chapter the basic presentation is analysed and discussed very carefully. A first-class press officer will be meticulous over these details. How a news release should and can be written will be dealt with in the next chapter.

The purpose of good, correct presentation is threefold: (1) to achieve legibility; (2) to make the release attractive to read; and (3) to minimize editorial work so that the release is capable of publication as it stands. The less a story is cut or re-written the less likelihood there is of its meaning being changed. But having said that it must be admitted that while a trade magazine may print the story exactly as submitted by the press officer the national newspaper will invariably do a re-write job to suit its own style and may well use the news release merely as a piece of information on which to base a story resulting from further investigation. In both cases, however, it is essential that the press officer issues his information in a thoroughly professional manner, and this really boils down to presenting the facts as an editor would like to receive them.

These three requirements therefore imply a knowledge of human psychology and an appreciation of editorial needs. Unfortunately so many news releases fail to meet these three elementary requirements. The presentation of a news release is as much a piece of marketing as the packing of a shirt in a plastic bag and a nice box.

Essential Elements of Presentation

The presentation can be divided into the following ten elements:

1. The basic sheet	6. Picture availability
2. Length, ending and authorship	7. Layout
3. Headlines, subheads and paragraphs	8. Running-off
4. Style and punctuation	9. Assembling
5. Embargoes and dating	10. Envelopes

1. *The Basic Sheet*

Sheet Size. A4 (297 mm x 210 mm) has become the universally accepted paper size for news releases. An advantage of this size sheet is that it makes it very easy to restrict the majority of news stories to the ideal of one piece of paper, a distinct advantage from the point of view of a busy editor. It is always psychologically easier to induce someone to read what is presented to them on one side of one piece of paper.

The Printed Heading. A news release which is merely duplicated straight on to plain paper without a printed heading looks dull and amateurish. A printed news release heading should quickly establish the identity of the sender. When a reputation has been won for good, interesting and accurate press stories instant recognition by means of a distinctive heading will be a desirable asset since the editor of even a small trade paper may receive as many as fifty different news releases of varying length in a single morning's post. The best headings are fairly simple and do not occupy too much space. A news release heading should simply distinguish that it is not a business letter or an advertisement heading. The wording should clearly state the name, address, telephone number and Telex number (if there is one) for further information, and a night or home telephone number can be helpful.

A PR consultancy has the problem of declaring the identities of both itself and its client, but from the editor's point of view it is the *client's* identity which matters even though further information is to be had from a consultant. It is therefore wrong, if common, for the consultant's name to predominate.

In fact it is best if the sender's identification is printed discreetly at the foot of the sheet, the only print at the top being perhaps a single word such as NEWS or INFORMATION or possibly NEWS RELEASE.

The effect is to give emphasis to the story, and since the story is reproduced in black it would contrast very legibly with neat, informative but unobtrusive coloured print. Moreover, since the subject of the news release will be clear from the headline and the openings words, this style of release heading is self-identifying so far as the client or organization is concerned.

1. *Length, Ending and Authorship*

The question of length occurs many times in this book. The more concise and precise the release is the more readable and acceptable is it likely to be. Nevertheless, with very technical products it may be proper to cover the subject in sufficient depth to make the story worth publishing. Discretion must be applied according to the topic and the media.

However, in this chapter we are concerned with length from the point of view of presentation, and length can sometimes be determined at the typing stage because if a second sheet is going to be required to carry a continuation of only a few lines it is usually possible to cut the story in order to keep it on one piece of paper.

Again, there is the question of extra work and extra costs. A PR department or press office in industry is seldom over-staffed and a few words running over on to a second sheet means an extra stencil or plate to prepare, an extra run on the machine and a third extra job in stapling the two sheets together.

Similarly, the PR consultant who charges his clients for the consumption of unnecessary reams of paper, as can happen over a period of a year, is not acting very responsibly if paper is wasted, so length of releases can be a matter of strict account management. In a consultancy it is essential to be cost conscious. There are only two people who can pay for wasted paper, the client or the consultant.

Finally, there is the question of editorial time and editorial needs. Editors receive so many hundreds of PR stories every week that they simply do not have the time to wade through pages of verbosity. The news agencies, which generally put out on their wire services stories of no more than 80 words, despair at the daily arrival of long-winded news releases which condemn themselves on sight.

Thus, when the facts are presented as briefly as possible, and the story can be read almost at a glance, there is seldom any need to go beyond the ample space provided by a single A4 sheet.

The *Ending* of the release and its *Authorship* are related to the length, and particularly to the more detailed release which does run to more than one sheet.

All news releases should close with the name of the writer. This is important when the story has originated from a consultancy, less necessary when it has come from an organization whose press officer is named on the printed heading. Closing the story with the author's name is a clear way of finishing and a good way of establishing personal contact and responsibility for the facts. However, a reporter in a newspaper office typing a story on small pieces of paper for several typesetters will need to mark *Ends* on the final piece. This is unnecessary on a news release of one sheet, as it will usually be set by one typesetter and the author's name marks the end of the story.

3. *Headlines, Subheads and Paragraphs*

Here we have three elements of a news release on which there seems to be hardly any agreed standard practice, yet when ordinary editorial needs are considered there can surely be no question about the *required* practice if good press relations are to be maintained. Let us examine each one in turn.

Headlines. Although it is tempting to invent clever, alliterative headlines, no-one will use them. Each editor likes to write his own, unless he is lazy or there is no better alternative to yours. The purpose of the news release headline is to quickly *identify* the story. The headline, which is not to be confused with the printed heading already discussed, has a practical purpose to perform, but it may never be printed if only because editors do not want to print the same headlines as their rivals. Sometimes employers and clients try to insist that the press officer should word the headline in some dramatic or persuasive manner, but the press officer must dissuade them from doing this as an advertisement-type headline suggests to some editors that the content will be the same. The headline should therefore create the right impression that what follows is a genuine, factual, news story.

While the foregoing is sound standard practice there can be occasions when the story of a seemingly dull or difficult subject can be given a lift and marketed by a bright and possibly humorous treatment such as MORE PARLIAMENTARY PIGEONS LOSE THEIR SEATS which was the headline to one of Peter Bateman's stories about the treatment of pigeon-infested ledges on the Houses of Parliament. Such headlines are part of Peter Bateman's inimitable literary style, rather than an attempt to concoct clever headlines. But this is an exception.

Subheads. Again, it is tempting to insert subheadings to add interest to a story, but they may be a nuisance to the editor who either does not use them, or likes to put them in where they suit him. So it is best not to use subheads, except in a very long release which has clearcut sections dealing with separate items such as a number of different models. Even then, it may be better to write individual releases on each subject rather than bury the various items in an omnibus story. Common sense must prevail to some extent. In all these matters the press officer has to remember that his story will be going to many editors who will each have distinctive styles of presentation, and therefore it is wise to present the basic story as baldly but as clearly as possible, leaving each editor to set it out as he pleases.

Paragraphs. The use of paragraphs and their presentation is imperfectly understood by some press officers, but the lesson can be learned very quickly by studying the columns of daily newspapers. Modern journalism calls for short paragraphs. They help people to read quickly, and to absorb the message clearly. Short paragraphs can be deliberately used to keep the interest flowing.

The setting out of paragraphs is not limited to their length, however. Most newspapers and magazines indent all paragraphs except the first, and news releases should adhere to this style. It is called book style. A news story with unindented paragraphs is a nuisance in that it requires just that extra bit of subbing.

4. *Style and Punctuation*

Capital Letters. Capital letters belong to titling or to proper names. Indiscriminate use of capital letters can be the bane of an editor's life. A company or product name should never be written *entirely* in capitals, nor should initial capitals be used for nouns as they are in German.

'The new range of Central Heating equipment made by ABC Ltd includes Solid Fuel, Gas-fired and Oil-fired Boilers.' It should be like this:

'The new range of central heating equipment made by ABC Ltd includes solid fuel, gas-fired and oil-fired boilers.'

Far too many news releases are written with needless capitals and it is plain to see the extent of editorial correction which is necessary.

Technical people are apt to refer to Cocoa, Radar, Timber, Steel, business people to Directors, Boards, Annual General Meetings and Dividends, but these capital letters are wrongly used and must not be used in news release.

Nor should emphasis be given by typing passages in capitals. All emphasis should be left to the editor since, as we shall see in the next chapter, it is not the place of the press officer to comment or invite testimony. The author of the news release must content himself with supplying factual material free of bias. Otherwise the news release becomes an advertisement. This distinction is sometimes, and understandably, difficult to appreciate by advertising people when they are employing press relations services.

Underlining and Quotation Marks. No underlining should appear anywhere in a news release, and preferably not even in the headline, because whereas to the writer underlining means a rule or line set there for emphasis, to the printer an *underlining is an instruction to set in italic type*. It is no business of the press officer to stipulate which words should be set in italics, except in the case of foreign words or Latin names in scientific matter. The academic style of underlining book titles does not apply to news releases.

Similarly, quotation marks can generally be avoided. The time to use quotation marks is when actual speech or material from another source is being quoted, always remembering that it is necessary to place quotation marks at the beginning of each paragraph and to conclude the entire speech or quotation with quotation marks. Otherwise it is not absolutely clear where the quotation starts and finishes.

Numerals and Symbols. A paragraph should never begin with a numeral unless a list of points is being made, and if the sentence cannot be recast satisfactorily the numeral should be spelt out. Except in special cases, numbers from one to nine should be spelt out, after which numerals such as 59 and 101 should be used until the numbers become so unwieldy that it is clearer to spell out many thousands and certainly millions. Five millions or £5 million is more readily understood than 5,000,000 or £5,000,000. The actual numerals should be given in dates, June 1st and not June First, and 1970, not one thousand nine hundred and seventy, and definitely not nineteen seventy. Similarly we write the 20th century as we do the 19th hole. The press officer has to be extremely careful that accurate and easily understood figures are given in news releases. An error can be disastrous once it is printed, and little can be done by way of correction. If the story has been widely distributed the error may be perpetuated for weeks, months, even years.

The same applies to measurements and signs where there is any risk of a mistake. It is advisable to avoid the signs and write 90 degrees and 100 per cent.

While on the subject, it is all too easy to be slapdash about the use of figures, signs and punctuation, and inconsistencies such as four wheel and 4-wheel are surprisingly frequent in the same press release. In the short space of a few hundred words the press officer should be capable of repeating numerical facts in the same way.

A sign which is badly abused is the ampersand (&) which should never appear in a sentence unless it is part of the normal way of spelling a company name. At best, it is a lazy device, sometimes resorted to by those who write quickly in longhand. The ampersand has its uses where space is scarce, that is in headlines and tabulated matter such as lists, catalogues and accounts.

Full points or Full Stops. Full points should not be used between initial abbreviations such as BSc, BBC, MCC and so on. If they were inserted, viz: B.Sc., B.B.C., M.C.C., the effect would be a spotty mess. Needless editorial work can again be eliminated by the omission of these points in the first place. A study of the press will show that the *Financial Times* index is abbreviated as the *FT* index, the Greater London Council as the GLC, the United States Army as the US Army and Member of Parliament as MP. This absence of full points in abbreviations is common to all types of publication, and although exceptions can be found the appearance of the text is always improved when the full points are omitted.

Full points remain a vital form of punctuation, and the so-called letter-writing style which omits all puntuation must not be used when typing a news release.

Punctuation Generally. The clarity of a news story can depend upon use of punctuation, and commas, colons, semi-colons, dashes and brackets are the signposts of written communication. The pedantic use of punctuation can impede reading, but the lack of essential punctuation can cause misunderstanding. Sometimes punctuation is omitted through carelessness, and stencils or plates must be scrutinized to see that parentheses are completely punctuated.

5. *Embargoes and Dating*

The date when a story may be published, the use of dates in stories, and the date when the release is issued are three things of great consequence to the recipient of press releases.

Embargoes. An embargo is an instruction to the press that the story should not be published before a certain date and perhaps even a certain time on that date. There are many genuine occasions when an embargo is vital, and this is often so in financial PR or when stories are being issued in different parts of the world where disparity in times could cause embarrassment if publication took place literally at the same time. The announcement of price changes or the publication of a speech are typical examples where it can be very helpful if an editor can have the news well in advance provided he respects the privilege and does not print the speech before it has been delivered.

But having admitted the necessity for embargoes, it must be emphasized that embargoes should be used sparingly and sensibly. Long embargoes, though, are bad and hardly ever justified. They usually have the effect of killing interest in the story. An embargo should be a privilege, enabling the editor to have advance knowledge or information which it would be foolish or improper to publish before the stipulated date and time. For example, lobby correspondents receive advance copies of white papers, the contents of which they must not divulge prematurely. However, if an embargo is unexpected and irrelevant it may even get overlooked.

Most stories should therefore be for immediate release, and if that is so it is pointless to print *for immediate release* across the top, unless it comes from one of those rare organizations which seldom issue a story without a stringent embargo. One suspects that some of the releases from commercial sources which bear dramatic embargoes or permissions for instant publication are produced by somewhat amateurish writers who are trying to capture some of the supposed glamour of a hectic Fleet Street newsroom.

Dates. If a date is important to the story it should be included in the narrative, and the month should read first and be spelt out in full, thus: November 12th, 1970. The month which is generally more significant and memorable than the day of the month and should be placed first. This significance is further borne out by the fact that press reports often refer to months only. Vague reference to 'today', 'yesterday', 'tomorrow' or 'recently' must be replaced by the actual date. Reliance should not be placed on the date of the release itself.

If the release describes a stand at an exhibition, the headline should state all the relevant details about name of exhibition, venue, *dates*, hall and stand number. In London or Birmingham there are two or three exhibitions taking place every week and editors cannot be expected to know when and where every exhibition is being held.

It should not be necessary for an editor to have to ring the press officer and ask 'when did it happen?'. Moreover, dated stories should be issued promptly so that their news value is not lost, and this implies knowing the last date or even time for copy for different types of publication. It may be that it is too late to write, reproduce and distribute a news release and that the story must be despatched by telephone, telex, UNS, PA or Reuters. In Chapter Seventeen we shall examine a BOAC news release of this nature.

Dating Releases. Apart from dates which are part of the information supplied, releases themselves should be dated. Some press officers insert the date at the beginning of the first page, others at the foot of the story. A consultant will also find it useful to combine his job number with the date in a coding at the foot of the page. However, this is not necessarily explicit to an editor unless the month is spelled out thus: XYZ1001/October 12th, 1980. There are, therefore, at least three methods of dating releases: (i) at the beginning, as with dating a letter; (ii) at the foot of the story and after the author's name; or, (iii) combined with a coding system which is useful for other purposes. Whichever method is chosen, dating is important to prevent out-of-date information being published, as can happen with magazines which file releases for future use.

6. *Picture Availability*

It may not be feasible to send photographs with every news release issued as this would be costly and wasteful. But the availability of pictures can be stated on the release, and since this is not publishable information these details should be set apart from the body of the story, that is, below the author's name. (Alternatively, the pictures can be identified and described on an accompanying order form.) Photo captions should not be incorporated in releases: they must be attached to the actual prints.

7. *Layout*

Spacing. All manuscript work should be double or one-and-a-half spaced in proportion to the size of the type on the typewriter.

Machines with very large typefaces should not be used for news release work since they will spread the story over more pages than, say, Elite type. Nor should a typewriter with italic type or all capitals be used. When a lot of text has to be read it is easier to read serif type. Electric typewriters conforming to this produce excellent results. A release produced from a typewriter with bold Elite serif type can be set out with one-and-a-half spacing and will look thoroughly legible while meeting the object of spacing which gives the editor space to make amendments and instruct the printer.

Margins. A right-hand as well as a left-hand margin is needed in a press release, although this is not usual with general manuscript work for articles and books. Both margins should not be less than 1½ inches (4 cm) to allow for editorial comment.

Continuations. When the news release consists of more than one sheet this should be clearly indicated at the foot of the page, and all succeeding pages should be numbered. If this is done more elaborate continuation references are redundant, but some people do put the title of the piece at the top of each page to make absolutely certain that scattered pages can be reassembled safely. This is really a matter of personal style and preference, but since a release is supplied as a complete story, the pages stapled together if there are two or more, there is no point in writing *More* at the foot. Use of the word *More* is convenient when a story is being produced in a number of loose sheets, as may happen in a newspaper office and the typesetter needs to know that more follows until the last piece of copy has *ends* at the foot.

8. *Running Off*

One Side of the Paper. All manuscript work must be typed or duplicated on one side of the paper only, and anything on the reverse side will be ignored. Editors and publishers always work from material on one side of the paper only; when type is being set the sheets of copy are held on the typesetting machine in such a way that it would be awkward for the operator if there was copy on the reverse side too.

9. *Assembling*

As we have already said, the ideal news story is one that is confined to one sheet of paper but there are times when a story does run to two or three pages. There are different ways of joining sheets together. The paper clip is dangerous and can come adrift in a pile of editorial material on the editor's desk. The most suitable is the small wire staple, provided it is properly depressed and not left humped. When folding the release for insertion in the envelope the stapled end should be enclosed within the folds, otherwise there is risk that the metal will rip the envelope during its passage through the post, or damage accompanying photographs.

It is also important to fold cleanly to avoid unnecessary bulk which can spring open a poorly sealed envelope. If mailings are frequent a folding machine is a good investment, and there are several makes on the market which handle work of various complexities.

This is possibly a good point at which to warn the press officer that secretaries are not always aware of the rough handling which postal packages have to suffer. Unless items for the post are securely packed and sealed they will stand little chance of surviving the hazards of the postal services. The onus is on the sender to protect whatever he mails.

10. *Envelopes*

The release should be folded as few times as possible so that it is as presentable as possible on arrival. There is no point in folding a foolscap or A4 sheet so that it will squeeze into a small business envelope. An A4 release needs to be folded only twice to fit a DL size envelope. A bulkier release, or a feature article, is best folded only once and posted in a larger envelope.

However, when accompanying a half-plate photograph (the size of print least likely to get damaged in the post by the string which postmen tie round bundles of letters for any one address) the release has to be folded once each way for insertion in a suitable envelope. A single sheet news release is preferable with photographs so that there is no danger of damage from the metal staple.

It is a simple matter to draw up a brief version of these recommendations and to see that every member of the press office staff has a copy to learn by heart, and stick on the wall if need be.

In this chapter the author has not hesitated to slaughter some of the sacred cows of press relations, such as embargoes, and the use of expressions such as 'for immediate release' and 'ends'. Most of these terms were derived from journalistic practices but the habits of the newspaper office are not necessarily applicable to individually produced press releases.

It is a mistake for press officers to add a note at the end of the story requesting a cutting if the story is printed and it is unnecessary to enclose a covering letter urging the editor to print the story. Many editors are generous about sending cuttings, or better still actual copies of the journal, but it is rather tactless to ask editors for favours. An exception, however, may be when the story is sent overseas and it is doubtful whether a press cutting will come through a press cutting agency. When despatching news releases a copy of the story and, if possible, a copy of the mailing list should be sent to the press cutting agency.

The best advice on the presentation of releases is to look at actual printed stories and see how they are presented.

CHAPTER FIFTEEN

How to Write
a News Release

In this chapter the technique of writing a news release will be based on a seven-point formula but before this is considered a few other points should be discussed.

The first thing to make absolutely clear is that a news release is just as much a specialized literary form as an essay, poem, short story, novel, textbook, letter, report, feature article or a piece of advertisement copy. Moreover, it has to be marketed.

According to the importance of the journal, every editor is confronted every morning with scores and perhaps hundreds of news releases. The majority of releases – often from famous sources – go into the bin directly the first few lines have been scanned.

A large number are discarded simply because they are obvious puffs, have been sent to the wrong publication or are too late. Many are too long and the subject is not apparent in the very first few words. The editor is not going to wade through three or four pages of turgid paragraphs to find out what the story is all about. We have only to read any newspaper story to discover how news is written, yet editors are invited to believe that the senders of news releases have never read a newspaper story.

A news release requires its own particular writing skill. It needs to be terse, factual, explanatory and totally free of superlatives or self-praise. It is the most unlearned aspect of PR, and the one that is most responsible for the antagonism towards PR that is expressed by so many editors. A news release is not a short article, nor is it a kind of advertisement. It is no exaggeration to say that 70 per cent of the releases received every morning by editors should never have been posted. There are two reasons for this miserable state of affairs. First, very few people employed in PR have ever had any training in the writing of news releases, let alone in PR itself. Secondly, the writers of news releases are the victims of clients and employers who insist that news releases should contain what they would like to see in print, not what editors are likely to print. The difference is enormous. There is only one answer to this: the writer must be so well trained and qualified that he has the status to be respected as a professional. This is what the CAM Diploma and membership of the IPR is all about.

News release writing has to inform in such a way that the information is seen by editors to be worth passing on to their readers. That implies a *double* communication, to and from the editor, so that a news release is not even a news story such as a reporter might produce. It has to compete with rival stories, and it has to be marketed on the strength of its news value and relevance to the journal concerned. The good presentation of the story, as explained in the previous chapter, is also part of this marketing process. The editor must be able to discern its qualities for himself.

It is therefore the job of the press officer to supply communication media with material which will help them to produce publications and programmes of interest and value to readers, listeners or viewers. This is his primary task, the one for which he should be trained and qualified. Of course, if the client or employer prefers to keep a hired hack to send out stories that please his vanity he cannot complain if press cuttings are rare or non-existent.

The onus is on the press officer to service the press and to create a two-way relationship so that editors come to him for stories because he is a reliable source of professionally prepared material. It is the press officer's responsibility to be accurate, and he enjoys the privilege of being better informed than the media.

Sometimes people ask why the IPR does not do a better job for PR. That is a non-question for the only people who can earn PR an enviable reputation are its practitioners. PR is judged by the people in it and the way they practise. Consequently, PR gets the criticism it deserves – like this from the editor of *Marketing*:

PR POPPYCOCK
We throw away something like 95 per cent of the releases received, and more than half of what we receive could not possibly be of the slightest interest to us. Indeed, a good proportion could not be of interest to anyone.

Let us take another instance. The London news agency which

supplies news to the UK national and regional press is the Press Association. By its very nature it is supplying mostly important 'hard' news stories, the kind that will appear on the home (that is, UK) news page of nationals and the front page of regional dailies. It has to be a very big PR story of national importance to get sent out by the PA wire service. Yet the PA is frequently put on the mailing list of, by PA standards, trivial product publicity stories. Ideally, the PA journalist would like to sub down from a maximum of 100 words. Also very few people go to the trouble to write a special brief story for the PA; instead, they send the PA the same voluminous three-page release that has gone elsewhere. They fill two six-foot dustbins daily with the rubbish that reaches them every morning from PR consultancies, PR departments and especially Whitehall PRO's. Most of them are written by ex-journalists who have obviously never had any training in PR.

Here is an example of an unusual story that was accepted by the Press Association and resulted in publication in almost every national daily and many provincial dailies plus the *New York Herald Tribune*, radio and TV. This Rentokil story is of course something of a change from 'hard' news. Note too that the length is as prescribed by news agencies.

FLEA CIRCUS IDEA SCRATCHED

The organisers of the Fourth British Pest Control Conference to be held in Jersey from April 21st-26th tried unsuccessfully to find a Flea Circus to entertain them at the Conference Banquet.

Conference Committee member Mr. Peter Bateman of Rentokil said We were prepared to grant safe passage for the performers for the occasion but it seems we've done too good a job in the past. Almost all fleas we come across today are cat fleas which nobody seems to have trained.

However, delegates and their wives are promised appropriate entertainment and the Conference itself, on the theme 'Pest Control for a Healthy Environment' has a suitably serious scientific programme with sessions addressed by world authorities on industrial, commercial and domestic pests. It will be held at The Hotel de France, St. Helier, Jersey.

Sometimes even bad news shows that we exist. As an example of the deliberate distribution of an unfavourable story here is one from the Shaw Savill Line:

```
It is announced today that the 26,000-ton Shaw
Savill passenger liner OCEAN MONARCH is to be with-
drawn from service on her return to the United
Kingdom in June and the vessel's summer cruise
programme has been cancelled.

Shaw Savill Line state that it is with the utmost
reluctance and only after very full consideration
that they have taken this decision, which is as a
result of operational problems with the ship.

Shaw Savill's other passenger liner, NORTHERN
STAR, will carry out her scheduled programme of
twelve cruises, commencing on 7 June. Certain of
her cruises still have accommodation available;
Shaw Savill will do their utmost to offer accom-
modation on NORTHERN STAR to passengers displaced
from OCEAN MONARCH. In addition special arrange-
ments have been made with Chandris Lines to offer
alternative cruises to these passengers.

For further information
Dennis Burges: Telephone 01-481 2525
               Home      01-992 4997
```

There are many good things about this very much to the point and delightfully short release. There may have been policy reasons, perhaps legal ones, for not disclosing the nature of the 'operational problems'. The use of caps for the names of the ships may be a house style, and may be acceptable in cruise brochures, but in a news release capital letters should be limited to the initial letters thus: Ocean Monarch and Northern Star. No editor would fail to get this message in a flash, there is probably little more to say, the story is publishable as it stands, and if editors do want more details the PRO gives both his office and home telephone number. It is quite unusual to come across a release such as this where the writer knows when enough is enough.

Even the experienced journalist needs further training to write good news releases and often graduates with no journalistic experience have become better press officers or PRO's than ex-journalists. There are lots of reasons for this if only that it depends what sort of press experience the journalist has had. More often than not the best experience that a journalist can bring to PR is a wide knowledge of the world at large rather than writing ability. The great anomaly of PR is that a great many journalists have been recruited by the business, yet the standard of news release writing is extraordinarily poor.

A singular problem does confront the news release writer. Seldom can we write an individual story for each separate publication, we have to avoid giving exclusives, and so our story has to be broadly pleasing and valuable to a number of editors. However, the mistake is sometimes made of trying to make a single version of a story, all things to all men, spreading it over many pages in the vain hope that different editors will go to the trouble of extracting the bits they want. It is the press officer's job to write what editors want, a technical story for the technical press, a much less technical story for the popular press. Studying the market and supplying what it is most likely to publish is what is meant by marketing a news release. It is this meticulous approach to press relations that makes PR so time-consuming, but it is the way to maximize press coverage.

Let us take a simple example. A common story is that of a new appointment. If one looks at the 'new appointments' columns in *The Financial Times*, *The Times* or *Campaign* it will be seen that most announcements are confined to a single sentence. It will be noticed too, if other paper are studied, that *The Guardian* and quite a number of others do not print these announcements at all. Yet it is practically normal for extensive biographies, accompanied by photographs, to be sent to a long list of publications. Why? Simply because the market for such stories has not been studied and understood. The stories, and beautiful salon portraits, may well please the subject of the story, but that is immaterial to a press relations exercise.

Here is an example of a good one-sentence appointment story:

```
Lord Beeching will take over as chairman of
Furness Withy & Company Limited from Mr. John
MacConochie on 1 January 1973.
```

It will be observed that in this example initial caps are *not* given to the job title.

Different versions of the story can be sent to other journals, more about the man's career for his professional journal perhaps, more about his life story and personal details for his local paper, and perhaps a whole article for the house journal.

There are occasions when one-off stories are necessary, or when the mailing list is limited to two or three local newspapers. Stories about prize-winners are often sent to their local papers. Here is one that was sent to papers in the Reading, Slough and Windsor area:

THOMSON HOLIDAYS FLY CROCODILE TO JAMAICA

Captain Morgan, the baby crocodile hatched at the Windsor Safari Park has, at last, gone home - to the Swamp Safari Park in Jamaica.

The crocodile hatched from an egg brought back to the UK by Thomson holidaymaker Anthony Hilbery of 2 Claremont Road, Windsor and has been in the care of Peter Waters at the Safari Park.

To grow to its full twenty-foot man-eating potential, the reptile needs the hot Jamaican climate and for this reason, Thomson Holidays and Britannia Airways were asked to help.

It would be wrong to suggest or expect that every release is intended for publication. The press officer will sometimes issue background information to which journalists may refer when writing about the subject. Releases sent to nationals may need to offer a number of story leads which can be followed up according to the policies of individual editors since rival newspapers will not wish to print exactly the same report. On the other hand, product publicity releases may well be printed as submitted, sometimes because trade and other specialist magazines are short-staffed and the editor is glad to print a well-written piece as it stands. But whatever the intention or fate of the news release the literary standard should be a publishable one, either because it makes it easier for journalists to extract the facts, or because it saves the editor time if subbing and re-writing do not have to be performed. Extensive re-writing of verbose stories can lead to the unintentional introduction of errors.

While emphasis will be placed on the application of a seven-point formula that is best applied to the product publicity story, the facility to write in such a disciplined fashion will enhance the ability to write any other kind of press story.

So, before proceeding to the formula let us first look at the various kinds of news release that the press officer may be called upon to write. They are six:

1. *One-sentence releases* – announcing new appointments, promotions, retirements, change of company name, and change of address.

2. *Publishable as it stands seven-point formula release* – as detailed below.

3. *Background story* – general information for filing and use when the journalist is writing about the subject.

4. *Summary and full technical story*. When a long detailed release is

justified it is helpful to editors to precede the main story with a short summary of perhaps a hundred words.

5. *Extended picture caption story*. A good picture may be the most publishable aspect of the release, and attached to it will be a story of perhaps half a normal sheet of release paper.

6. *Digest of a speech or a report*. Rather like the summary and full technical report, this kind of release is helpful to the editor in highlighting or summarizing the contents of an accompanying document such as a speech, annual report, brochure or catalogue.

The Frank Jefkins Seven-Point Formula for Writing News Releases

The following seven points form a logical sequence for the presentation of facts in a news release. The formula is also useful as a guide to the sort of information without which a story cannot be written, and as a check list to ensure that a story contains all the necessary factual elements. With the aid of this formula a rough draft release can be produced very quickly. Inability to base a release on this formula will immediately reveal the inadequacy of the material on which the writer is trying to produce a story. Woolly stories, using many words to say very little, are the result of not using such a formula or plot. Here, then, are the seven points to follow:

1. The *subject* of the story.
2. The name of the *organization*.
3. The *location* of the organization (which may be different from the address for further information).
4. The *advantages* of the policy, scheme, action, product or service.
5. The *applications* to which the subject may be put.
6. The *details* of specifications, prices, colours, sizes and so on.
7. The *source* of further information, samples, price lists, or address of showroom, information centre of the maker.

These seven points can be memorized by the key words: *Subject – Organization – Location – Advantages – Applications – Details – Source*. The initial letters give us a mnemonic, SOLAADS.

It is usual for press officers to give their names, addresses and telephone numbers for 'further information', but it is also useful to close the story with a paragraph which says 'XYZ is made and marketed by the ABC Co. Ltd of 112 Orchard Way, New Hoxley,

Exshire, EX4 7MA.' Use of this closing paragraph also provides the means of stating the full company name so that there is no need to clutter up the opening paragraph with some long-winded monstrosity such as 'The XYZ Company Limited, a member of the OMS Group Inc of Chicago,' which no-one is going to print. Moreover, it gets in the way of the story and obscures the subject.

While this may look like the framework for a release of seven paragraphs this is not so. The formula represents the *sequence* of information, even of a long release running to more than one page. The secret of a good release, however, is that the opening paragraph should summarize the whole story. (Look at any newspaper report and it will be seen that the essence of the story is given in the first paragraph, succeeding paragraphs providing amplification.) The opening paragraph is therefore the most important part of the news release, and will be dealt with separately in the next chapter as it is of supreme importance.

There is nothing difficult about writing a publishable release when this formula is used for it imposes the discipline of presenting in a logical sequence a coherent assembly of facts expressed in the fewest necessary words. There is no requirement for dramatic prose, although apt words and correct terminology call for a first-class vocabulary and understanding of the subject matter. While an advertisement may demand superlatives and repetition, a news release does not. Adjectives should be expunged. Brief statements like 'in three popular shades' which may be all right in an advertisement must be detailed as 'in shades of pink, blue and green'. In other words, a good news release is one that states cold-blooded facts without comment.

The Seven-Point Formula In Use

To explain the use of the formula in practical terms here are two step-by-step demonstrations, one for a building society story and the other for one about a new air travel service. The SOLAADS mnemonic is set at the side of the breakdown of information, and this outline provides a useful guide to the facts required before the story can be written.

A Building Society Savings Scheme
Let us assume that this is a fairly simple story about a new savings scheme whereby the lender who leaves a minimum sum in his account for six months receives a higher rate of interest. The seven-point formula is applied like this:

1. S   New savings scheme – leave minimum sum for six months, earn higher rate of interest.
2. O   Name of building society.
3. L   All large cities, towns, branches and agents.
4. A   Higher interest. Hedge against inflation. Tax paid. Easy withdrawal.
5. A   Saving up for special occasions – holiday, wedding, anniversary, new furniture or to meet accounts that fall due such as rates or school fees.
6. D   Details of scheme – how to join, interest rates, when and how paid.
7. S   Head Office address for details.

An Air Travel Service
In this case let us assume that an airline is announcing a new route which is time-saving and cheaper.

1. S   Air travel using new route.
2. O   Name of the airline.
3. L   Airport from which the new service operates.
4. A   Shorter journey – fewer stops – cheaper.
5. A   Business travel.
6. D   Aircraft. Times. Days. Fares. Services (e.g. meals).
7. S   Airline office in London.

When one tries to apply the seven-point formula it is necessary to determine the subject. And the subject could be different according to the media. If, for instance, the press officer was working for a central heating firm his stories could have a variety of subjects such as the company, the equipment it manufactures or the fuel or fuels used, according to the type of story and the class of media. To take the instance still further, if oil suddenly became the cheapest fuel and the company made an oil-fired boiler, the boiler would be the primary subject. But it is not merely a question of topicality: the subject should be chosen for its reader interest and reader value. Company names are pretty dull subjects, and that is why they need to be pared of their 'company limited' frills. *Ford's new Capri* is infinitely better than *The Ford Motor Company's new Capri*, and those three short, sharp words combine as a total subject which is impossible when the full company name is recited.

What, then, is the subject? No doubt the managing director would plump for the name of the building society. But that is not the subject: it is the new savings scheme, and better still it is the extra rate of interest. (Variations on a possible opening paragraph for this story will be found in the next chapter.)

Below is a draft showing how this building society story might be written, applying the seven-point formula. It is not claimed that this is a perfect news release. The reader may profit from attempting his own final version.

New Savings Scheme

An extra one percent interest is offered to savers who leave a minimum deposit of £250 for six months at any of the 300 local branches of the British Building Society of Ipswich.

The minimum deposit of £250 may be built up with regular weekly or monthly savings, or £250 or more may be invested as a lump sum so that the extra interest is earned sooner. If the minimum sum has not been withdrawn after six months, an extra one percent will be added to the usual 10 percent interest (tax paid).

Depositors are offered a means of saving for short term needs such as holidays, weddings or new furniture, or for regular payments of bills such as rates, school fees or insurance premiums. A minimum sum of £250 can be left in the account for six months, gain its extra interest, and be withdrawn one day later.

Accounts may be opened at any of the 300 branches of the British Building Society, all addresses being in Yellow Pages and local telephone directories. All accounts qualify for the scheme from the day of the first deposit, which may be made personally or by post. Freepost envelopes are supplied to regular postal savers.

This new extra interest savings scheme is announced by the British Building Society - a member of the Building Societies Association - of 80-90 New Suffolk Street, Ipswich, IP2 6DO, telephone Ipswich 80001, from whom an explanatory leaflet may be obtained.

John Smith,
Press Officer.
Telephone:
Date   Ipswich 80001.

Fig. 15.1

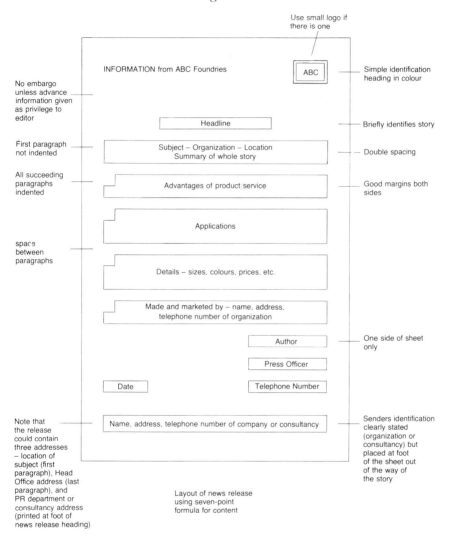

Layout of news release
using seven-point
formula for content

The facts are stated simply and without superlatives, without persuasion, and the reader is left to decide whether the proposition is a sound one or not, whether he wishes to enquire at a local branch for more information, or whether he would like to write for a leaflet. He is not told to visit a branch or write for a leaflet *now*, as he might in an advertisement. The story is not padded out with the history of the society. There is no puffery, it is a story publishable as it stands, and it merits publication as it is news of interest to a very large number of readers of many publications. Since the society has 300 branches it is of national interest. And the release is only one page long. Since the scheme is in force there is no need for an embargo, and there is no point in announcing it days ahead so that an embargo is required. Nor is it necessary to say *for immediate release* since that is obvious. By giving the author's name and the date at the end of the story there is no need to insert *ends*. The last paragraph is used to give the full name, address and telephone number of the organization, and to offer to the reader an explanatory leaflet. The name of the press officer and his telephone number is given so that the editor can seek further information if he wishes it.

To combine the advice given in the previous chapter on presentation and this one on the actual writing, the plan of a model news release is given in Figure 15.1.

CHAPTER SIXTEEN

The Opening Paragraph

In the previous chapter a seven-point formula or model was set out for the writing of publishable news releases, and great importance was placed on the opening paragraph. Two important statements should be emphasized.

1. The secret of a good release is that the opening paragraph should summarize the whole story.

2. If all that is printed is the first paragraph the message has been published.

The subject should be stated in the first paragraph, but preferably in the first sentence and ideally in the first three words if not the first word.

In most cases, the opening paragraph should contain the subject, organization, location and brief highlights of the story. By making use of the seven-point formula the form and content of the opening paragraph becomes a natural discipline. When editors make their rapid appraisal of releases a glance at the opening paragraph will be sufficient to tell whether the story has a possible use or whether it will join the great majority that are discarded. This is so whatever the subject matter.

A great mistake with some releases is that they open with a rambling sentence, even a rambling paragraph, and nowhere in these hundred or so words is there any mention of the subject of the story let alone the substantial introduction recommended in the preceding paragraph. This is no exaggeration. It happens all the time. Here is an example:

```
In all spheres of industrial activity it is widely
recognized that for increased productivity and
```

```
improved overall efficiency Materials Handling
Methods must be scientifically organized, using
the latest techniques, such as unit loads, con-
tainerization etc.
```

Unlike an essay, a news release does not require an 'introduction', and that is the main fault with the example given above. It applies an essay style which is misplaced in a news story. The three capital initial letters are unnecessary, and 'etc' should not appear in a sentence.

In the previous chapter it is pointed out that different versions of the opening paragraph are possible and here are some variations:

```
1. A new high interest savings scheme is announced
   by the British Building Society of Ipswich
   which has 300 branches in the UK. If a minimum
   of £250 is not withdrawn for six months, an
   extra one percent will be added to the current
   interest rate.
2. If a minimum of £250 is not withdrawn for six
   months an extra one percent will be added to
   the interest on deposits with the British
   Building Society of Ipswich which has 300
   branches in the UK.
3. A minimum of £250 deposited for six months with
   one of the 300 UK branches of the British
   Building Society of Ipswich will now earn an
   extra one percent interest.
4. An extra one percent interest is offered to
   savers at the 300 branches of the British
   Building Society of Ipswich on a minimum
   deposit of £250 not withdrawn for six months.
5. An extra one percent interest is offered to
   savers who leave a minimum deposit of £250 for
   six months at any of the 300 branches of the
   British Building Society of Ipswich.
6. The British Building Society of Ipswich
   announces that it will now pay an extra one
   percent on minimum deposits of £250 not with-
   drawn for six months on accounts at any of its
   300 UK branches.
```

Examples one to five show how an opening paragraph can be improved by re-writing. In 32 words the whole story is told in example five so that the potential lender absorbs the information in the sequence of the greatest interest and value *to him*. The sixth example presents the same information in the sequence which is of greatest interest to the *sender*, although this version would be acceptable to the financial press.

However, too many otherwise very good releases, assume that the company or product name is inevitably the principal subject. There could be more than one subject in the opening paragraph and priorities need to be defined. This can be seen from the following set of opening paragraphs.

```
1. Sanders' new frozen sardines are ready to serve
   on toast, with salads or on their own so that
   their real flavour can be appreciated. Being
   frozen, they do not have to be preserved in
   oil, nor are they tinned but come in cellophane
   packets.
2. Frozen sardines in cellophane packets is the
   new fish delicacy from Sanders of Hull. Free of
   oil and preservatives, they retain their
   natural flavour, and are ready to serve on
   toast, with salads or on their own.
3. The natural flavour of sardines can now be
   enjoyed with Sanders' new frozen sardines. Fresh
   from the cellophane packet, and free of oil and
   preservatives, they are ready to serve on
   toast, with salads, or on their own.
```

There are three subjects here, the packers, frozen sardines and the natural flavour of sardines.

It will be noticed that in this invented example the name of the organization is not given in full. There is nothing more boring than the release which begins with *'The ABC Company Ltd., a member of the XYZ Group (Inc), the world's largest makers of the best hot air. . .'* The place for full names and addresses is in the last paragraph.

Now let us turn to some actual first paragraphs taken from releases which have been issued by a variety of organizations. Here is one from a three-page story that was impeccably produced with a good printed heading but which was far too long. It suffered particularly from a generalized and subjectless opening paragraph:

```
Another progress mark in the time-scale which
later this year will bring into operation
```

```
Britain's most advanced institutional catering
system has now been reached with the completion
of three custom-built assemblies designed to
provide refrigeration for a five tunnel blast
freezer complex; a 1,069 m³ low temperature
store and various small coldrooms.
```

The meaningless opening paragraph, with its mysterious semi-colon, is not the way to write a news release that will attract the editor's attention and interest. The writer appears confused between the style required for writing a news release and that for an article.

The National Westminster Bank has most modest yet distinctive news release headings. Across the extreme top edge of the sheet is a narrow silver band bearing the familiar logo and the words National Westminster Bank Press Release. With this good start opening paragraphs in Nat-West stories are to the point:

```
Customers visiting the Bridgend branch of National
Westminster Bank during the next week will be
forgiven if they think they've walked into the
local rugby club premises by mistake.
```

For sheer stark brevity this one for Rentokil's hygiene service is acceptably dramatic:

```
The worst toilets in Britain are those in some of
our older Primary Schools.
```

Sometimes newspapers themselves issue press stories and here is one from the Liverpool press:

```
Merseyside's two independent daily newspapers -
the Liverpool Daily Post and its evening stable-
mate the Liverpool Echo - have moved to a new
£8.8-million headquarters which incorporates some
of the world's most advanced thinking both in the
design of the building itself, and of the equip-
ment it houses.
```

One of London's most fascinating sources of press information is Christie's, but the following was unusual even for them:

```
On Tuesday, December 3rd, in a sale of Contempor-
ary Art, Christie's are to sell a set of ten
Pirelli calendars. This is the first time a com-
plete set has ever been offered for sale and the
```

first time Christie's have ever auctioned Pirelli
calendars.

Let us look more closely at the all-important opening paragraph. Because a news release is a short, brief piece of writing, the first paragraph must do its job succinctly. If the reader is not spurred to continue reading beyond the opening words the rest of the story need never be written; it must be interesting and compelling.

Notice, too, that our opening paragraph is not introductory. It does not lead up to story, but tells the gist of the story at once. *It gives the story away*. Some news release writers try to play games with the reader, as in this case:

When Italian soccer teams go training this Spring,
many of the footballs they will be using will not
be of the conventional leather type.

Teasers are tiresome. Better to write:

When Italian soccer teams go training this Spring,
many of the footballs they will be using will be
made from USI Europe's EVA powder Microthene.

Newspaper stories are written in the style of the seven-point formula, with the opening paragraph summarizing the whole story.

CHAPTER SEVENTEEN

Some News Releases Analysed

It is now proposed to reproduce a number of releases, in part or whole according to their length or usefulness for quotation purposes. In previous chapters recommendations have been made which are not always apparent in these examples, and while they are not serious blemishes (and it would be remarkable if everyone did everything in exactly the same way!) the following comments are offered for consideration when these examples are being read.

1. Underlining is unnecessary, unlikely though it is that the press officer's headline will be used.

2. Location of organizations is seldom given, yet it should not be taken for granted that editors will know, especially when the address on the heading is that of a consultancy.

3. Address of organization is frequently missing from releases, yet it is very important information which may or may not be on the printed heading.

4. Full points are used in abbreviations when press practice is to dispense with them. They take up needless space.

Finally, several of these releases include 'For immediate release' and 'Ends' which are superfluous bits of jargon.

However, before examining the better releases let us look at a release which the author considers his prize example of what not to do. All the story says is that the firm has changed its address, and this could be said in even fewer words than the first paragraph of the actual release which needlessly ran to three sheets. This release seems to be a prime example of failure to let well alone, of anxiety not to miss the opportunity of saying more than that the firm has moved.

TRI-WALL CONTAINERS ON THE MOVE!

Tri-Wall Containers Limited, who for the past five years have been operating from offices in Curzon Street, London, W.1., will, from the 11th November, be directing their sales effort from new offices at One Mount Street, London, W.1.

Since the company introduced TRI-WALL PAK material to Great Britain in 1963, operating from limited accommodation, there has been some expansion of staff, and the new location will allow even better customer service, and give the company space to demonstrate its materials and containers.

The company has remained in the heart of London because the management believes that it is of paramount importance to be at the centre of the business world as this offers ease of access for customers availability of business services, the position as a focus of national and international travel and telecommunications systems, which are great advantages to a small company supplying a service throughout Great Britain, while possessing very valuable overseas contacts.

Service is provided by Packaging Engineers and associate companies throughout the country, and facilities are available in many European countries and North America to assist with trial and other shipments if required.

Service begins with design and advice on associated aspects of packaging and is carried through samples, testing to the supply of any quantity of simple or complex packs, at short notice, on reliable delivery.

TRI-WALL PAK is a lightweight, triple-fluted, corrugated fibreboard, specially developed for the export packaging market. It is an economical and reliable substitute for timber and plywood, and is used for numerous applications in providing the protection required by goods being exported either by sea or by air. Apart from direct cost savings, it offers cost reductions in labour, storage

I

space, and freight, while allowing advertising
through printing on the outside of the container.

TRI-WALL and TRI-WALL PAK are the trademarks for
triple-flute corrugated board manufactured to the
specifications of Tri-Wall Containers Limited.
Manufacture, arrangements for fluting, fabrication
sale and use are protected by U.S. patents
2,759,523; 2,949,151; 2,969,170; 2,985,553;
3,036,752; 3,096,224; 3,122,976; 3,186,283;
3,199,763; 3,290,205; and U.K. Patents 805,320;
1,018,241; 1,053,095. Other patents pending.

Tri-Wall Containers Limited is jointly owned by
the British firm of Tillotson and Son Limited,
Ashleigh, Heaton, Bolton and the American Company,
Tri-Wall Containers Inc., Plainview, New York.

Comment is superfluous, but the reader may find it an amusing if
breathless experience to read this release aloud.

The first example, issued by J. C. Bamford Excavators, is historical
in that it was issued in November 1973 when the oil crisis produced a
petrol rationing scare.

CHANGE OF STYLE TO SAVE FUEL

Mini cars have replaced the expensive four litre
Jaguars driven by directors of J. C. Bamford
Excavators, the Staffordshire based manufacturer
of earthmoving equipment.

The switch in style is part of the company's
contribution to voluntary fuel savings. The
chauffeur car service and demonstrations of
excavators on sites throughout the country have
also been stopped.

The four JCB aircraft have been grounded
indefinitely and can be used only for export
service if there is no scheduled flight as an
alternative.

Anthony Bamford, director, said today: 'No one
will be allowed to drive a car with an engine
bigger than two litres. The field representatives
have been instructed to cut the number of journeys
in their Marinas and to observe the suggested 50
miles an hour speed limit.'

'The cancellation of demonstrations and the

```
self-imposed restriction on the aircraft will un-
doubtedly mean the loss of orders. If the crisis
lasts for several months the effect will be
serious.'
Issued 28 November 73 by T. John Foster, MIPR,
MInstM, Promotions Manager.
```

In many respects this is an excellent release, and it follows much of the advice given in this book. Note the correctly indented paragraphs and the absence of a capital 'D' for director. The opening paragraph sums up the whole story very well in three lines that give subject, organization and location.

In Chapter Fourteen reference was made to the embargo as a privilege, enabling the editor to have advance knowledge of information which it would be foolish or improper to publish before the stipulated date and time. Unfortunately, embargoes are abused by both sides, press officers using embargoes for trivial reasons and editors sometimes overlooking or ignoring the stricture. There is no law which says the embargo must be obeyed, and it is no more than a gentleman's agreement subject to responsible editors understanding the embarrassment or serious consequences that would be caused by premature publication.

The following instance of an unjustified embargo was repeated in the Observer column of the *Financial Times*:

Chicken counting

I am indebted to the far-sighted British Textile Machinery Association for a Press release about U.K. participation at a trade fair in South Carolina, which opens tomorrow. The release, not due for publication until November 2, points out that 'the stand of Mather and Platt, of Manchester, attracted considerable interest.'

That was taking an embargo too far, the irony of the *FT* comment being that the above is quoted from the issue of *October 24!*

Because of this abuse of the embargo, the next example of a news release not only carried a typed embargo but was also rubber-stamped NOTE EMBARGO in huge letters. It is a brief, well-detailed story and opportunity is given for follow-up through a bank official.

```
            EMBARGO: Not for publication
            before 0015 hours, Friday 14
            February, 1975.
Nat-West to buy majority stake in Swiss Bank
```

National Westminster Bank has agreed terms with
Nestlé Alimentana SA, Vervey, for the purchase of
a controlling interest in Handelsbank in Zurich, a
leading privately-owned commercial bank in
Switzerland.

Subject to the necessary consents in both the UK
and Switzerland, National Westminster Bank is to
acquire 55% of the equity of Handelsbank in
Zurich, whilst Nestlé Alimentana is to retain an
approximate 19% shareholding. The proposed
purchase does not affect the balance of the shares
which are held by leading industrial and financial
groups in Europe. For the time being National
Westminster Bank does not intend making any
significant changes in the management and
personnel policies of the bank.

Handelsbank in Zurich, which had a consolidated
balance sheet total of S.Frcs. 1,417 million
(£235 million) as at 31 December 1974, provides a
full range of commercial and investment banking
services from its main office in the centre of
Zurich and has a subsidiary in Nassau; it is
engaged in universal banking activities with
emphasis on securities administration.

National Westminster Bank sees this investment as
a further and particularly significant extension
of its representation in the major financial
centres of the world.
End

Issued by John Duncan Chief Information Officer
          National Westminster Bank
          22 Old Broad Street EC2N 1DU
Enquiries to:
Eric Ruddell Chief International Executive
Planning, Co-ordination and Special Relationships
International Banking Division
Telephone No (Office) 01-606-6060 Ext 2648
             (Home)   01-850-4452

There are one or two generalities (e.g. 'leading', 'full range' and 'universal') in this piece, but these could be deliberate since the writer has correctly judged the strength of the story, but he has left the door open for a fuller story by inviting editors to contact Eric Ruddell. The strategy is excellent. One small quibble: it uses the old-fashioned 'whilst' although most publishers prefer 'while' just as they prefer 'among' to 'amongst'.

It is interesting to see what happens to a release and here is a story that recorded an historic moment for Pan Am when their first jumbo jet came to London. The release read:

```
                    FOR IMMEDIATE RELEASE
       PAN AM TO INAUGURATE BOEING 747 SERVICE TO
               LONDON ON DECEMBER 15
```

Pan American World Airways will introduce the 362-passenger Boeing 747 jet transport into regularly scheduled service on December 15 with an inaugural flight from New York to London, William H. Lyons, Director for the United Kingdom, announced today.

The first flight will initiate daily 747 service in each direction between New York and London. The flight will continue on from London to Frankfurt. Then on December 12, one week after the inaugural, Pan Am will expand its New York-London 747 service by adding a second flight, providing both morning and evening 747 flights daily between New York and London.

'The inaugural of Boeing 747 service into London will be Pan Am's most significant contribution to the history of air transportation since it started flying Boeing 707 jets across the Atlantic nearly a decade ago', said Mr. Lyons.

'Not only will the wider aisles, broader seats and increased passenger services make the new aircraft the most comfortable jet ever introduced, the new aircraft has already enabled us to offer less expensive bulk fares.'

He also pointed out that the aircraft's sophisticated navigational and other equipment will make it the safest, most reliable jet in operation and added: By introducing a service

capable of carrying more people in fewer aircraft
Pan Am is contributing to the alleviation of aircraft congestion both in the sky and at large
airports. For instance, the 747 is expected to
enable Pan Am to cut aircraft movements at
Heathrow from 22 flights each day this summer to
16 next summer.

In anticipation of the arrival of the giant jets,
Pan Am has already opened two new London
facilities: Heathrow Airport's largest foreign
airline cargo terminal featuring equipment geared
to 747 container handling and its own spacious
town terminal at Semley Place near Victoria. This
terminal, Mr. Lyons said, is already proving quite
popular and promises to help alleviate much of the
airport check-in congestion in the era of the
Superjet.

By the time of the 747 arrival in London both the
terminal and Pan Am's London Airport check-in desk
will also be fitted with 35 Panacheck check-in
computers. By eliminating paper work and human
error, the system is capable of processing each
passenger in a fraction of the time it presently
takes. Pan Am is also training its Heathrow staff
for the first arrival and expects to expand its
central London staff and facilities.

Then there is a three-paragraph description of the number of flights
around the world and the dates they will commence followed by:

Pan Am was the first airline to order the 747. Of
33 Boeing 747s Pan Am has on order, 25 will be in
service by August, 1970, and the remaining by June
1971.

AUGUST 27, 1969

This is a long two-page release but it is thoroughly factual and, for a
change, the quoted material is informative. Too often quotes from
company personalities are invented banalities.

To illustrate what happens to a release, and to vindicate what has been said in the previous chapter about the importance of the opening paragraph, here are the reports which appeared in the London *Evening News* on August 27 and in the *Financial Times* on the same day. Note how each newspaper has adapted the story as a legitimate piece of reporting.

THE FIRST
FLIGHT OF
HEATHROW
JUMBO JET

BY GARRY MAY
Evening News Air
Correspondent

BRITAIN will get its first look at the jumbo jet when Pan American Airways starts its daily service into London from New York with the 362-seat Boeing 747 on December 15.

The new service will go on to Frankfurt and provide one flight a day in each direction.

Pan Am will introduce a second Boeing 747, giving both morning and evening flights, on December 22.

Daily services between New York and Paris start on December 18 and polar route services from America's west coast to London and Paris on March 20 next year.

The huge four-engined jets, with more than double the capacity of Boeing 707's, will enable Pan Am to cut its flights into Heathrow from 22 to 16 a day next summer.

BOAC introduces the new jet early in January and when other major airlines follow air traffic congestion at Heathrow will be eased.

Mr. William H. Lyons, Pan Am director for the U.K., said today: 'The new aircraft has already enabled us to offer less expensive bulk fares.'

More than 180 jumbo jets have been ordered by 28 airlines, including twelve by BOAC.

Substantially, Garry May's piece was written for him by Fred Tupper, the Pan Am PRO, although he probably did not bargain for the air correspondent's patriotic additions.

The *Financial Times* 'legitimatized' its version even more, which only goes to show that you cannot believe all you read in the editorial columns. The story was issued from Pan Am's Piccadilly, London, office.

Jumbo jet
service
By a Special Correspondent
NEW YORK, August 26.

THE first scheduled airline service flight of the Boeing 747 'Jumbo' jet is to go ahead on December 15, Pan American World Airways confirmed today. The inaugural flight of the 362-passenger liner will be from New York to London and on to Frankfurt.

The flight will initiate a daily new York–London–Frankfurt 747 service. A daily 747 service between New York and Paris will begin on December 18.

But of course it is a compliment if a journalist puts his own by-line on a press officer's story or a newspaper pretends it did not get the information from a PR source. Some press officers dislike journalists taking credit for their work, but this is a narrow outlook. A good news release is one that the journalist receiving it might have written himself. Nor is he being lazy in reproducing a good release word for word for that is the highest accolade a press officer can receive. The trouble with so many releases is that no journalist would ever wish to put his name to them.

In 1972 Thomson Holidays launched one of the most unusual and successful tourist ventures – cheap weekend visits to Moscow. Here is one of the releases, together with a selection of headlines which indicate the volume of coverage obtained.

```
Date: 22nd February, 1972.
FLY EAST WITH THOMSON HOLIDAYS

A Winter weekend in Moscow is the dramatic new
holiday offer announced by Thomson Holidays today.

Holidaymakers will be able to fly from Luton to
Moscow by Britannia Airways Boeing jet to spend 3
nights in the Russian Capital for just £29.

First departure is on November 2nd and flights
will continue until 22nd March. On a three night
holiday, with prices starting at £29, clients will
leave Luton at 10.00 hrs. on Thursday and return
at 19.30 on Sunday. Those wishing to spend more
time in the Soviet Capital can leave Luton on a
```

Sunday morning and return on a Thursday evening.
Prices for the 4 night visit start at £31.

Accommodation will be in the new Hotel Intourist
just a short walk from Red Square. All rooms have
private facilities and the price includes 3 meals
per day, and transfers to and from Moscow International Airport. Also included in the price are 2
excursions - a visit to the Kremlin and a tour of
Moscow.

Commenting on this exciting new venture, Bryan
Llewellyn, Managing Director and Chief Executive
of Thomson Travel Holdings Limited said that it
was the policy of the Company to introduce carefully planned new items to the holiday programme
each year, offering real value for money.

This is a good release marred only by the superlatives 'dramatic' and 'exciting'. Some of the headlines were:

Now Moscow for £29 (*Reading Evening Post*)
Cut-price Moscow air holidays (*Western Morning News*)
Moscow's warming (*Evening News*, London)
Three nights in Russian capital for only £29 (*Evening Chronicle*, Newcastle)
£29 Moscow! (*Travel News*)
Better red than Med? (*Sunday Times*)
Russian Weekend (*Daily Record*, Glasgow)
Moscow Holidays (*Birmingham Post*)
Moscow weekend for £29 (*The Guardian*)

There is a special reason for quoting this variety of headlines – and they are only a small selection – and that is that they demonstrate the pointlessness of inventing clever headlines. Each newspaper will create its own.

The next release comes within the category of releases which summarize a document, in this case an issue of the *Advertising Quarterly* published by the Advertising Association.

CREATIVITY THEME OF SPRING ADVERTISING QUARTERLY

For the first time in its ten years of publication, Advertising Quarterly devotes a complete

issue to a single theme - creativity. The Spring
issue consists of articles by prominent special-
ists in the agency and media worlds, covering such
topics as creating corporate identity, making
commercials, (radio as well as TV), mail order,
agency organisation of creative talent, and
creative responses to consumer attitudes.

Ralph Kanter, marketing director of the Thomas
Cook Group, gives an account of how an old-
established international travel company has
created a face for the times, with help from a
leading advertising agency. Alan Martin-Harvey
makes a personal plea for the press at a time when
the creative balance seems tilted towards television. And Peter Bostock, creative director of
J. Walter Thompson, London, describes an in-house
research project designed to show how creative
people spend their time when working - or not
working - in the office.

James Garrett contributes a critical assessment of
the state of play in the TV commercials business,
and Tony Hertz does the same for radio. Two top
executives of a leading American agency, Lester A.
Delano and Donald L. Kanter, detect growing
resistance to over-advertising in the United
States, and offer creative solutions. Graham
McKorkell takes a look at mail order advertising
in its creative aspect - and finds that very
little has changed.

Between them, the contributions to the Spring
issue of Advertising Quarterly illustrate the
range and variety of creative thinking in the
advertising industry - by no means confined to the
typewriter and the drawing board.

Advertising Quarterly, published by the Advertising Association, is available on subscription at
£5.00 a year. Single copies are £1.50 each.

- ENDS -

```
FOR FURTHER INFORMATION CONTACT:
                    Winifred Stacey
                    Public Relations Officer
                    The Advertising Association
                    Abford House 15 Wilton Road
                    London SW1V 1NJ
```

The above gives a useful digest of the contents of the magazine, and the same technique could be applied to releases about holiday tour brochures, catalogues, speeches, conferences, annual reports and other lengthy documents.

It will be noticed that in this example a name is quoted – Advertising Quarterly – but there is no attempt to present it in any special way. Some writers use inverted commas, others capital letters, while under-linings are not uncommon. Unless there is risk of confusion (e.g. Queen Mary launched the 'Queen Mary'), the simple style adopted in the last release is adequate. If an editor wishes to use italics, bold face, capitals or inverted commas he may do so.

One fault may have been spotted by the perceptive reader, and it has been brought out by the quoted reports from the press. Paragraphs are indented in the press, with the exception of the opening paragraph which usually follows 'book style'. Yet almost every quoted release is set out with unindented paragraphs, possibly because the press officer has not instructed his typist how to type a manuscript. In the following example of a release the seven-point formula is applied and the correct style of presentation is used. Note the absence of 'For Immediate Release' and 'Ends' which are superfluous. Normally, use of the word 'you' is not recommended in releases, but this was a publishable story sent to women's page and women's magazine editors.

```
     NATIONAL DISTRIBUTION FOR NECCHI LYDIA 544
               AUTOMATIC SEWING MACHINE

The new Necchi Lydia 544 automatic sewing machine
is being distributed through a national network of
some 250 agents, a number of whom have branches in
department stores in addition to their own shops.
There are more than 30 Necchi agents in London,
and the rest are in 200 towns throughout England,
Scotland, Wales and Northern Ireland. All these
agents will give free demonstrations.
```

With this new sewing machine each stitch is clearly pictured on the selector knob, and all you have to do is turn the knob to the stitch you want and sew. There is no needle position lever, no zig-zag width lever, and there are no separate cams for different stitches. The Necchi Lydia is so automatic that in a single afternoon you can make a dress including basting, button-holes, sewing on buttons or zip fastener and embroidery, too, without any hand sewing.

And with the new speed control, not just foot control, there is a choice of five speeds to make sewing even easier. The free-arm is so slim it is small enough to take the sleeve of a child's garment only $2\frac{1}{2}$ inches across.

This machine will produce every kind of domestic or household sewing. Every stitch will be used, each is as useful as the other, and you do not have to pay for stitches which you will rarely if ever use. It will sew tiny straight stitches, zig-zag frayed edges, cord pillow cases, blind-stitch hems, stretch-stitch elastic, tack, make button-holes, shell edge or embroider - automatically without having to make complicated changes of attachments, discs, cams or gadgets. The recommended price is 85 guineas.

The Necchi Lydia 544 is marketed by Necchi (Great Britain) Ltd., 69-85 Tabernacle Street, London EC2.

(Telephone: 01-253 2402).

N.1008/January 26 1970   FRANK JEFKINS, PRO

This Necchi story was sent out on a consultancy heading which said at the top NEWS from NECCHI (GREAT BRITAIN) LIMITED.

In a release from Rentokil we see how facts can be presented succinctly with good use of short paragraphs:

27th March, 1974

CENTRAL HALL PIGEONS EVICTED

A fire engine with a 100 ft. turntable ladder was used by Rentokil's pest control team to reach the

ledges of the Central Methodist Hall Westminster
on March 14th so that they could apply a soft,
plastic pigeon repellent jelly.

The Central Hall, the Cathedral of Methodism, is
currently receiving a face-lift and Rentokil are
following the stone cleaners to prevent pigeons
fouling the building or causing a nuisance to
passers-by. The soft plastic jelly does not harm
the birds but produces a wobbly sensation if they
try to land on it.

Wherever Westminster's pigeons now hold their
meetings it will not be at the Central Hall - and
they no longer have safe seats at the Houses of
Parliament either, Rentokil's bird men have
treated them as well.

ISSUED FOR: Rentokil Limited
              Felcourt
              East Grinstead
              Sussex
PRESS ENQUIRIES: P. L. G. Bateman, M.I.P.R.
                        East Grinstead 23661
              Home- East Grinstead 25615

Newspapermen work at night and it is a sound idea for the PRO or
press officer to make himself available by giving his home telephone.
Lady press officers tend to be less willing to do so.

Finally, here is another story with evidence of the coverage
achieved:

Dickensian Era at Nat West Bank

Customers at the National Westminster Bank at 11
High Street, Biggleswade, can be forgiven if, from
17-28 February, they think they've stepped back
into the 19th century as they enter the branch.

For staff members will wear Dickensian style
costumes in a banking hall decorated with cur-
tains, posters and antiques designed to give an
atmosphere of that period.

It's all part of a customer contact exercise, one
of a series being held at Nat West branches

throughout the country. The glass security screens
in banks, although very necessary, restrict any
opportunity for close personal contact between
customers and counter staff.

In an effort to break down this personal communication problem, more than 1,000 of Nat West's
3,300 branches have so far mounted an exercise
since a successful experiment in April 1973.

At Biggleswade a member of the branch staff will
sit at an enquiry desk in the banking hall to tell
customers about the variety of services provided
by the bank. These range from Trustee and Executor
services to advancing personal loans, farm and
business development loans and supplying passports
and foreign currency.

The bank can always provide customers with
suitable introductions to experts in many departments and can provide any financial service very
quickly. It is concerned with farming, shop and
house building and buying, factories and business
ventures.

End

Press cuttings came in from papers as diverse as *The Sun*, *Daily Mail*, *Luton Evening Post*, *Irish Independent*, *The Royal Gazette* (Bermuda), a South African and several European papers. A film crew from the American NBC TV network visited the bank, and Anglia TV covered it too. A freelance photographer took pictures which appeared in magazines all over the world. And it made a full-colour picture front page story for the Nat West house journal, *Bankground*.

The above are examples of releases that were written and posted to selected publications, but sometimes the story is so urgent that it can only be telephoned to news agencies. Such was the case with an historic story on the night of October 3, 1958. It is composed with admirable concision and precision and is a model of the sort of story agencies like PA and Reuters appreciate.

BRITISH OVERSEAS AIRWAYS CORPORATION

The British Overseas Airways Corporation
announces that it will inaugurate its Trans-

Atlantic pure jet airliner scheduled service today Saturday 4th October 1958.

Authority to operate this service has now been received from the British Ministry of Transport and Civil Aviation and also from the Port of New York Authority.

A de Havilland Comet 4, under the command of Captain R. E. Millichap and with the Chairman of B.O.A.C., Sir Gerard d'Erlanger, on board, will leave London at 0930 hours British Summer Time for New York today.

A second Comet 4, under the command of Captain T. B. Stoney and with the Managing Director of B.O.A.C., Mr. Basil Smallpiece, on board, will depart from New York at 0700 hours Eastern daylight time today for London.

The two aircraft are expected to pass each other over the Atlantic at approximately 45 West longitude.

The story could not be released until the Press Branch of BOAC knew that the Port of New York had given its permission to operate the service. Permission was not received until late that night.

CHAPTER EIGHTEEN

Pictures and Captions

Photographs cost a lot of money and can absorb a disproportionate part of the press relations budget unless properly controlled. Many mistakes are made over pictures. Releases are sometimes accompanied by too big a selection of too large prints, and that can be a waste of money. Photographs are not always necessary for every journal to which the story is sent. Sometimes, especially if the mailing is large, it is more practical to tell editors that pictures are available. These strictures are made at the beginning of this chapter because while every user of press relations services loves to see a picture published, not every picture sent out has even a chance of being reproduced. Profligate distribution of pictures is a vice of bad PR.

Another common fault is the quality of pictures, both in composition and in suitability for reproduction. And there are still some newcomers to the business who are capable of mailing snapshot size prints, captioned on the backs with a ballpoint pen, and sent through the post unprotected by card.

Peter Ransley, when editor of *Plastics & Rubber Weekly*, made some quotable comments on pictures. He said:

'Pictures are very important. They're the first thing a reader looks at. Yet the standard of industrial PR pictures is always low. . . Pictures should be taken with the lowest common denominator of reproduction in mind – newspapers. Yet many are technically not good enough for newspapers. And many show little imagination. Uninteresting pictures of a complete piece of machinery instead of a close-up of some of the guts of it that would bring out an important points. Pubs, laboratories, hospitals unrealistically bare of people; a stand at an exhibition which closed six weeks ago; a view of a new office block, minute, from several hundred yards away. I think one of the biggest single improvements that could be made in press relations work is in the quality of pictures.'

Of course, Peter Ransley was right, but it is not entirely the fault of press officers. Press officers do not always buy their pictures wisely, and seldom understand the limitations of the photographers they use. A photographer can take only the picture he is instructed to take by a press officer who knows what pictures he wants and what kind of picture he needs for the distribution he has in mind. The press officer will need to spend much time sorting out which photographers are best for particular work – studio portraits, table top, industrial action, speakers at meetings, interiors, and so on. Few photographers are equally good at all these specialities. A good photographer is worth his price.

The selecting and instructing of photographers is itself a highly skilled business which has to be learned in the hard school of experience. The press officer who masters this side of his business is well on the way to becoming a very successful practitioner.

An Eleven-Point Guide for Pictures and Captions

The following eleven points provide a practical guide to pictures and captions for press relations purposes:

1. Subject material
2. People in pictures
3. Copyright, reproduction fees and delivery
4. Size of prints
5. Sharp, contrasty, glossy prints
6. Pictures available
7. The caption
8. People's names
9. Never use a paper clip
10. Protect pictures in the post
11. Colour pictures

1. *Subject Material*

Pictures should be taken for pictorial effect as well as for information value. Composition and lighting can enhance comparatively dull subjects like technical components. Glamorous models are usually more of a hindrance than a help in the majority of PR pictures, unless perfectly relevant and natural. True, there have been some PR gimmicks such as bikini-clad girls at a filling station to announce a new petrol. But it remains a fact that more people will look at a picture of a child or an animal than at a piece of cheese-cake.

2. *People in Pictures*

Human interest in pictures can often be a big asset. Holiday guide books issued by resorts usually carry pages of advertisements which look more like those for estate agents than hoteliers. The tables are always empty of people, white napkins frigidly set out as if all the guests have died in their beds. In external pictures no-one is seen entering or leaving and no cars are parked outside. Contrast these pictures with those in the brochures issued by holiday camps or agents for holidays abroad which are bursting with happy holiday-makers. People make pictures.

The people in pictures should usually be doing something suitable, and be intent on what they are doing, not grinning up into the camera. Pictures taken of factory operations will look more authentic if the operators are seen in profile or backview.

If it is desirable to make a scene – such as an airport – look natural, busy people should be asked to walk into the picture, and to do so naturally, ignoring the camera. The photographer should make sure that ordinary people photographed like this have no objection to their picture being published.

Permission to photograph people, or to use pictures containing people, is something which may have to be established to avoid legal problems. Normally it is quite safe to print pictures with people in them provided no opinion or testimony is attributed to them.

It is necessary to avoid offending professional men and women or amateur athletes and sportsmen and women if pictures appear to be giving them publicity. This is a point to bear in mind when pictures may be used for a variety of purposes involving press relations and advertising. What might be admissible in press relations might not be in advertising, yet there might be a temptation to use the same pictures. This problem has occurred when people of amateur status have been featured in a magazine article, but to picture them in an advertisement for that issue of the magazine would have been extremely embarrassing if not dangerous to their amateur status.

3. *Copyright, Reproduction Fees and Delivery*

When commissioning photography it is essential to ensure that the copyright is assigned to either the organization or the client as the case may be. Photographers earn income from reproduction fees on pictures for which they retain the copyright. As a result, it is not uncommon for those unfamiliar with copyright to obtain prints of pictures taken by newspaper or press agency photographers, and then to pass them on to the press officer with instructions to issue them to the press. Such pictures cannot be reproduced without a fee to the owner of the copyright, and editors will not do this with a picture supplied from a PR source. They will expect the picture to be free of copyright, and this is possible only when the organization concerned owns the copyright.

Similarly, one has to be careful about using pictures in any kind of printed material. Unless copyright belongs to the organization a reproduction fee will be due to the owner. Higher reproduction fees are charged when a picture appears in advertisements or advertising material, than when it is used for editorial purposes. Although a PR consultancy may produce an educational leaflet it could be classed as advertising literature, especially if distributed through a showroom or on an exhibition stand. In this context, 'picture' may be read to mean any illustration whether it be photograph, drawing, diagram or cartoon. It is a point to remember when wishing to reproduce a newspaper cartoon in a house journal: if it is a staff journal the publishers may be kind and agree to a token fee provided full acknowledgement is given. But newspapers do earn a very considerable income from syndicated material.

One also has to be careful of organizations which make a speciality of photographing businessmen in their offices: when the time comes to want to use the picture because, say, the man has been promoted, the print charge may be too exorbitant to justify its wide distribution, while purchase of the copyright may be as high as £100. The photograph itself may be excellent but this kind of photograph, which plays upon the plausibility and vanity of the businessman, is of no practical use to the press officer who has a budget to keep to and needs 25 half-plates in a hurry.

Before commissioning a photographer it is crucial to find out when he will deliver. More often than not the press officer needs a same-day print service, otherwise the story is dead and the pictures worthless. Some photographers are specially set up to provide rapid service and go so far as to provide a regular messenger service. But on the whole this is uncommon, as most photographers are small units, and if they do their own processing there may be delay of up to seven days before the contact prints or proofs arrive. It depends on the purpose of the photography whether this delay matters or not; it is also another case of the press officer having to understand how to buy photography.

From these remarks it will be seen that the press officer must maintain strict control over photography. Pictures can be very valuable and costly property. For example, when a large number of prints are required (and provided the original is first-class) it is possible to have quantities of repro-prints run off at about a third of the cost of ordinary prints. Again when having photographs taken the photographer may charge by the 'shot', and it is very tempting to be wasteful instead of working to a clear programme of planned 'shots'.

It is advisable to make sure that photographers retain the negative safely and can supply prints to order and the press officer must keep a photographic library so that he knows exactly what pictures exist, and who took them. The simplest record system is a ring file containing sheets on which are stuck prints and captions with the negative numbers and the photographer's name and address typed below. This is handier to use than a bulky guard book.

The consultant will also find that for accountancy purposes he should always issue written orders bearing the job number so that the photographer can include both order number and job number on his invoice. This saves time in checking invoices and authorizing payment.

4. Size of Prints

It is advisable that pictures no larger than half-plate size be used for general press relations work. For special work – fashion, for example – big prints are justified. If it is an exclusive article, a set of large prints is desirable. But on the whole, half-plate prints of good pictures are perfectly suitable for most press needs. There is very real risk that larger pictures will be damaged in the post, and therefore rendered useless.

Larger than negative size pictures are required because they are easier to see by the editor, easier to retouch if necessary, but most important of all blockmakers and platemakers, when re-photographing the picture, like to reduce from the original to the actual size of the plate. Blemishes lessen upon reduction.

It is sometimes mistakenly thought that if large pictures are sent to an editor he is more likely to print large pictures in his journal. The size of the photograph has no bearing on the size of the picture eventually reproduced.

5. *Sharp, Contrasty, Glossy Prints*

To reproduce well, especially on cheap newsprint, a picture must have good gradation of tone, otherwise the printed picture will be very poor. Unless a picture is first-class to begin with it will reproduce badly, even with skilled retouching. For reproduction purposes photographs should be black and white (not sepia), glossy not mat, and not glazed since glazed prints finger-mark easily and are liable to suffer cracked surfaces.

'Sharp' is an expression not always appreciated, and it is surprising how many people are content to accept a picture that is out of focus. A sharp picture enlarges well, and reproduces perfectly. Sharpness is not always possible in a news picture taken in hurried circumstances but it is essential in a picture taken with deliberation.

An editor is bound to reject a fuzzy, dull print which he knows will print badly. One of his problems is how to secure a regular high standard of picture reproduction.

6. *Pictures Available*

There are several ways of letting editors have a preview of the series of pictures available without going to the needless expense of mailing all the pictures to every editor. Miniatures can be sent, or sheets of lithographed reproductions, but one of the best ways is to reproduce the pictures at about snapshot size on whole-plate or larger photographic paper. Such pictures can serve a double purpose because for some magazines they will be reproducible as they stand, while editors of other journals, newspapers mainly, can request enlargements.

7. *The Caption*

First let us deal with the controversial question of whether captions should be fixed to the packs of pictures or flapped so that they can be folded down to be read leaving the picture visible. Both methods are in use, and there is something to be said for each. Many editors favour the first method, but the second is advocated by the IPR and in other textbooks. It is sensible to set out here the advantages and disadvantages of each method and possible reasons for their adoption.

Flapped Captions. Flapped captions are obviously very convenient to a person studying a picture since he can see both caption and picture together and refer from one to the other. Flapped captions probably owe their origin to the vast picture libraries in newspaper and magazine publishing houses, and this suggests that flapped captions are ideal for reference prints, but not for prints that will be used by an art editor and eventually a platemaker. When the caption is flapped there is always the risk that it will get ripped off and then the identity of the picture is lost.

An interesting development is the *double caption*, the top one fixed to the back of the print, the bottom one being flapped but perforated so that it may be detached.

Fixed Captions. Fixed captions have the distinct advantage that they are reasonably permanent. The fixing must be done carefully. Too much adhesive will spread with disastrous results. Some glues will crimp a photograph if it is on lightweight paper. Captions may also be attached with two strips of sellotape, one at the top, one at the bottom, but captions should never be caught with a single piece of tape so that they dangle precariously and can be separated from the print. If the caption stays with the picture identification is certain, and the wrong caption will not be applied. And since the caption is a source of information for the benefit of the journalist composing the actual caption which will appear in print there is no question of a detachable one being useful to send to the printer.

Direct Captions. Yet another method of captioning is to duplicate the wording direct on to the back of the photograph, and for this purpose a Banda spirit duplicator is generally used. This method has the merit of maintaining the identity of the picture even after it has been marked up with the required reductions for reproduction. These instructions to the platemaker are drawn on the back of the print. Sometimes they will be drawn over a caption which is pasted to the back of the print, but it can happen that a separate caption, whether flapped or fixed, may be taken off so that the instructions can be made on the back of the print itself.

Direct captions are used by those who frequently distribute pictures, the BBC for instance, and it is a good method when pictures are likely to be used soon after issue. But for pictures with a longer life and ones which may be held in stock, the attached caption can be replaced if the information has to be revised. The rule is that direct captions are well worth using when the expected life of the caption is short, and duplicating is perfect. It is, of course, a time-saving method ideal for urgent news pictures.

The only kind of caption which may provide actual copy for typesetting is the extended caption story, that is the sort which forms part of what is known as a picture-and-caption story. Here it is wise to submit the extended caption in news release form in addition to the fixed caption.

Wording of the Caption. The caption itself should consist of a title, a briefly worded description, and the address and telephone number of the source from which further information may be obtained. Usually, the text of a caption can be contained in about 50 words, but there may be exceptions to this. Accuracy of detail is absolutely essential. Photo captions are apt to survive a long time and may be referred to long after news releases have served their purpose. In addition, as a separate paragraph away from the information, it pays to identify the source by means of a rubber stamp on the back of the print itself. This is a precaution in case a caption is removed. Photographers should be instructed not to put their rubber stamp on the backs of prints as this is of no interest to editors.

Pictures suffer a strange life, and captions must be capable of standing up both physically and informatively to the diverse demands that many people may make upon them at various times over a considerable period.

There is surely nothing more foolish than the photograph which dangles by a piece of sellotape from the foot of a news release, a practice to be observed quite often in the press rooms of exhibitions. The picture is very easily parted from the news release, and since it bears no caption the picture is useless.

Equally useless is the photograph bearing no caption but having an identifying rubber stamp which has the effrontery to ask the editor to please mention the company's name!

After so much criticism this is the place to commend the practice of running off captions on headed caption paper. This is done very well indeed by P & O who print the company name in the house style shadow type logo and clearly set out the full address of the PR photographic library followed by the telephone number.

An aspect that is easily overlooked is that an editor may not like the picture he has in front of him, but would like to print something else on the same subject. If it is easy for him to pick up a telephone and ask for another picture he will do so, but if there is no address or telephone number on the caption he will use somebody else's picture. Pictures have to be marketed too, and the printed caption heading used by P & O is an excellent piece of press *relations* thoughtfulness, or good marketing if you prefer to call it that.

8. *People's Names*

It is vital to get names, initials, spellings, ranks, titles, jobs, qualifications, decorations and honorary positions correct. To be absolutely certain it is wise to go back to the most reliable source, such as the man's private secretary. It is frighteningly easy to get personal details wrong, especially when they are given over the telephone. Names like Davis and Davies, Philips and Phillips, and many others call for the utmost care. Most people like to see their names in print but they are not amused by misspellings.

Equally, it is vital to be accurate about personal descriptions. This is seldom easy because people's titles, jobs and positions may change.

Remember, too, that editors are relying on the press officer for thoroughly reliable information. The press officer may think that there is nothing to caption writing and dismiss it as a chore, but it is one of the most serious tasks he can perform.

9. *Never Use a Paper Clip . . .*

Or any other means to attach a picture to a letter, news release or MSS. Any sort of fastening will inevitably damage the picture and these marks will mar the picture when it is being re-photographed for plate-making purposes.

10. *Protect Pictures in the Post*

This may be unbelievable but editors do receive many pictures in crumpled envelopes with no protection whatsoever. Photographs should be protected by card, or despatched in specially made card-backed envelopes.

11. *Colour Pictures*

Finally, to complete this chapter, a word about colour pictures. Except on rare occasions when perhaps an editor wants a cover picture, colour photographs are of no use for media relations purposes. Colour pictures can be useful for other PR activities such as house journals, literature, exhibition displays and especially for slide presentations at seminars, but for normal press work black and white pictures are required. So, unless there is a special arrangement with an editor to supply colour pictures, the press officer will restrict himself to black and white photography.

However, the web-offset four-colour magazine does make colour photography a very different and exciting proposition for the press officer, and more use of this process could be made in the future.

CHAPTER NINETEEN

Feature Articles

A news release is broadcast, but an article is written specifically for one publication. It should bear an author's name and be exclusive to a single publication, although other articles on the same subject can be written by the same author for other journals and may appear concurrently. For example, the subject of holidays in Spain could form the theme of any number of original articles, each one being exclusive to a particular journal.

Such articles are not written speculatively. Editors do not sit back and wait for articles to appear out of the blue. Issues are planned and contents are commissioned. They may be written by staff writers, freelance contributors or by PROs and press officers. An editor may go to a literary agent in search of a suitable author. This means that there is no point in a press officer sitting down and writing an article which he then offers to an editor. Nor is he likely to be very successful in placing one of those articles which someone within the organization has decided to write without so much as the slightest invitation.

There is a very substantial market for good articles from PR sources, but chiefly for technical articles for trade, technical and professional journals which do not have large staffs. On the whole, national newspapers, women's magazines and other big circulation journals prefer to have articles written by their own staff writers, or by commissioned professional contributors, and will rarely publish features from PR sources unless perhaps they are written by well-known or authoritative writers.

The press officer can therefore achieve publication of feature articles in one of three ways, and the third can be sub-divided into a further three sections.

1. They may be written by staff writers.

2. They may be written by outside contributors.

3. They may be supplied by the press officer, either written by himself, or by a freelance author specially engaged, or by people within the organization.

Let us consider each in turn.

Articles by Staff Writers

Regular feature writers working on newspapers and magazines usually have to produce at least one article a week, and it is no mean feat to write interestingly on fifty or more different topics in a year. If a press officer can succeed in giving a staff writer a first-rate idea for an article it will be very welcome, but it must be an idea worthy of the writer, feature and journal.

The press officer should study the press and collect the names of writers who either write about the organization's subject, or could be interested in some aspect of it. Thus, the press officer will become aware of the staff writers to approach when appropriate topics occur.

Similarly, he will note the special correspondents who have columns to fill, the motoring, industrial, gardening, property, shipping, aviation, science and other correspondents whose contributions may appear in many publications. It is not unusual for the editor of a specialized journal to be a special correspondent and contributor on his subject to other journals such as national newspapers. All these people are constantly seeking ideas and subject matter.

The more the press officer knows about the needs of these staff writers the more useful he can be both to them and to his organization. There are some very real press relations to be cultivated here in the realm of ideas for articles. Of course, it may entail rather more than just handing over an idea: the press officer must be willing to devote time to escorting the staff writer to the scene of the story which may be a factory, site or installation.

For the press officer commencing in a new post it will be a long and painstaking task to get to know all the staff writers who may be interested in material about his organization, but the most satisfactory state of affairs is when staff writers know that you are a valuable source of material and come to you for material to write about. The press officer who provides a service and does not seek favours will have his service used and be given the favours.

Articles by Outside Contributors

These are more numerous and less easy to contact because they may write less frequently for the same journals, and correspondence will have to be forwarded to their private addresses. But as the various publications are studied it will become apparent that there are writers who specialize in certain subjects, and that they should be kept supplied with information and possible themes for future articles. Freelance writers of all kinds abound, and if the press officer bothers to offer them information facilities he may well find that they tend to write about his organization and its services or products simply because he alone takes the trouble to feed them with facts. The enthusiastic press officer will seek out these writers and make a point of offering to help them with facts, ideas, pictures, samples, facility visits or whatever may be of use to them.

There are some press officers who regard freelance writers as time wasters, nuisances to be put off and ignored. Provided they are not amateur writers producing speculative articles, they can be extremely valuable. It does pay, however, to check that their work has in fact been commissioned and will be published.

In addition, there are also text-book authors, and script writers for radio, films and television who work independently and are glad to know of reliable sources of information.

Supplied Articles

Here we come to the kind of article which is most satisfying to the press officer because he has more complete control over its content. When helping staff and freelance writers one has to concede the treatment to them, and it may not necessarily be as the press officer would wish. But if he writes it or edits it himself he can take more responsibility for what is published.

There is no reason why a press officer who knows his subject and writes well should not write articles in his own name, and establish himself as a writer in his own right. Press officers should be big enough to be able to put their own names to articles.

But he may be too busy to write every article himself, or it may be a subject requiring an expert on the subject, and then he will need to use his file of freelance writers. The careful creation of a file of specialist writers on appropriate topics who can be commissioned to write articles is an important part of the organization of a press office. With these additional writers the press officer can augment his staff and efforts; moreover, although his budget may not permit an addition to his full-time staff, the occasional use of freelance writers can be a convenient way of easing the staff problem when he is exceptionally busy.

Within the organization there are likely to be experts, either willing or unwilling to write articles. Sometimes the too willing ones have to be restrained because it can be embarrassing when an important member of the scientific, development or design team takes it into his head to write an elaborate technical article running to ten thousand words which he is confident the press officer can get published for him. Such enthusiasts must be dissuaded. Conversely the man whose name would look well on a company article is often disinclined to prepare a manuscript. Between these two extremes, which are very common, the press officer has to operate so that he can obtain articles by the right people, prepared in a way that is acceptable to editors.

The correct procedure is simple, and when this is explained to authors within the organization it is usually accepted as the professional procedure. Editors do accept articles which have been written speculatively, but that is exceptional. The majority of articles are first of all discussed with the editor, and if he likes the idea he will commission a piece. The press officer will therefore approach an editor with an idea, giving a brief synopsis, suggesting illustrations, and asking how many words the editor requires; how many pictures will be used; when copy is required; and in which issue is the article going to appear. When an editor writes back and says, yes, he likes the idea of the article, and wants 1500 words with three photographs by the middle of next month for the issue of the month after, then the press officer has a definite instruction to go ahead and prepare the article. If it is to be written by someone within the organization that person must understand that he is virtually under contract to supply an article of a given length on a certain subject by a specified date and that space has been allocated for the article in a particular issue.

But will this executive do what is expected of him? It would be remarkable if he wrote more than one article in a year. He may put off writing the article, always intending to do it 'next weekend'. This is where the press officer reveals his special ability. He can offer to edit the author's rough notes; he can 'ghost' the article – that is, write the article for the executive or have it written by a freelance – and this is often the way in which famous or busy people do 'write' their articles; or the article can be prepared as the result of an interview when the executive dictates his views in reply to questions. This last method, using a tape-recorder, is a popular solution.

Once the press officer becomes known within his organization for the publication of articles he may have to beware of executives who do not understand that these articles are exclusives, and cannot be offered to other editors once they have been published. In this respect, an article is very different from a news release.

However, it is possible to syndicate an article when its appearance will be in journals with non-competitive circulations such as provincial newspapers or possibly house magazines. For example, an article on a business topic might be offered to all the chamber of commerce journals published throughout the UK, and there would be no harm in an identical article appearing in several of these journals published in cities many miles apart.

It is also possible to paraphrase a basic article and produce a number of exclusive articles for different journals, using the same information but varying the applications and case histories according to the readership of each journal. Here is an example of how this has been done.

A manufacturer of louvre windows enjoyed a very useful series of articles in journals read in local government, confectionery production, and laundry and dry cleaning circles. The technicalities of how the windows were made and how they operated were identical, but the applications to various kinds of building and the interviews with people working in these buildings were quite different.

It does cost more to write an article than a news release, but when a series of articles results the cost of fares and hotel expenses as well as the press officer's time becomes a very good investment. Sometimes the work cost can be diffused even more cleverly when the field research and pictures provide further material for house journal articles, picture-and-caption stories, annual reports, training manuals, and slides for training programmes and client presentations. From this general list it will be seen how a single press relations effort can contribute to the entire PR programme for an organization, entering right into the functions of finance, production and marketing. Within the press officer's own sphere, the material for one article in a specialized journal may, later on, be used together with the material on other subjects in a comprehensive article which reviews the achievements of the organization in many different fields.

When commencing work on an article the press officer should consider what possibilities exist for facts and pictures to be used for other PR purposes. He may, for instance, take the opportunity of obtaining 35 mm colour slides because these will be useful for future

PR activities such as exhibitions or seminars, even though he has no immediate use for colour pictures for press relations purposes.

Articles and Advertisements

PR techniques can be employed to do all that is required to get the product off the ground in an economic and beneficiary way.

An example of this occurred with a company supplying the hospital service. A certain hospital in Kent had a hygiene problem, but traditional methods of finance meant that a small sum of money was allocated annually to deal with this problem. No-one had really considered whether the expenditure achieved anything and year after year the same ineffective work was carried out, having been put out to tender with a budgeted limit on cost. The fact that the hospital had suffered this problem for 90 years had not struck anyone on the management committee as being stupid.

An enterprising company, convinced that it had a method of totally eradicating the nuisance for ever, and not merely for a year, put up a scheme costing far in excess of the annually budgeted sum, won the contract and carried out the work successfully. At the time this was a phenomenal achievement in the British hospital world. The press officer published an article in *The Hospital* which brought hospital administrators from all over the UK to see the miracle in Kent. Treatments in other hospitals for the same or similar problems were later published in other journals such as *Hospital Engineer*.

By press relations methods a service of great public value was made known to those responsible, and the company's reputation was notably enhanced as it became recognized by the health authorities as the specialist organization for this particular kind of work. The cost of producing the articles was negligible compared with the cost of inserting display advertisements which could not have told the story with anything like the same degree of authenticity and conviction. Later, this success in the hospital field was included in the company's advertising to the municipal and health authorities.

Enough has been said, then, in this chapter to show that the signed exclusive feature article is not only a major part of press relations practice but a major medium of PR practice in general.

There is, however, one other aspect of advertising in relation to PR articles which needs to be discussed here. It has been shown that articles can, in special circumstances, do a better job than advertising, perhaps serving as the vanguard of advertising. Sometimes an alert advertisement manager will discover that an article from a PR source is to be published, and he will think that here is an opportunity to sell advertisement space.

It happens all the time: companies in all foolishness buy such space and have advertisements facing their articles. The advertisement is unnecessary and a waste of money. But worse than this, the advertisement looks as if it is there because of the article, and the article looks as if it is there because of the advertisement. It looks like a double blackmail. The advertisement, *in that issue and in that position*, must destroy much of the authenticity of the article which depended so much on its editorial independence. A totally unnecessary and irrelevant element of commercial bias is introduced by the advertisement at a time when the content of the article is novel and acceptance is bound up with faith in the statements of the technically qualified author, a very different matter from being persuaded and convinced by the claims of an advertiser who is entitled to put the best face on things.

However, there may be times when an accompanying advertisement is justified. This is when the advertisement can do what the editorial cannot, giving more information, making persuasive sales appeals, offering catalogues or samples, and inviting response by means of a coupon.

Unfortunately, some marketing people cannot see the validity of this argument because they regard press relations as no more than an extension of advertising. *But the average reader makes very clear distinctions between the two* and rightly or wrongly it is the reader's point of view which matters here.

How to Write Feature Articles

Article writing is utterly different. It is not an extended news release. Instead, it is an original piece of writing based on carefully researched material, in which the personality of the writer can emerge and a much richer vocabulary can be used. There should be no plugging of company or product names, except that such names may be introduced where they fall naturally into the account which is being written. Once again it is necessary to market this piece of writing. A copy of the journal should be studied so that the article is written in the appropriate style. Even among journals of a similar kind it is seldom that exactly the same article will be equally suitable for all of them. This often applies to length, one magazine running long articles, another preferring short ones, one using lots of pictures, another having few or none. These are questions to be discussed with the editor before commencing the article, and a good reason for not preparing speculative articles.

Here are five reasons why an article may fail:

1. The identity of the reader (or market) has not been defined.
2. There is no plot or coherent sequence of information.
3. The article is woolly because the writer lacks sufficient information to be selective and so write concisely and precisely.
4. The vocabulary is poor and there are too many clichés and stock phrases.
5. The writer lacks the facility to write easily so that the article is pleasant to read, but this facility is the result of practice.

However, the PRO or press officer is a literate communicator and it should not be difficult for him to write a feature article. The main problem is having enough to write about. In practice, it is easier to write an article than a news release. Very few people can write a good news release, partly because they tend to write short articles!

As a guide to the writing of articles the following is a useful seven-point formula:

1. The opening paragraph.
2. The problem or previous situation.
3. The search for the solution.
4. The solution.
5. The application of the solution.
6. The closing paragraph.
7. Check sources and obtain approval.

Concentrating on items 3, 4 and 5 for the moment we have the basis for a mental or written questionnaire with which to conduct our research. This will probably require a visit to, for instance, the factory where our machine has been installed and is working, and this will entail one or more interviews. The interviews must be by appointment and with people who have the power to give information. However, it is wise to make sure that the supplier of information will permit publication, and he should be told when and where the article will appear. It is best for the writer of the article to contact the customer's PRO or managing director and obtain clearance on the understanding that a draft of the article will be submitted and anything may be deleted, amended or added. If this promise is made information is likely to be more forthcoming.

We have suggested that a customer has made successful use of some

K

equipment, and this case study is to be the substance of the story. There can be many variations on this sort of product use story. In every case there was a point when the advantages of the new product or service were not being enjoyed. There was a problem, which has now been solved.

Presumably some effort was made to seek a solution: how did the customer find out about our product or service? Did he seek the advice of a consultant, a friend or his trade association, visit an exhibition or trade fair, or read an advertisement?

We already know quite a lot about the solution since it is our firm's or our client's product or service, but we still need to know how it has been applied by the customer and with what results. For example, a new kind of dish-washing machine was bought by a hospital which had problems of labour shortage, need to maintain high standards of hygiene, and need to protect large utensils which became battered under ordinary scouring methods. The machine, with its nylon brushes, proved its worth and at the end of a year there was a very good story for the manufacturer's PRO to write for the hospital press. There was a happier kitchen staff, and shining, perfectly hygienic utensils, their shape retained and costly replacement made unnecessary.

Researching a feature article is a matter of discovery, and often the information discovered is unexpected, fascinating and ideal for a feature article. But the PR writer has to probe and probe, politely but insistently, showing interest in an industry or business which may be foreign to him. People are flattered when a stranger takes an intelligent interest in their jobs and problems, their plans and achievements. It is essential to collect all the relevant details at the time of the interview because the writer may never have the chance of a second visit.

We have now reached the point where a lot of interesting information is required about the results which have been achieved with the product or service. It may be statistical or the statements and views of individuals. On one occasion the author was visiting a sugar refinery to write an article about the control of wasps. When introduced to the manager of the packing room he asked 'What has been the effect of the wasp control service?' Overhead was a glass skylight, and the manager pointed to it and said 'Last year that was black with wasps. This year you can see the sky.' Then the manager produced the Red Cross book and turned the pages to the previous year showing the large number of treatments recorded for stings. Then he turned to current pages and showed that none of the staff had been treated for stings. Before setting out to visit this plant in Norfolk the author had no idea what information he was going to find, but by talking to people the facts were volunteered. So when researching material for feature articles it is a common experience to start with a more or less blank mind, perhaps wondering if there really is anything worth writing about, yet by adopting the discipline of hunting for the *problem, solution* and *results* the article begins to create itself around this simple plot. The word *problem* may not seem to fit every kind of topic, but in practically every case there must have been a very different situation before the product or service was bought and used successfully.

Now we have to top and tail our piece, that is write the opening and closing paragraphs, and this is best done when the heart of the article has been written. Unlike the news release the opening paragraph of a feature article must not summarize the complete story. Instead, it has to grasp the reader's interest and make him want to read on. A question may be posed, a quotation used, an anecdote related or some other device employed to make the reader curious and anxious to know more. Ideas for the opening paragraph may come from the main part of the article. The closing paragraph has to finish the article on a note that satisfies the reader, and again an original touch is required.

Finally it is not only courteous but a sensible precaution to invite those who have supplied information to check the piece for accuracy. There is a deadline to meet so return of the article must not be delayed. A simple method of expediting return is to say that unless the draft is returned by a certain date approval will be assumed and the article will be despatched to the editor. It is important to have this co-operation so that everyone is happy with the published article. The writer can also keep faith with the editor by assuring him that the contents have been checked.

One last consideration: if any other organization, product or service is mentioned care must be taken to see that no objection can be taken to these references. For instance, if the article was about a repair service, and a well-known product was the subject of a repair the inference could be that this product had broken down and was inferior. Naming names, without permission, could lead to legal proceedings if it could be shown that the reference was harmful to business. However, an article may be made all the more interesting and comprehensive if other products can be mentioned because they are complementary to one's own or a natural part of the story as long as no risk is involved. For example, an article about a new dock would make more realistic reading if the names of cranes, forklift trucks and straddle carriers were given as well as the identity of the computer system which was one's special interest in writing the article.

CHAPTER TWENTY

Professional Codes
of Conduct

Professional PR requires professional expertise and behaviour. A PR practitioner may carry out his work with skill, knowledge and experience, which is the theme of this book. He can also behave towards his fellow practitioners and be seen by the media, his clients and employers and the outside world to behave in a professional manner. That is the purpose of the IPR Code of Professional Conduct and the PRCA Code of Consultancy Practice.

A member of the IPR and the representative of a member firm of the PRCA has to sign an undertaking to uphold its Code. Membership of these bodies therefore implies acceptance of high standards of professional conduct and practice.

A major advantage of being admitted to membership – one cannot simply join – is that the PR practitioner or his firm becomes subject to the Code, whereas non-members do not. A non-member has no ethical obligation to resist the unethical wishes or instructions of his client or employer, nor is he obliged by a signed undertaking to behave in a fashion which earns respect for himself and his profession. In his relations with the media, clients or employers, and others this acceptance of professional constraints gives the practitioner the strength to assert that he cannot and does not lend himself to questionable practices. This means in effect that every member is obliged to do a PR job for PR, and collectively this is the best way in which the IPR and PRCA can project understanding of PR and so maintain its good name. The image of PR rests with the individual member.

1. Interpretation of the IPR Code of Professional Conduct

Over the years the Institute's Code of Professional Conduct has often been revised and extended. This should be regarded as normal. No set of rules for the behaviour of members can afford to remain rigid in a fast-growing profession which is itself intricately involved with the changing standards of society.

To help IPR members to interpret and uphold the Code, the Professional Practices Committee has prepared this interpretation explaining the operation of the Code's 17 clauses.

No such brief commentary can hope to cover all the problems of interpretation which might arise under the Code. Members can always obtain advice from the Professional Practices Committee by writing to the Director of the Institute.

Clause 1   *Standards of professional conduct*

A member, in the conduct of his professional activities, shall respect the public interest and the dignity of the individual. It is his personal responsibility at all times to deal fairly and honestly with his client or employer, past or present, with his fellow members, with the media of communication and with the public.

Clause 1 is intentionally drawn in broad terms. The expression 'the public interest' is used in statute law and the term 'the dignity of the individual' echoes wording used in the Universal Declaration of Human Rights. Both phrases have yet to be interpreted formally in a public relations context, but there are few members who would not in practice recognize any flagrant violation of the principles which they express.

'The public interest' can be assumed to mean the interest of the public as a whole, as opposed to the sectional interest of a public relations practitioner's employer or client, or indeed his own.

Which of us can claim to judge what is or is not in the interest of the public at large? It is, in theory, possible that the Institute might one day have to decide whether public relations action in support of some particular cause was promoting, say, immorality. In so unlikely a case, the Institute would certainly be guided by the climate of public opinion and the law in force at the time.

In practice, the more likely danger is the use of *methods* which are against the interests of the public. It is possible to envisage an unscrupulous practitioner lending himself to the fostering of ill-will between racial communities, or trying to conceal the future ill effects of an industrial process known to cause pollution. Such conduct would be contrary to Clause 1.

The 'dignity of the individual', if taken in its fullest sense, is equally a matter which can be judged only subjectively. Yet members in the National Health Service, for instance, will have no doubt of their obligation to respect the privacy and feelings of a patient or his relatives.

At a lesser level, perhaps, no member who respects the dignity of the individual would contrive a situation – perhaps in a press or radio interview – where a person was artificially held up to ridicule.

Dealing 'fairly and honestly' with clients, employers, fellow-members, the media of communication and the public is an all-embracing requirement. It applies particularly to consultants' public relations proposals, plans and reports.

In one example which attracted some publicity, a member was found to have represented to his client that he had arranged for his Scandinavian director secretly to edit an English language section of a foreign newspaper with a view to trying to place favourable articles. The statement was found to be incorrect; had it been proved correct, the member concerned would have been in breach of the Code in other ways!

Fairness and honesty must run through all public relations practice, from the way in which information is given to the financial world to the manner in which the employee communications aspects of redundancy are handled.

Clause 2   *Dissemination of information*

A member shall not knowingly or recklessly disseminate false or misleading information, and shall use proper care to avoid doing so inadvertently. He has a positive duty to maintain integrity and accuracy.

The object of this clause is to make it plain that not only is it the member's moral duty to be honest and accurate, but that it must be his positive concern to ensure that all information issued, whether by himself or by those who work for him, is correct.

It forbids any form of deception in the issue of information and also lays upon the member the responsibility to ensure that no unchecked or unconfirmed material is released. This responsibility can range from avoiding misleading phraseology in financial documents to not stating as facts unproved claims for the performance of consumer goods.

Clause 3   *Media of communication*

A member shall not engage in any practice which tends to corrupt the integrity of the media of communication.

This clause is aimed at protecting the freedom of the press, including radio and television, to publish news and views as they think fit. Any influence, or attempted influence, on the decision-making processes of the press is expressly forbidden. This is one of the most serious forms of professional misconduct, whether it takes the form of straight or disguised bribery or hints of 'advertising considerations'.

Common sense should rule the provision of entertainment for the press, which can rarely be criticized as applying undue pressure. A meeting over drinks to get to know a specialist writer and his requirements is as acceptable as providing lunch during a press facility visit; on the other hand, a case of whisky for an editor before – or after – he has published a story is not permissible.

Clause 4   *Undisclosed interests*

A member shall not be a party to any activity which deliberately seeks to dissemble or mislead by promoting a disguised or undisclosed interest, while appearing to further another. It is his duty to ensure that the actual interest of any organization with which he may be professionally concerned is adequately declared.

The main purpose of this clause is to prevent the formation of 'front' organizations which appear to have a particular – and usually apparently laudable – objective, while in fact concealing vested interests of one kind or another.

An example would be the setting up of a body to campaign for more relaxed abortion laws on a social reform basis without revealing that the sponsors were running a chain of abortion clinics. A less extreme example would be an information bureau appearing to deal with a particular raw material, but which was covertly sponsored by one company and acted in its interests rather than those of the industry as a whole.

Actual cases of deception on similar lines have occurred and there are various situations in which the temptation to set up a 'front' organization might exist.

Disclosure of interest is a necessity in any body which seeks to impose professional standards and perhaps particularly in public relations where accusations of misrepresentation are not unknown.

There are, of course, numerous promotional associations which set out quite openly to publicize a variety of products or services. Because the objects of these associations are clearly defined – often in the titles – and their sponsorship is made plain, there is no doubt about their aims and backing. The Professional Practices Committee would be happy to advise any member who might have doubts about the acceptability, under Clause 4, of forming a particular promotional body. Normally, the test is simple: is the interest which it is designed to further clearly and specifically identified?

Clause 5   *Confidential information*

A member shall not disclose (except upon the order of a court of competent jurisdiction) or make use of information given or obtained in confidence from his employer or client, past or present, for personal gain or otherwise, without express consent.

Any professional adviser, if his advice is to be of value, must receive the full confidence of his client. Public relations practitioners in the financial field are entrusted with figures and information which could make them a fortune on the Stock Exchange. Those concerned with marketing – and indeed almost all public relations practitioners in some degree – hold information which competitors of their employer or client would wish to obtain. It is not merely ethically right, but a practical necessity, for practitioners to respect these confidences if public relations is to hold the status the Institute believes it should.

In practice this means keeping a constant watch on security in the office. At least one financial public relations consultancy requires every executive and secretary to read and acknowledge a formal letter of warning regarding the buying or selling of personal shareholdings in client companies. If a practitioner changes employment, or takes on a new client whose business competes with that of a former client, great care must be taken to distinguish between what is useful experience in the field and what is information received in confidence by virtue of the public relations man's professional status. The bracketed phrase 'except upon the order of a court of competent jurisdiction' distinguishes the professional position of the public relations man from the position taken up by journalists, who believe they have an obligation – not, of course, recognized by the law – never to disclose their sources. The Institute does not ask or wish its members to defy the law, and their position in this matter is exactly the same as that of doctors or lawyers.

Clause 6   *Conflict of interests*

A member shall not represent conflicting or competing interests without the express consent of the parties concerned after full disclosure of the facts.

The question of conflicting or competing interests is one which affects every consultant. Competition needs no clarification. Conflict is perhaps rather less obvious, but could arise if, for instance, a practitioner were to be retained by a local authority and by an organization campaigning for improvement of amenities in the same area; or by a trade association of manufacturers and another of retailers in the same industry.

There is *no* rule that members may not represent conflicting or competing interests, only that they may not do so without the consent of those concerned, after full disclosure of the facts.

In some fields, clients often feel that the consultancy's special knowledge of their needs outweighs any danger caused by sharing its service with other organizations of the same type. This is so, for example, in the City, where merchant banks and others are themselves familiar with conflict situations, and where a highly confidential relationship between consultant and client is normal practice. In the context of consumer marketing, on the other hand, clients usually dislike their consultancy to represent a competitor.

Although the bigger the consultancy the more frequent are the possible clashes of interest, it is easier for a large consultancy to ensure that a different team works for each client. This, of course, is the way in which firms in other professions deal with this problem.

Clause 7   *Sources of payment*

A member, in the course of his professional services to his employer or client, shall not accept payment either in cash or in kind in connection with those services from any other source without the express consent of his employer or client.

As a public relations man is paid by his client for writing and issuing a feature, it would be wrong for him to accept an author's fee from a paper which publishes it. That is the simplest example of the malpractice against which this clause is aimed.

However, it does not preclude a consultancy, for example, receiving a trade discount from a supplier, such as a printer or photographer, provided that acceptance of this discount is approved by the client. If it is not agreed by the client, then the discount must be passed on.

This clause, however, does forbid the member from receiving rewards from suppliers or others as an inducement to place his employer's or client's business with them.

In Clauses 5, 6 and 7 the words 'express consent' are used. To say 'I know my client would not mind' or 'he is aware of the situation and did not object' is not enough, either ethically or as a defence against any complaint that the Code has been breached in this respect. The practitioner's client or employer must be made aware of the facts and formally accept the situation.

Clause 8   *Disclosure of financial interests*

A member having a financial interest in an organization shall not recommend the use of that organization, nor make use of its services on behalf of his client or employer, without declaring his interest.

This is an extension of Clause 7 to cover the situation in which, for instance, a consultant has an associated graphic design studio or photographic or model agency; or in which a staff public relations man is privately a partner in a printing or catering concern.

There is nothing wrong in the member having such an outside interest, but it is improper for him to use it or recommend its use without, firstly, disclosure of the interest and, secondly, the client's or employer's specific agreement.

Clause 9   *Payment contingent upon achievements*

A member shall not negotiate or agree terms with a prospective employer or client on the basis of payment contingent upon specific future public relations achievements.

One of the most-discussed problems in the profession is the evaluation of the results of public relations activity. If there is any broad agreement on this it is that the basic need, in an ideal situation, is for sophisticated research to check regularly on changes in attitude among the audience concerned. The problem affects all practitioners, but only consultants are likely to face it in the context of payment.

Confusing the situation is the ghost of the old-time press agent, who often charged his clients per column inch of press mentions obtained on their behalf. Even today it is not unknown for some form of payment by results to be suggested. The basic argument against this is that the client is buying the professsional skill and knowledge of the consultant. The success of the wide range of methods used to further the client's interests cannot fairly be judged by specific results over a given period; nor do corporate public relations campaigns, for example, depend for their success solely upon specific achievements. A further point is that many outside factors may be involved in determining whether the intended results are realized. Moreover a payment-by-results basis of operation is a potential inducement to corruption of the media.

Of course, at the end of the day the client has to decide whether he is getting value for money. This assessment is likely to depend upon the attainment of a variety of objectives ranging, perhaps, from improved employee relations to a defence against a take-over bid. The results which have been obtained need to be evaluated and management decisions made on future action and expenditure. This cannot sensibly be done on the basis of a prior agreement to pay a fixed amount for the achievement of such results as can be physically measured.

Members of the IPR are as much professionals in their own field as are accountants and solicitors. We do not pay a solicitor an agreed portion of the damages he might obtain in a court action; we pay for skilled work, having initially agreed what needs to be done. That this should also happen in public relations is the purpose of Clause 9.

Clause 10   *Supplanting another member*

A member seeking employment or new business by direct and individual approach to a potential employer or client shall take all reasonable steps to ascertain whether that employment or business is already carried out by another member. If so, it shall be his duty to advise the other member in advance of any approach he proposes to make to the employer or client concerned. (Nothing in this clause shall be taken as inhibiting a member from the general advertisement of his services.)

The Institute does not want to rob the business of fair competition between its members, but professionalism, with all the sharing of knowledge and struggle for higher standards that the word implies, is essential. Members are hardly likely to behave as professionals if they are trying to steal the bread from each other's mouths. Hence Clause 10.

There is no harm in a member writing or telephoning to offer his services or capabilities to a potential client or employer, but he must first find out whether that employer or client is already using the professional services of a fellow member. If so, he must first advise the member of the approach he proposes to make.

In the case of employed fellow members this is not difficult to check from the Register of Members. In the case of consultants, however, it is not so simple for they do not always publish the names of their clients in the standard reference books. A check can be made with the Public Relations Consultants Association provided, of course, that they are members of that association.

The blanket coverage circular – particularly if it contains a phrase inviting the recipient to disregard it if already satisfactorily served – is not prohibited by this clause: 'direct and individual' communication is its specific concern. Likewise, there is no restriction on press advertising or other public promotional activity.

Clause 11   *Rewards to holders of public office*

A member shall not, with intent to further his interests (or those of his client or employer), offer or give any reward to a person holding public office if such action is inconsistent with the public interest.

Clause 11 simply reflects the fact that Institute members are citizens before they are public relations practitioners and must not improperly make use of the services of a public office-holder.

That does not mean that it is *never* proper to employ, or pay a fee to, a public office-holder; there are many respectable precedents for this both in and out of public relations.

For example, if an employer has premises which cause pollution or a consultant specializes in environmental problems, then to engage as an adviser an MP or a member of a local authority who has particular knowledge of such matters would not be improper, provided the public interest was not put at risk.

If, however, that adviser were then asked to be concerned with a specific issue with which he had to deal in the course of his public duties, there would be a clear risk of his acting in a manner inconsistent with his public responsibilities.

The moral problem facing both the Institute member and the office-holder may not be resolved by a simple declaration of the interests involved. It would clearly be wrong, for instance, to offer to pay the chairman of a planning committee for advice on a client's planning problems if eventually he were likely to hear an application from that client; nor would it be an adequate defence to say that it was the chairman's duty to declare his interest.

An Institute member does not breach the Code simply by employing or retaining a public office-holder, but he would do so if he tried to persuade that individual to act in his employer's or client's interests contrary to the public interest.

Clause 12 *Employment of Members of Parliament*

A member who employs a Member of Parliament, of either House, in connection with Parliamentary matters, whether in a consultative or executive capacity, shall disclose this fact, and also the object of the employment, to the General Secretary of the Institute, who shall enter it in a register kept for the purpose. A member of the Institute who is himself a Member of Parliament shall be directly responsible for disclosing or causing to be disclosed to the General Secretary any such information as may relate to himself. (The register referred to in this clause shall be open to public inspection at the offices of the Institute during office hours.)

Clause 12 simply requires an Institute member who employs or retains a Member of Parliament, of either House, *for Parliamentary purposes*, to register the fact formally with the Institute. If the member is himself an MP or peer, he has a personal responsibility for registering.

The Institute is thus provided with a register which reveals to the public the names of Members of Parliament involved directly or indirectly in public relations practice. In other words, professional conduct in this sphere must not only be good, but be seen to be good!

It is hardly necessary to add that this in no way diminishes the traditional responsibility of a Member of Parliament to declare any personal interest which may have a bearing on his public duties.

Clause 13 *Injury to other members*

A member shall not maliciously injure the professional reputation or practice of another member.

Injury to the professional reputation or practice of a member is most likely to arise in practice under the temptation provided by competition between consultants: for instance, by informing a member's client of any real or imagined shortcomings in the member's practice of public relations.

It is probable that 'maliciously' in the context of Clause 13 could be proved by any such behaviour carried out with an improper motive; indeed, an improper motive could often be inferred from the circumstances.

Clause 14 *Instruction of others*

A member who knowingly causes or permits another person or organization to act in a manner inconsistent with this Code, or is party to such action, shall himself be deemed to be in breach of it.

Clause 14 is an important safeguard to professional standards. No member can excuse breaches of the Code by pleading that they were committed by, for instance, a member of his staff, who might not be a member and by reason of his subordinate position might in any case be under pressure to comply with his senior's instructions.

A member must not be a 'party to' a breach of the Code. He must resist it and dissent from it. For example, a member who is a director of a consultancy must not acquiesce or join in any decision of the board which is in contravention of the Code.

If this were not so, a member would have the excuse that the breach was carried out by a corporate body which would not, of course, be amenable to the Institute's discipline.

Clause 15 *Reputation of the profession*

A member shall not conduct himself in any manner detrimental to the reputation of the Institute or the profession of public relations.

Clause 15 applies to all forms of behaviour which could harm the reputation of the Institute or the profession.

Quite apart from the fact that certain jobs, possibly estimable in themselves, cannot easily be compatible with professional status, a member is unlikely to be able to hold a position on the staff of a newspaper or other medium without harming the reputation of public relations for professional detachment and the reputation of journalism for objective assessment.

However, there is no 'black list' and each case must be decided on its merits.

Many other circumstances are covered by the clause. A member who writes an article or makes a speech in which he seriously denigrates the profession, or the Institute which represents it, would be in breach of Clause 15. So would any member who was found guilty of a major criminal offence.

Clause 15, in fact is designed to protect the profession and Institute in all matters which, while not part of public relations practice, reflect on their collective good name.

Clause 16   *Upholding the Code*

A member shall uphold this Code, shall co-operate with fellow members in so doing and in enforcing decisions on any matter arising from its application. If a member has reason to believe that another member has been engaged in practices which may be in breach of this Code, it shall be his duty to inform the Institute. It is the duty of all members to assist the Institute to implement this Code, and the Institute will support any member so doing.

Clause 16 requires members to uphold the Code, and – as a duty – to help the Institute to deal with possible breaches. The Institute has an effective procedure on disciplinary matters, but in the last resort it is helpless without members' co-operation. The Professional Practices Committee can often give guidance to members which – if they follow it – will ensure they keep within the Code.

Where disciplinary proceedings have to be taken, the Institute must depend on the co-operation of everyone concerned: it does not possess the powers of a court of law to compel witnesses, and without evidence the Institute may be rendered powerless against an individual who has harmed the profession by his conduct.

Clause 17   *Other Professions*

A member shall, when acting for a client or employer who belongs to a profession, respect the code of ethics of that other profession and shall not knowingly be party to any breach of such a code.

This most recent clause to be added to the Code recognizes the public relations practitioner's responsibility for understanding and respecting the code of ethics applicable to a client or employer who is a member of one of the established professions.

It is specifically aimed at ensuring that members of the professions are not aided or persuaded to act in breach of their own ethical codes by the application of public relations techniques. The restraint laid upon doctors, architects and others over the use of publicity to attract business is an example of a likely area of difficulty.

If in doubt about the interpretation of this – or any other – clause, members may seek the guidance of the Professional Practices Committee, writing first to the Director.

2. Public Relations Consultants Association Code of Consultancy Practice

1. A member firm has a general duty of fair dealing towards its clients, past and present, fellow members and the public.

2. A member firm shall not knowingly seek to displace another member firm's relationship with a client, other than in fair competition or at the behest of the client.

3. A member firm shall cause all its clients to be listed in the Annual Register of the Public Relations Consultants Association.

4. A member firm shall cause all its directors, executives and retained consultants who hold public office, are members of either House of Parliament, are members of local authorities or of any statutory organization or body, to be recorded in the relevant Sections of the Annual Register of the Public Relations Consultants Association.

5. A member firm shall not offer or give nor cause a client to offer or give any inducement to such persons as described in Article 4 above who are not directors, executives or retained consultants with intent to further the interests of the member or of the client if such action is inconsistent with the public interest.

6. A member firm shall not engage in any practice which tends to corrupt the integrity of channels of public communication or legislation.

7. A member firm shall not negotiate, propose or agree terms with a client or prospective client on the basis of payment of fees being contingent upon specific achievements.

8. A member firm shall not propose to clients any action which would constitute an improper influence on organs of government or legislation.

9. A member firm shall not engage in any practice nor be seen to conduct itself in any manner detrimental to the reputation of the Public Relations Consultants Association or the reputation and the interests of Public Relations Consultancy.

10. A member firm shall not intentionally disseminate false or misleading information and is under an obligation to use reasonable care to avoid dissemination of false or misleading information.

11. A member firm shall not purport to serve some announced cause while actually serving an undisclosed special or private interest.

12. A member firm shall safeguard the confidences of both present and former clients and shall not disclose or use these confidences to the

disadvantage or prejudice of such clients or to the financial advantage of the member firm.

13. A member firm shall only represent competing interests with the consent of all those concerned.

14. A member firm shall not, without the client's consent, accept fees or other valuable consideration from anyone other than the client, in connection with services for that client.

15. A member firm shall inform a client of any shareholding or financial interest held by that firm in any Company, firm or person whose services it recommends.

Code of Consultancy Practice – Definitions

Definition of Practice

Public Relations Consultancy practice, in the context of the PRCA, may be defined as the provision of specified technical and creative services by an individual or a group of individuals, qualified to do so by reason of experience and training, and having a legal, corporate identity, registered for the purposes of business in the United Kingdom. The whole or principal income of the corporate body so formed will be by way of professional fees paid for its services by clients under contract to the consultancy.

Definition of a Client

A client is an organization, corporate body, individual or group of individuals which retains the professional services of a public relations consultancy for an agreed programme (or project) of advice or activity, for a specific period on terms previously agreed between the consultancy and the client and binding on both.

Definition of Services

The services provided by a public relations consultancy may comprise, in all or in part, the following:

Establishing channels of communication with the client's public or publics, management communications, marketing and sales promotion related activity, advice or services relating to political, governmental or public affairs, financial public relations, personnel and industrial relations, recruitment training and higher and technical education (this list is not intended to be exhaustive).

Not all public relations consultancies will claim competence in every area; some will confine their practice to certain industries or interests, whilst others may offer consultative but not executive services. However, all Members of the Association who do not offer a full range of services to clients but specialize in certain areas must be competent to recommend to their clients a full range of services from other members, if required by the client to do so.

Sections 1 and 2 are reproduced by permission of the Institute of Public Relations (20.1) and the Public Relations Consultants Association (20.2).

References

20.1 Institute of Public Relations, 1 Great James Street, London WC1 3DA
20.2 Public Relations Consultants Association, 44 Belgrave Square, London SW1X 8QS

Part Four
Case Studies

Four
Case Studies

Flymo Air Cushion Mowers

Background

The Flymo (short for 'flying mower') air cushion lawnmower was developed by a Swedish lawnmower manufacturer, Karl Dahlman, who was fascinated by the British hovercraft and inspired to replace wheels with a cushion of air. His invention won a gold medal at the 1963 Brussels Inventors' Fair.

In 1964 the power mower industry was in its infancy. The cylinder mower, or reel mower, was then the most popular powered machine. The market was then approximately 250,000 per annum.

In this year Flymo Limited was started in the UK by Charles Bramall, who is now chairman of the Flymo Group, which in turn is now a member of the Swedish Electrolux Group of Companies.

Within four years the power mower market had doubled whereas the Flymo mower sales had trebled. Flymo continued to gain an increasing share of the quality power mower market and is now the leading rotary mower manufacturer in this important segment where sales are estimated at nearly one million.

In the UK, Flymo have about 1600 authorized distributors and dealers, and the Group markets its products through a further 3500 distributors in Scandinavia, the continent and elsewhere overseas.

Today, the main production centre is at Aycliffe, near Darlington, Co. Durham, England. It is the base for exports to more than seventy countries, but there is also production in West Germany, Australia, New Zealand and South Africa.

Marketing policy

The keystone of Flymo's successful marketing policy was, and still is, the setting up of a system of authorized distributors who, in turn, support a network of carefully selected sales and service dealers, located in each buying centre.

The dealer's first consideration is customer satisfaction by giving a home demonstration of a Flymo mower. He ensures that the prospect buys the right mower for his kind of lawn, and good after-sales service is maintained.

Together, these distributors and dealers have been trained and further courses are mounted each year to keep them up-to-date with new products, marketing and servicing methods. This is a two-way marketing communication effort with feedback coming from the trade at seminars and discussion groups. There is thus a continuous check to see that the market gets the kind of mower and service that it wants. No such network had previously existed in the power mower industry. The result is that Flymo has a national network of distributors providing before, during and after-sales service.

In every country on the continent and in Scandinavia, the Flymo Group have set up their own companies or have an authorized distributor. The same marketing policy applies in all countries.

The company was ahead of its time with such policies which guarantee customer satisfaction in advance of the growing tide of consumerism and recent statutes designed to protect the consumer's rights against irresponsible retailers and manufacturers. In fact, Flymo are convinced that it is the controlled marketing policy and their insistence on its implementation which is the real reason for the company's success. It is even more important than the revolutionary air cushion principle on which most of their products operate.

Advertising

The main selling points of Flymo air cushion mowers are that they are light and easy to use, versatile, and capable of swiftly cutting all kinds of grass.

In 1964 the AB market was the target. Since then the appeal has broadened to include C1/C2. The chief media continue to be the *Sunday Times, Sunday Express, Daily Telegraph, News of the World, The People, Homes and Gardens, Ideal Home* plus special issues of the gardening press. The popular Sundays are used to promote the Minimo air cushion mower.

Large spaces have been used in these publications between March and June. Attempts have been made to extend the selling season and, depending on the weather and the sales situation, February has been included at one end and July–August at the other. At least £100,000 is invested in press space which includes regional and local advertising based on 50–50 dealer co-operative schemes. About £15,000 is invested in point-of-sale display material and literature, with special attention to its placing.

Because there are now nine air cushion products, one reel mower, Flymo oil, and a lawnrake, it is impossible to have an effective campaign on purely product advertising. The answer is the editorial style advertisement with numerous items on lawn culture. The selling points are presented in a practical, factual and credible way, and existing customers as well as prospects are educated in the continually improving methods of lawn care. The advertisement itself becomes part of the after-sales service. But 'mood ads' have also been developed, putting over the idea of enjoying the weekend.

Literature

Large quantities of price lists and give-away leaflets are not used. Believing that a mower should be sold according to the needs of the customer, and not necessarily by its appearance or price, sales literature has been restricted to helpful advisory folders on the 'which mower for which type of garden' principle. This helps to avoid waste too, but mainly it helps to guide the customer towards making the purchase which will give the most satisfaction. However, stuffer leaflets are provided for use as direct mail shots, for use on exhibition stands, and as reminders for dealers to send out when invoicing.

Display

At one time posters were produced, but these were found to be wasteful since they were not easily displayed where mowers are usually sold. Swing tickets and crowners for the mower handle (which are themselves good display frames) have proved to be both practical and popular with dealers. Once in position it tends to stay on view. Use of this and occasional special POS material is included in training courses for distributors.

Press Relations

Flymo have had exceptional success with gardening writers. The initial reaction to the new mower in 1964 was overwhelming in the UK. While some correspondents thought the Flymo was just a gimmick, most journalists recognized the usefulness of the air cushion mower for all types of garden and wrote up how gardeners could mow more easily, more quickly, especially in awkward places. Flymo have kept faith with the press by supplying news stories well in advance, and the facts have been presented in a brief professional way.

Although this is primarily a marketing study it is included here because the marketing strategy has been PR-orientated throughout, mindful of both good dealer and customer relations.

Organization: Flymo Ltd
                      A. Cooper, Publicity Manager
Advertising Agency: Butler & Gardner Advertising Ltd
                      J. Hardman, Account Director
PR Consultancy: Eridon Ltd
                      E. Woolnough, Account Director

The Inaugural Flights of British Airways' Concorde

To cut the flying time of subsonic air travel by half – flying to the USA in less than four hours and to Australia in less than fourteen – would seem to be the last word in commercial aviation. But until 1975, the story of Concorde was one of political discord.

After 12 years of acrimony, during which time designers, engineers, test pilots and salesmen of the British Aircraft Corporation, the French Aerospatiale, BOAC (as it then was) and Air France were patiently preparing the droop nose delta wing supersonic plane for eventual service, the time came for a change in PR direction. The PR role of the operators moved from the defensive as reality was accepted. Concorde was going to have development flights in 1975, and it was going into service in January 1976.

This coincided with the merger of the two British state airlines, BOAC and BEA, and the new British Airways – thanks to Concorde – was born with the image of the international airline with the world's most advanced passenger aircraft. It was a time for thinking big.

In spite of a financial forecast of a possible operational loss of £25 million if Concorde went into service, there were other considerations. In itself it was to be a massive PR undertaking on an international scale.

Britain needed a success story. At home, a severe morale booster was needed to help counteract the effects of economic depression. Abroad, it was necessary to show in places such as the USA, Australia and Japan that Britain was not finished. If Concorde had been abandoned the British and the world at large would have regarded this as an admission of failure. To go on was to flaunt British achievement in the eyes of the despondent and the doubtful. British Airways PR programme embodied these points within its overall strategy but always the interests of the airline were the motivating factor. The French were going ahead anyway, and with fewer qualms. Seldom, then, has an otherwise commercial PR programme been formulated with such a Drake's Armada-atmosphere about it.

Moreover, it has to be remembered that after all the talk and half-promises, only two airlines, the national ones where the plane was built, had actually come through with their options. America had not only failed to order Concorde, but had dropped plans to build a rival machine, and had powerful special interest groups intent on preventing Concorde from even landing in the States.

Between July 7 and September 13, 1975, 130 development flights were flown and 6500 invited passengers were carried. The objectives were to give the various manufacturers the opportunity to conduct tests, and for the airline in conjunction with the manufacturers, to test the aircraft under simulated commercial conditions. Feedback was obtained by means of questionnaires completed by the 'guinea-pig' passengers, and much was learned about such aspects as diverse as the air-conditioning, seating and catering. The passengers were influential people who were able to experience the quite different qualities of air travel when flying at 1350 mph at 52,000 feet in Concorde, and a lot of important friends were made for both the aircraft and the airline all over the world.

The passengers were selected by a joint committee representing the Department of Trade and Industry, British Aircraft Corporation and British Airways. They included air correspondents from almost every country in the world, Ministers, MP's, prominent customers, and dignitaries and personalities such as Dr. Donald Coggan, Archbishop of Canterbury and Group Captain Douglas Bader. The development flights took them to Gander, Beirut, Bahrain, Kuala Lumpur, Bombay, Singapore and Melbourne. On more than one occasion,

Concorde flew to Gander and back twice in one day, an unheard-of feat for a commercial airliner.

The first of these flights on July 7 was also used as a dummy run for the inaugural flight on January 21, 1976, and, with the splendid co-operation of Cable and Wireless in Bahrain, Allan Solloway organized full press room services which even included a supply of cold beer for the press men arriving to temperatures of 100°F.

For another special flight, a public ballot was held for seats, and there were half a million applicants which, of course, made a good press story. The winners flew to 40° West in mid-Atlantic during the summer bank holiday.

Another exercise was a press reception in a Concorde mock-up at Heathrow where the first flight to Bahrain was simulated and jour-nalists sampled the food that would be served.

During 1975, British Airways also intensified its output of news about the aircraft, this being distributed through the company's worldwide PR network which has major information centres in Berlin, Hong Kong, Johannesburg, Montreal, New York, Rome and Sydney. From July until January, Concorde was maintained on the news pages, radio bulletins and television screens by means of a controlled output of stories. They not only provided continuity of the Concorde story, but had a valuable PR spin-off for the airline as a whole. The stories concentrated on exclusivity, and a few examples were the special unveilings or introductions of the new uniforms for the Concorde cabin staff, the specially commissioned Royal Doulton crockery, the seats, and the identities of the first crew.

Meanwhile, the PR Department, headed by Alan Ponsford, was planning to achieve maximum worldwide press, radio and TV coverage of the inaugural flight to Bahrain on January 21, 1976. Before Christmas it was necessary to collaborate with the BBC and ITN to plan TV coverage of the take-off. This also meant a series of meetings on both London and Paris with the French to synchronize TV cover-age since at the same time as the BA Concorde took off from Heath-row the Air France Concorde would be taking off from de Gaulle airport for Rio de Janeiro. The PR plan was to achieve a split-screen presentation of the two aircraft taking off simultaneously! There was some scepticism about this, worry that it could hold up air traffic over Paris for two hours, but the problem was solved eventually. However, British TV proposed to make recordings at 11.30 a.m. (take-off time) and screen the pictures at 12.30. The *Sunday Express* deplored this and demanded live coverage. Although British Airways would have preferred the earlier showing, they may have benefited from a larger audience at the more convenient lunchtime screening.

With the corps of newspaper air correspondents, and ITN, BBC, NBC and ABC British and American broadcasting teams, some 40 journalists were given seats on the Bahrain flight so that they could make first-person reports. In addition, a group of journalists representing the regional press, were flown out in advance so that they could write up the plane's arrival and then fly back on Concorde's return flight to London with a further story for their countries' evening paper chains.

The rest of the 100 passengers included Henry Marking, managing director of British Airways, who hosted the journalists, and special guests such as the Duke of Kent, Group Captain Leonard Cheshire and Sir Max Aitken. Fare-paying passengers included Lord and Lady Leathers (who had booked tickets when supersonic travel was first announced 11 years previously!) and the Duchess of Argyll. Another passenger was Philip Croucher of Rembrandt Philatelics who organized a first-day cover philatelic service.

Media coverage had to be arranged not only at the departure point and during the flight but also at the point of arrival. Moreover, with the journalists and cameramen covering the flight itself with in-flight stories, facilities were required upon landing for the immediate transmission of stories and pictures to Britain, the USA, Australia, Canada and most European cities. This was organized by Allan Solloway, deputy chief of news services, who had already learned much from the experience of the dummy run in July. He arranged the services of teleprinter operators and open lines through Cable and Wireless, and hired the services of a processing organization in Bahrain so that still pictures could be processed and transmitted from Bahrain to the Press Association in Fleet Street who circulated them. The pictures of the Duke of Kent and Henry Marking, taken by the British Airways' photographer Harry Stewart during the flight, were reproduced all over the world.

Transmission of stills was comparatively easy compared to TV material, which had to be flown to Kuwait. Allan Solloway hired a Beechcraft from Gulf Air and all the TV cameramen had to do was disembark from Concorde, pass quickly through the terminal building, and board the charter plane. Just before Concorde was due to arrive the message came through that Kuwait was fogbound and the Beechcraft could not be used. Very co-operatively, Gulf Air wheeled the plane into the hanger and brought out a Fokker Friendship which had a bigger range. But the fog lifted, and the British and American

TV cameramen flew off to Kuwait where their film was processed, the normally severe security at the transmission station was waived, and the pictures were transmitted by satellite to the UK and the USA.

The national and international coverage was enormous and immeasurable. It was Britain's big day out, and the British relished the excitement. Even the ear-witness accounts of noise, as reported in press, radio and TV interviews, were favourable. This was an occasion when independent radio, especially London Broadcasting, showed its importance to the PRO.

With permission to land at Dulles Airport, Washington, and for Atlantic flights over a fairly long trial period of 16 months commencing May 24, 1976, the British were cheered up yet again.

The London–Washington inaugural flight was different in two respects. While the January 21 flight was a *departure* story, the one on May 24 was an even more dramatic *arrival* story. The British and French 'planes timed their arrival so that there was a spectacular taxi-ing in of both aircraft. This delighted the Americans who, being fond of showmanship, let their welcome and applause diminish or destroy their supposed hostility. The roads to the airport were jammed with sightseers. But it is true to say that although British Airways aimed to hearten the British public, both flights won great coverage and admiring interest in the USA.

In setting up the Washington flight there had been the gamble that if America had given the Concorde an unfriendly welcome, British Airways' subsonic business – built up over 30 years – could have been damaged. As an insurance, possible reactions were tested by a market research exercise which showed that reactions were less hostile than British Airways had expected. In the event, far from harming normal business, the Washington inaugural flight enhanced British Airways' reputation in the States.

Organization: British Airways
Personnel: Alan C. Ponsford, Group public relations director
            Allan Solloway, Deputy chief of news services
            Michael Pickering, Public relations executive, Overseas division
            Norman Lornie, Public relations manager, USA
            Harry Stewart, Head of photographic services

ITT (Europe) Corporate Communications Programme

The International Telephone and Telegraph Corporation (ITT) is an international group of companies owned by an American parent, but run autonomously by local management, the European unit being ITT Europe Inc. with its headquarters in Brussels.

In Britain, the ITT companies include Abbey Life Assurance, Ashe Laboratories, Excess Insurance, ITT Consumer Products, Rimmel, Sheraton Hotels, Standard Telephones and Cables, and Standard Telecommunication Laboratories. ITT may be described as a multinational conglomerate. Each national company conducts its own PR but the Brussels office monitors and co-ordinates communications and was responsible for development and implementation of the corporate communications programme described in this case study.

While the task of advertising is basically to make known in order to sell, the public relations task is often to overcome apathy, hostility, ignorance and prejudice, and this is a classic PR case study in that while ITT had been commercially highly successful very little was understood about ITT itself. For some years it had been the victim of misunderstanding, suspicion and outright hostility. For example, *The Guardian* had attacked ITT for more than two years while Anthony Sampson had described ITT as 'a symbol of irresponsibility and secretiveness, a caricature of the malfunction of multinationals'. In Brussels it was recognized that the attacks were symptomatic of the problem that ITT simply had not done a good PR job for itself.

First, it was necessary to see the company in relation to changed economic and political conditions in Europe following economic slow-down, inflation, rising labour costs, consumerism, cuts in government spending, reduction in discretionary spending power and unemployment. All this was creating a situation of disenchantment with capitalism, labour unrest, and national protectionism. The multinational, especially American, was regarded as a form of economic imperialism.

Second, in the case of ITT, two 'scandals' had given the company an unfair and unfortunate image which people of all kinds, from Leftists to business people, all too readily accepted, goaded on by both the mass and the quality media.

ITT was accused of complicity in the downfall of the Allende regime. It was admitted that the company was probably over-zealous in talking about possible ways of preventing its Chilean interest being expropriated without compensation. It has publicly expressed regret that a false impression was created, but it has emphatically denied contravention of any national or international legislation, and it has produced evidence of its long history in Chile and its contribution to the Chilean economy.

ITT has also denied accusations that it attempted to influence the settlement of a US anti-trust case by making a contribution to the Nixon re-election fund. In fact ITT offered to pledge a sum of money to the San Diego Convention and Visitors Bureau (unconnected with any re-election fund) provided that the new Sheraton hotel should be designated as presidential headquarters during the Republican Party convention. In the event, the convention was held in another city and the contribution was return to ITT. In any case, the sum involved was typical of the promotional support given to a new hotel. There was nothing untoward or secretive about it but, in the atmosphere of Watergate suspicions, accusations were easily inspired.

Third, as a result of the so-called 'scandals' in North and South America, ITT faced a curious communications problem in Europe where half of the corporation's worldwide business was handled. Before the Chilean affair, less than one in fifty Europeans had heard of ITT, and they knew the corporation for its growth record and its reputation for good management. After Chile, one in five were aware of ITT, but chiefly as a guilty American multinational. Apart from those who did know and understand ITT (its employees, customers and sub-contractors) it was seen in terms of the attributes least liked – big, multinational and conglomerate. This information gap in Europe produced fear, hostility and suspicion, the classic anti-PR situation with which corporate PR has to contend.

Before anything could be planned, image and attitude research was required. What did people think of ITT? Whose attitudes mattered most? What misunderstandings were common and needed to be answered? What media and tactics should be employed? These considerations had to be taken country by country. While a company's favourable impact on the balance of payments would be irrelevant in Germany, it is very important in the UK. A pan-European PR solution was impossible.

Fortunately, ITT had initiated a regular image/attitude research programme in 1969, taking a sample of 480 opinion leaders. The surveys were conducted by Conrad Jameson and Associates in partnership with the *Financial Times* who had exclusive rights to certain data. The existing research programme was used to define attitudes of the target audience for the PR campaign. This target audience consisted of business and industrial leaders, professionals and academics, senior civil servants, and the media. A random sample was taken from the Kompass Register and lists of civil servants, professionals and academics. This target audience study was conducted as an omnibus survey with non-competing firms sharing the cost. The study was repeated over a maximum of ten countries with concentration on the six countries, Germany, France, UK, Spain, Belgium and Italy where ITT had 80 per cent of its European business.

The questionnaire had three main sections. First, questions were asked about attitudes to business in general including American-owned multinationals and their benefits and disadvantages to the economy. Then a check was made on the awareness levels and attitudes towards ITT. One of the results of this second section was the development of an ITT Awareness Index indicating understanding of (1) areas of business engaged in by ITT; (2) businesses ITT is in; and (3) awareness of subsidiary companies. The third section sought to discover the publications read by respondents, and this part of the survey was conducted jointly with *Newsweek*.

The research produced evidence of misconceptions which were particularly valuable to ITT's advertising agency, KMP, when producing the copy for the UK corporate advertising campaign. Typical misconceptions were:

> ITT was not interested in exports – was probably a net drain on the balance of payments.
> No autonomy – subject to New York decisions – local managers either local puppets or Americans.
> Multinationals milk rather than feed the host economy.
> Acquired companies have their assets stripped, staff fired and company milked.
> Only interested in profit, short-term policy stifling talent and creativity.
> Multinationals export all their profits and do not invest in their host country's future.

These particular misconceptions are taken from the UK survey.

A package of inter-dependent corporate PR programmes was devised, rather like a 24-hour cold cure capsule. The components of the campaign were planned to have an impact of different intensity at different times and its key components consisted of the following five activities:

1. A Fact File – *Facts about ITT in Europe*.

2. A corporate newshandling programme.
3. A speakers programme.
4. Corporate advertising.
5. A quarterly external house magazine – *Profile*.

Reverting to the target audience, its definition has to be seen in relation to the corporate communications programme set out under the above five headings. It excluded two segments, the extreme Leftists who would not be convinced by *any* argument and those who were already well disposed, while the 'man-in-the-street' was reached at the subsidiary company and product level. Thus, the programme was aimed at the top end of the population triangle.

An important facet of the PR strategy was the deliberate involvement of ITT top management in Europe. Two meetings were held in Brussels, one in December 1973 to discuss the problem and the proposed solution, and one in February 1974 to review and approve the five-point programme as finalized after the December discussions. Fifteen members of top management attended these meetings along with ITT Europe PR director, David Barker and assistant director Nigel Rowe. At the first meeting some eight hours were spent on discussing the dimensions, character and causes of ITT's PR problem in Europe, and the strategy and action proposed by the Brussels PR office team. One result of this was the enthusiastic support of the ITT senior officer in the UK, Kenneth Corfield, deputy chairman and managing director of Standard Telephones and Cables, which resulted in the launching of an impactive corporate advertising campaign in the UK well in advance of any other country. This particular advertising campaign would never have been launched but for top management support and involvement at the highest levels at all stages of its planning and development.

Let us now consider each element of the capsule in turn.

1. *Facts about ITT in Europe.* To put a face on the faceless giant, a 24-page A4 size fact file was produced to act as a cornerstone of the campaign. First published in English, editions in German, French, Dutch, Italian and Spanish were later produced. The publication was fitted with a pocket at the back for filling with supplementary and up-dating material. The contents included ITT policy, structure, management and research in Europe; technical, statistical and financial facts; and details of ITT companies, products and services. It was set out with commendable concision and precision.

2. *A Corporate Newshandling Programme.* The corporation refers to 'press' or 'media' relations as *newshandling*. All publications relevant to

ITT's target audience in Europe are listed in a master media file. Waste mailing is eliminated by this careful choice of media. Most stories are released by the press offices in the various ITT companies in fifteen different countries, the Brussels office restricting itself to releases on specific issues. For example, press tours of ITT plants are arranged in Brussels with the agreement and help of the local PR people.

A press coverage evaluation formula is used, a points system being applied to coverage, quantity and quality. This is adopted right across Europe to track press coverage in each country. It also presents evidence of failure to get coverage.

An example of a specific effort by the Brussels office was the way in which Nigel Rowe handled *The Guardian*'s persistent antagonism to ITT. This culminated in an article by Adam Raphael provoked by the corporate advertising campaign, and a vigorous 'letters to the editor' debate followed. But this was not all: cuttings of *Guardian* ITT stories during the previous two years were studied and a letter of protest was sent to the editor, seeking a meeting to discuss the newspaper's unwarranted bias. The editor at that time, Alastair Hetherington, replied that he could not meet the ITT representatives but offered a meeting with Adam Raphael, the features editor and the deputy editor. At a two-and-a-half-hour meeting in the London offices of the paper, the collection of cuttings on ITT was discussed by Nigel Rowe and *Guardian* staff. Afterwards, the editor was thanked for the meeting and presented with a file of cuttings. This resulted in one of the most extraordinary feats of press relations: Adam Raphael volunteered to surrender his space for an ITT reply based on key issues.

On February 7, 1975 nearly half a page was devoted to an article with the displayed heading:

> Who the devil does ITT think it is? This is the theme of ITT's current advertising campaign designed to defend its image, and the subject of a recent article on this page by Adam Raphael. We invited Nigel Rowe, ITT's Assistant Director of Public Relations, to reply.

In this remarkable PR feature article the author gave chapter and verse about the 'scandals' and closed by giving the Brussels address from which further information could be obtained. Towards the end of the article, Nigel Rowe said:

> 'This lack of knowledge of ITT's corporate character and real positive impact upon the countries in which we operate, much of which is due, frankly, to our own lack of attention to it in the past

L

has provided fertile soil for accusations. This has given rise to a great deal of emotion – suspicion, fear and hostility.

'Because of this situation, we know we must be much more open and outward going with facts and information. Hence our current advertising campaign in leading media in the UK, our recently produced 20-page fact-file *Facts about ITT in Europe*, our new quarterly external publication *Profile*, and our desire to foster an open dialogue with such people as readers of *The Guardian*.'

These remarks made out a splendid case for corporate PR and could well have provided an inspiration to other large organizations whose management had been shy about communications.

Peter Earl, PR director of ITT's major UK company, Standard Telephones and Cables, saw to it that thousands of reprints were run off for distribution to the staff of the UK companies.

3. *A speakers programme*. This was a more long-term component of the capsule since staff speakers had to be found and prepared, lecture notes and visual aids produced, and dates and venues arranged.

4. *Corporate advertising*. This was the responsibility of Terry Quinn in Brussels, the British campaign being produced by the KMP agency in London. The agency rightly insisted that no advertising should appear without pre-testing for there was a risk of ITT overestimating the level of interest in the corporation as a result of the bad publicity that had been received. Specialist Research Services conducted folder-technique interviews, proposed ITT advertisements being compared with other corporate advertisements, and alternative copy approaches being tested.

Six different treatments were tested before the campaign finally appeared. The first ad gave too little information, the next too much, cartoons were tried but found to be too flippant, then the bold headline approach was brought in and finally this was coupled with brief factual copy, the whole advertisement being typographical. Shock headlines such as 'Who the devil does ITT think it is?' and 'Does ITT give a damn about Britain's balance of payments?' were reversed white on black and occupied the left-hand half of double-spread magazine advertisements and the top half of full-page newspaper advertisements. Four advertisements were placed between the Autumn of 1974 and the Spring of 1975. In June 1975 a wrap-up advertisement appeared which reproduced miniatures of the four ads above the headline 'What more can we say?', and this carried a coupon offer of *Facts about ITT in Europe*. Such was the response that David

Barker was able to say 'Altogether we were well satisfied with the campaign which we believe completely fulfilled its objectives.'

Let us see how each of the four ads set about achieving its objective:

1. *Who the devil does ITT think it is?* The first ad was intended to put a face on the faceless giant by relating some of the British companies, products and brand names to ITT. Its information was probably a surprise to many people, a good many of whom thought of ITT as an electronics manufacturer.

2. *Does ITT give a damn about Britain's balance of payments?* The copy asserted that far from being a drain on the economy ITT made a net contribution of £11 million in 1974.

3. *Why would ITT want to invest in Britain at a time like this?* Psychologically, this was one of the best of the series, appearing as it did when inflationary uncertainties were everybody's worry, and one of the causes of an investment slow-down. The copy confirmed ITT's confidence in Britain's future and read as follows:

> For many years now, ITT companies have been investing in the British economy.
>
> Since early 1970, for example, their investments in buildings, equipment and machinery in the UK has totalled £43 million, much of it in Government designated development areas.
>
> Not to mention the £76 million that went into British research, development and engineering during the same period.
>
> All of which is long-term investment, with export and employment implications stretching into the 80s and beyond.
>
> But what about 1975 itself?
>
> And what about all those gloomy forecasts about Britain's future?
>
> As far as ITT is concerned, there were good reasons for investing in Britain for the last 50 years. And there are equally good reasons this year.
>
> So ITT companies plan to invest at least another £12 million on buildings, equipment and machinery in Britain during 1975.
>
> Which represents not only a £4 million increase on the ITT average over the last five years, but also a pretty unambiguous vote of confidence in Britain's long-term future.

This message was writ large in a single column of type half a page deep.

4. *Why should ITT care tuppence about British technology?* The fourth advertisement in the series nailed the myth that all US-controlled

multinationals do all their research in the States, leaving Europe dependent on imported technology.

The media list consisted of *The Times*, *Financial Times*, *The Guardian* and *The Observer* plus magazines such as the *Spectator*, *New Statesman* and the *New Scientist*. Because its cost did not fit the budget and its readership dipped too far below the target audience tip of the triangle to be cost-effective, the *Sunday Times* was not used.

5. *Profile*. Launching a sponsored external magazine to be read by busy people already inundated with reading matter is a great challenge to its designers and editors. It demands a recognizable character, originality and the ability to be welcomed issue by issue. In the case of ITT, it was imperative that the magazine should not be a propaganda sheet and neither should it be a glossy entertainment.

Designed by Richard A. Hill of Comark Europe SA, a Brussels consultancy, and edited by Mike Wade of ITT Europe's PR staff, it has a 20-page A4 format and typography that is fresh yet typical of the European business journal. The content has articles by personalities such as Peter Ustinov, George Mikes, Pierre Salinger, Jacques Tati and Northcote Parkinson, and a minimum of ITT material. The character of ITT is well projected.

It took ITT staffs all over Europe five months to assemble a 55,000 mailing list, which has been increased by the demand provoked by the corporate advertising and other facets of the communications programme. By the third issue the circulation was nearly 80,000. In 1975, the cost of production was 40p a copy.

Profile is printed in five language editions. The cover is printed in a bulk run in four colours, a fifth run being required for each of the language versions, the wording being reversed white on the fifth colour chosen for each issue. It is printed sheet litho, but set in letterpress type and made up from repro pulls, this helping with the complicated proof-reading in language versions. The articles are specially 're-created', not translated, in the four languages.

While a twenty-four-hour cold cure capsule is expected to act within a short time, the ITT corporate communications programme for Europe was expected to take at least twenty-four months, and in some cases longer, to perform its task of making the corporation known, understood and appreciated by influential opinion leaders in fifteen countries. Nevertheless, the results at the end of the first six months were a pretty good indication that the selected components and the methods of application were producing a snowball effect.

The corporate advertising campaign and press comment in the UK alone brought in some 2000 letters and 1000 'phone calls, 99 per cent complimentary, requesting copies of *Profile* and the facts-file. Newspapers such as *The Guardian* and *Financial Times* published the facts in feature articles. A second edition of *Facts about ITT in Europe* had to be run off within four months of its publication. *Profile* produced some outstanding compliments from important people who had read it from cover to cover.

Perhaps even more complimentary was the frequency with which articles were quoted or reprinted in newspapers and magazines, while summaries of articles were wired by the news agency UPI to the USA, Europe and the Middle East. *Profile* contents became long-lived since they were often reproduced up to three months later. *The Times*, the *New York Herald-Tribune* and *FEM* are among the journals which have reproduced Profile material, crediting the source and extending the ability of the magazine to communicate with its target audience.

This was only the beginning and to some extent represented only the initial thrust of the UK corporate advertising, the facts-file and the external house journal. In March 1976, an up-dated edition of *Facts* was published, and since it gave much of the data called for under OECD guidlines ITT believed it was more informative than probably any other information disclosure by a multinational company. The 1974–75 press advertising campaign described here was the forerunner of the next which was pre-tested during the summer of 1976 and launched in the UK business press during the Autumn. The second series of press ads contained revised figures, but continued to focus on ITT's contribution to Britain's balance of payments, exports, technology and so forth. At the time of writing, the campaign had not been extended to the European press outside the UK, but this had been contemplated.

In the second advertising campaign, the reversed white on black headline area was greater making headlines such as 'Just How Long Term is ITT's Commitment to Britain?' even more dominant and topical. Taking up less space the tersely written text copy occupied two columns.

Organization: ITT (Europe) Inc., Brussels
Personnel: Vice-president public relations: David Barker
               Assistant PR director: Nigel Rowe
               Advertising manager: Terry Quinn
               Editor: Mike Ward
               Consultant: Richard A. Hill, Comark Europe SA
               PR director, Standard Telephones and Cables, London: Peter Earl

The Open University

Background

The Open University received the Royal Charter in May 1969, and started in rented premises at 38 Belgrave Square, London. The OU moved to Walton Hall, Milton Keynes, in September 1969, and the first phase of the Walton Hall campus was opened the following year by Lord Mountbatten. Within five years it became Britain's largest university with 56,000 part-time home-based students. It was Harold Wilson's brainchild in 1963, the object being to provide a 'second chance' university with no conventional entry requirements, hence the name *Open*. Study is by means of well-produced correspondence courses, radio and TV programmes, study groups and summer schools.

While the OU has been an undoubted success, and the standards of its tutorial material and techniques have often been envied by those teaching in conventional full-time universities, it has for various reasons tended to attract teachers, other professionals and housewives rather than working-class students. The heavy and often inconvenient demands on time, and increasing problems of cost, have been deterrents.

Nevertheless, these were the first three paragraphs of an OU news release issued at the London press conference on January 29, 1976:

> 'Graduates from the manual and routine non-manual occupations have gone up by from six percent last year to nine percent. Although teachers remain the largest occupation group, their share continues to decrease. They have declined to 53 percent of graduates from 60 percent last year and 86 percent in 1972, the first year of graduation.
>
> 'Women, another group often considered as educationally disadvantaged, make up an increased share of new graduates. They are 34 percent this year compared with 31 percent in 1975 and as regards occupation, housewives are still the second largest group with an increased share up from nine percent to 11 percent.'

The press operation has tended to draw attention to working-class applicants and graduates in order to overcome the resistance of such people to applying for a university place.

For its own purposes the OU defines *public relations* as 'the state of mutual understanding and respect which exists between the university and various sections of the public'. *Publicity* is very rightly regarded quite distinctly as 'any printed, broadcast or verbal information (accurate or otherwise) about the university'. *Advertising* is seen as 'any publicity in journals or on television for which the university pays'. *Editorial coverage* is defined as 'any publicity in journals or on the broadcast media for which the university does not pay'. And *press liaison* consists of 'activities undertaken in order to secure accurate editorial coverage'.

The Information Services Department is organized like this:

DIRECTOR — *Administrative Secretary* — *Receptionists*

PRESS	PUBLICATIONS	VISITORS	GENERAL INFORMATION
Senior Press Officer & Deputy Director	Publications Officer & Editor of student journal	Visits Officer	Information Secretary
Regional Press Officer	Assistant Publications Officer		
Press Officer	Editor of staff journals		
Secretary	Secretaries		

The chart demonstrates the range of activities controlled by the director of information services to which may be added his supervision of advertising conducted by advertising agents and opinion research undertaken by a research firm. The regional press officer and the press officer have equal status under the senior press officer, as do the assistant publications officer and the editor under the publications officer.

The case study will draw on material from 1974–76 and concentrate on the particular episode in the OU's PR work leading up to the kind of press conference and news release already mentioned. It should be remembered that this is closely related to the advertising campaign run during January and February to recruit students for the following academic year. Unlike other universities, the OU's academic year follows the normal calendar year with courses starting around February and examinations being held in October.

But as will be seen, the publicity effect is an on-going one from the previous year, and the OU depends upon maintaining and continuing the momentum achieved in its growth years. Even so, there are inevitable peaks and troughs in publicity effort and resultant interest which do not make OU PR simple to sustain.

There is, however, bound to be clearer and greater understanding of the university during the burst of editorial publicity and press advertising during the recruitment drive months of January and February. In fact, a Harris survey in 1974 showed that in the peak five weeks, when there were 70,000 requests for the *Guide for Applicants*, and 18,000 applications for places, *awareness* of the OU increased from 54 per cent in January to 65 per cent in March.

Again, a Harris survey in January 1975 showed that 55 per cent of the adult population has 'heard' of the OU, but this can be superficial. For example, one gap in public understanding continues to be about the very name of the university.

From the start, the OU has had to face three inter-related PR situations: political controversy – it was a Labour Government which had initiated the OU; academic scepticism from those who clung to belief in classroom teacher–student relationship; and plain public ignorance. After all, a *university* is not exactly a popular topic even if it is intended for everyman. By concentrating on the defeat of ignorance, which is what PR is mostly all about, it has been possible to minimize the first two problems.

A measure of the success gained in breaking down public ignorance has been that during the university's first six teaching years demand for places has greatly exceeded the number that could be awarded, and all the time the syllabus was being extended with new subjects. In 1976 the OU was providing one in 13 of all new British graduates, 5450 graduates gaining their first degree with the university.

The New Graduates Editorial Publicity Campaign

There is nothing intangible about this PR campaign. The objectives are clearcut: to exploit existing newsworthy material in order to achieve maximum editorial publicity which will reinforce the advertising and leaflet campaign to attract students. When the advertising breaks in the *Radio Times* in January, followed by insertions in the *Daily Mail*, *Daily Express*, *Daily Mirror* and some forty regional newspapers, readers need to be encouraged by testimonial stories and pictures about men and women who have just been awarded OU degrees.

But finding these stories begins during the previous June, and involves all the thousands of students who are likely to complete their studies in the October examinations!

In June the senior press officer asks the university data processing manager for information about the prospective graduates. In 1975 there were 7095 of them. This is a mass press relations exercise which is unlikely to be repeated in other organizations, but because it is a model of planning and precise execution it is admirable for inclusion in a book with this title.

So, in June the data processing manager is asked to supply listings, by serial number within regions, of all prospective ordinary and honours graduates showing full name, title, address, occupation code, age, sex, terminal age of education and educational qualifications, together with peel-off address labels. All this is required by October. (In addition, a more precise breakdown of overall characteristics of the graduates is called for by December, based on the examination results.) The press office now has to work within the constraints of inelastic time limits which are linked to the examination dates, the announcement of examination results, and the press conference or press conferences in January.

In November, just after those likely to graduate have sat their examinations, a letter and questionnaire form is sent out to each one. It is university policy that it will not release the names and addresses of students without their permission. The letter begins:

Dear Student,

I am writing to ask you as a student who may graduate next year for your help in publicising the University's 1976 group of graduates.

We believe the press, radio and television will be interested – as they have been in the last three years – in publicising your achievement.

If you agree to help, could you please fill in the form on the reverse side of this letter as completely as possible and return it in the prepaid envelope. . .

From half to two thirds of the students contacted usually return the form and agree to publicity. The details they supply then have to be transcribed onto 13 regional lists of newspapers and television and radio stations and sent out to the 900 such outlets in the UK.

But that is only the beginning: all the forms – 3700 in 1975 – have to be scrutinized for special news value, and assessed against a pyramid of editorial needs. A handful of exceptionally interesting graduates are required for personal appearances at the national press conference at the end of January. Then another twenty or so graduates are needed for national stories in addition to the five or six present at the press conference. Third, a pool of perhaps a dozen graduates are wanted so that they can be offered on an exclusive basis to television.

The national press conferences are usually held at a hotel near Fleet

Street, when some 40 journalists are addressed by the vice-chancellor. His remarks and journalist's questions occupy about half-an-hour, and then the press interview the graduates who also pose for pictures.

So far, the pyramid has considered only the needs of the national media. During the scrutiny of forms the OU press officers are also on the lookout for stories for the regional press, radio and TV.

The checking of individual forms, the transcribing of the information from the forms to a master list by an agreed formula by the secretarial pool, and the checking of the lists, followed by the deletions of those students who fail their examinations, *has to be done in three weeks*. Yet by the day preceding the press conference the press office will hold – hopefully – accurate press information on every new graduate who has permitted its release.

A typical timetable for the operation is this one that was used for the January 1974 press conferences in London and the regions:

GRADUATE PRESS CONFERENCE TIMETABLE

November 19	Potential graduates mail out
21	Book London venue
25	Invitations to national education correspondents and selected journals
28	Deadline for regional press invitation list
December 2	Invitations to regional press
11	Briefing for regional directors
Mid-December	Graduate print-out identifies graduates and gives examination statistics as requested
January 3	Deadline for issuing invitations to selected graduates to attend conferences
10	Set up BBC arrangements
14	National graduates story and examinations story – preparations begin
20–21	Embargoed stories mailed out to national and regional press
24	Press conference
25	Service requests for graduates from regional press.

Reverting to the scrutiny of the forms and the 'pyramid process', the five graduates selected for the London press conference on January 29, 1976 were a docker, Mr. Ron Littell; the proprietress of a hairdressing shop, Mrs. Dorothy Lee; an electrician in a cigarette factory, Mr. Pierce McDermott; a freight terminal supervisor, Mr. Thomas Kane; and Mr. Ted Graham, MP for Edmonton. They came from different parts of the UK, and on this occasion only a national press conference was held. From the Edmonton MP who studied while travelling on the London Underground, to the local postman in Peebles, OU graduates filled the press that week with their stories and pictures. From the *Daily Telegraph* to the *Morning Star*, the *Jersey Evening Post* to the *Highland News*, the coverage was widespread. Local radio and regional TV stations also carried the stories.

A week later the press advertising appeared in the national and regional newspapers. Response to these advertisements cannot be calculated without taking into consideration the market education provided by the preliminary editorial coverage. The amount spent on advertising by the Open University is very small – only £27,000 for this recruitment campaign – but its value must be enhanced by the opportunity prospective applicants have of identifying themselves with the graduates whose press stories that read like these two:

Degree for fire officer

Five years of studying between being called out to fires has paid off for West Midland fire officer, Peter Wilson.

Mr. Wilson has·just won a B.A. degree from the Open University.

As a youth his family could not afford to let him take up the grammar school place which he hoped would lead on to university.

Mr. Wilson, 49, was deputy chief officer of the former West Bromwich Fire Service when he enrolled for the course.

Now he is head of project and forward planning for the West Midlands Fire Service into which seven brigades merged in 1974.

He is believed to be one of only three B.A. holders among Britain's 40,000 firemen.

Mr. Wilson said: 'Now we'll perhaps have the first proper holiday for years – most of my spare time was previously spent studying.'

(*Birmingham Evening Mail*)

Mother gets her BA . . .
despite Swaziland trip

A Welshpool mother of two young children who had spent four years of intensive study on an Open University BA course, found that the whole exercise was jeopardised last summer when her engineering husband was suddenly posted to Swaziland – just when she was due to take her final exam.

But Mrs. Janet Elizabeth Ellis of Pyllygo House, Welshpool, found that the Open University administrators were up to the challenge. They sent out her papers to Swaziland and laid on a chapel building and a Minister to act as invigilator.

Mrs. Ellis sat the examination, passed with flying colours and got her degree. Now she is on her way home from Swaziland.

(Charles Quant, *Liverpool Daily Post*)

Sometimes the search for a good picture at the press conference leads right out of the hotel as in 1976 when the MP had his hair styled in a ladies' hairdressing salon by another graduate who was a hairdresser.

In addition to the graduate publicity generated in January and February there is a second burst of press activity at the graduation ceremonies in the summer. This latter publicity is valuable in the general sense for all the courses whereas the earlier coverage is important because it precedes the applications period.

Another operation is called 'short fall publicity' and this is aimed at some dozen towns where in the past recruitment has been disappointing. In these places the OU carries out a special campaign consisting of press coverage, advertising, open evenings at study centres and other activities prior to the main campaign. This gives residents in these towns the incentive to apply earlier than the rest of the country and so get a better chance in the queue of applicants.

The OU PR campaigns are planned differently from year to year, and examples here have been drawn mostly from the 1974–76 period. But whereas in 1974 the OU held 13 simultaneous press conferences throughout the country to announce the new graduates, only one national conference was held in 1975 and 1976.

Organization: The Open University
Personnel: Director of information services: John C. Greenall
               Senior press officer and deputy director: Kevin Moloney

Index